D0208446

COPY-EDITING
THE CAMBRIDGE HANDBOOK

COPY-EDITING

THE CAMBRIDGE HANDBOOK

JUDITH BUTCHER

Formerly Chief Subeditor, Cambridge University Press

SECOND EDITION

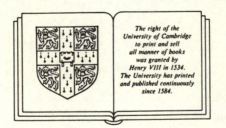

The right of the
University of Cambridge
to print and sell
all manner of books
was granted by
Henry VIII in 1534.
The University has printed
and published continuously
since 1584.

CAMBRIDGE UNIVERSITY PRESS

CAMBRIDGE

NEW YORK   PORT CHESTER

MELBOURNE   SYDNEY

Published by the Press Syndicate of the University of Cambridge
The Pitt Building, Trumpington Street, Cambridge CB2 IRP
32 East 57th Street, New York, NY 10022, USA
10 Stamford Road, Oakleigh, Melbourne 3166, Australia

© Cambridge University Press 1975, 1981

First published 1975
Reprinted with corrections 1976
Reprinted 1978, 1980
Second edition 1981
Reprinted 1983, 1986, 1987, 1989

Printed in Great Britain at the
University Press, Cambridge

British Library Cataloguing in Publication Data
Butcher, Judith
Copy-editing. – 2nd ed.
1. Proof-reading – Hand books, manuals etc.
- I. Title
808'.02 PN162 80–41722

ISBN 0 521 25638 0 desk edition

CONTENTS

Contents

Contents

Contents

ILLUSTRATIONS

PREFACE TO THE FIRST EDITION

Copy-editing is largely a matter of common sense in deciding what to do and of thoroughness in doing it; but there are pitfalls an inexperienced copy-editor cannot foresee. Some years ago I wrote a handbook for use within the Cambridge University Press, so that new copy-editors could benefit from the accumulated experience of their predecessors rather than having to learn by making their own mistakes; and it has now been suggested that such a book might be of use in other firms.

It is impossible to write a handbook suitable for every publisher or every kind of typescript. This book is based on my experience at Penguin Books and the Cambridge University Press, where copy-editors work on the premises and see a book through from the estimate stage until the proofs are passed for press. Freelance copy-editors and others working to a more limited brief – or sponsoring editors who wish to do their own copy-editing – will be able to make use of the parts relevant to their own job; the things to be done remain the same, although the same person may not do them all.

As I am not writing primarily for authors, I have not, for example, explained the reasons for choosing one system of bibliographical references rather than another. By the time the book reaches the copy-editor the system is chosen, and his job is to make sure that it works efficiently, by eliminating certain faults in it. Publishers now realize more and more, however, that authors must be briefed early and adequately. If your firm does not already have a good set of notes on style for its authors, do prepare one: not all authors will be prepared to follow your instructions, but many of them will be grateful for any guidance you can give.

It is difficult to decide how to arrange a book of this kind, but it seemed best to cover first the things that are common to all books, and to leave the more complex material until later, rather than to adopt a more strictly logical order. Chapter 1 outlines the copy-editor's function.

Chapters 2–5 cover this in more detail in relation to the three stages at which the copy-editor works on the book: the preparation for an estimate or the setting of specimen pages; the main copy-editing stage, at which the text and illustrations are prepared for the printer; and the proof stage. Chapter 6 discusses some difficult points of spelling, capitalization and other things collectively known as house style. Chapters 7–9 treat the various parts of the book in more detail: preliminary pages, headings, tables, notes, indexes and so on. Chapters 10 and 11 cover more complex material such as bibliographical references, quotations, poetry and plays; chapter 12 books with more than one author or in more than one volume. Chapters 13 and 14 deal with specialized subjects: science and mathematics, classical books, books on law and music. The final chapter gives some points to look out for when preparing reprints and new editions.

Many people have given me good advice during my years in publishing; and it would take too much space to thank them all individually. I am especially indebted to those who have written parts of this book: Michael Coles compiled the chapter on science and mathematics, Gillian Law wrote the section about books on law, and Jeremy Mynott the one on classical books; Mrs M. D. Anderson made the index.

The author of this kind of book lays himself open to the charge of not following his own precepts. Alas, both my copy-editor and I are fallible, and I should be grateful if you would let me know of any errors, omissions or better ways of doing things.

PREFACE TO THE SECOND EDITION

I have taken the opportunity to include the new British Standard proof correction marks and to revise the information about US copyright legislation. Innumerable smaller changes have been made throughout the book.

I

Introduction

Four kinds of work will be done on a typescript before the printer sets the first word in type: editing, copy-editing, typographical design and printer's marking-up. (I use the word 'typescript' rather than 'manuscript' to refer to the book before it is set in type, because a printer cannot now be expected to work from handwritten copy.)

The sponsoring editor (or acquisition editor) will look at the book as a whole: its content, scope, level, length and organization. He will see whether it is written clearly, without ambiguity or repetition, and whether the illustrations are necessary and suitable; and will also look out for inaccuracies and anything that might involve his firm in legal proceedings for libel, defamation, obscenity or breach of copyright. The sponsoring editor will discuss with the author any revisions he thinks necessary; and when the agreed changes have been made, the typescript will be copy-edited. Copy-editing – which may be carried out by the sponsoring editor, a copy-editor, or in some cases by the printer – aims to remove inconsistencies and any remaining errors, ambiguities and faults of organization. The designer will give the necessary instructions about the appearance of the book: page depth, type sizes, and so on. Finally the printer will mark up the typescript in accordance with these instructions.

The copy-editor's main aims are to remove any obstacles between the reader and what the author wishes to convey, and also to save his firm time and money by finding and solving any problems before the typescript is sent to the printer, so that production can go ahead without interruption. He is usually involved at three stages of a book's progress: before the printing cost is estimated, before the typescript is sent to the printer for setting, and when the author returns his proofs. Some copy-editors also send the author his proof, and may read a set of proofs themselves, either checking it against the typescript or reading it for sense.

If a printer's estimate is required before the book is copy-edited, the copy-editor can usefully look at the typescript before it is passed to the

1

designer. This early view has three advantages. First, the copy-editor can list the editorial factors that the designer must take into account: for example, the need to distinguish certain passages from the main text, the use of unusual symbols, whether headlines are required, or the number of categories of subheading (see chapter 2). Secondly, he can help the printer's estimator to work more accurately by making sure that the typescript is complete – or by giving details of what is not yet available – by numbering the sheets of typescript in one sequence, identifying the various kinds of headings and any material that is to be distinguished typographically, and by marking the approximate position of any text illustrations and tables. Thirdly, the copy-editor is able to diagnose early any general problems or faults in the author's system of subheadings, bibliographical references, capitalization or use of italic, and has time to propose remedies to the author while the estimate is in progress, and at the same time to mention any points of house style that he plans to incorporate into the typescript.

When the estimate has been approved, the copy-editor will put into effect the remedies the author has approved. He will also watch out for ambiguous or misleading English, spelling, punctuation, paragraphing and inconsistencies (see chapter 3). The printer cannot be expected to put these things right unless he is given specific instructions; and if he is, he is likely to charge for the extra work.

If the copy-editor later sees the author's corrected proof, he is able to ensure that the author's alterations are comprehensible and consistent with the book's style, and that they can be incorporated without great difficulty or expense. He tries to see that the cost of corrections is allocated fairly as between author, printer and publisher, and to ensure that any additional material, such as an index, is legible, well organized and consistent.

The good copy-editor is a rare creature: he is an intelligent reader and a tactful and sensitive critic; he cares enough about perfection of detail to spend his working hours checking small points of consistency in someone else's work, but he has the judgement not to waste his firm's time or antagonize the author by making unnecessary changes. Most authors are extremely grateful for the amount of work the copy-editor does to remove the imperfections from their work, but a few refuse to have anything changed; and it is important to tell the author in advance what kinds of change one proposes to make, and why. If the author is going to object, it is much better to find this out before a great deal of unnecessary work has been done – work that will take almost as long to undo if the author insists – and, above all, before the book is typeset. Some publishers return the typescript to the author after it has been copy-edited, and one should certainly do this if the author is at all uneasy about the changes one is making. However, it delays the book; and one may need to look at every sheet of the typescript again afterwards, to make sure that the author has not made inconsistent changes.

It is very helpful if the author and copy-editor can meet, even if they may have to conduct later negotiations by correspondence. It is sometimes difficult to convey in a letter that one is not trying to find fault, and that one is not simply being obtuse in querying the author's brand-new and over-subtle system of bibliographical references. The copy-editor must show great tact; and he must also see the faults in proportion to the author's achievement. I say this because it is easy for a copy-editor, who is after all employed to look for faults, to regard his authors as incompetent and difficult, instead of trying to see things from their point of view.

The copy-editor is not usually an expert on the subject of the book, though he must be able to interest himself in it in order to try to put himself in the position of the intended readers. The author is usually so familiar with his subject, and has spent so much time on his book, that he cannot see it as it will appear to someone else; and the copy-editor will often see where the author has repeated himself or omitted a step in his argument, expressed himself ambiguously or failed to explain a point or spell out an abbreviation.

One may be able to suggest better ways of organizing the material. This may mean having *less* formal organization rather than more: some authors erect an elaborate scaffolding before starting to write, but if they have constructed the book well it will stand on its own when it is finished. A lot of subheadings and numbered paragraphs may make a book look more formidable without necessarily making it any more helpful; it is worth asking oneself whether points in the argument, or headings, need be numbered or lettered unless there are cross-references to them. Sometimes material may be more effectively presented in a different form or a different place: for example the data presented in a table may be clearer as a graph, or vice versa.

If the book has illustrations, the copy-editor will compare each one with the relevant text, to see that it will do its job effectively, is placed in the most appropriate position and is correctly referred to. Sometimes

3

an author borrows an illustration without making it fully suitable for its new purpose; sometimes he finds a better illustration at a late stage and forgets to change the text. The copy-editor will see whether parts of some of the photographs could or should be omitted, and whether the author's rough sketches for diagrams or maps will be clear to the draughtsman who will prepare drawings suitable for reproduction.

The copy-editor tries to ensure that the printer receives complete, clear and self-explanatory copy. As well as seeing that the sheets of typescript are numbered in one sequence, identifying the various kinds of heading, and marking the passages that need to be distinguished typographically, he will make sure that the typescript is entirely legible, that all ambiguous or unusual characters are identified, and that any corrections or additions are made in the right place. He will realize that the printer will not be able to place each illustration and table exactly where the author wants it: some illustrations may have to be printed on different paper; others may have to be moved because there is not room for them on the relevant page. As well as warning the author about this, he will change the references in the text from 'as follows' to 'in table 5' (or whatever the number may be).

Although the copy-editor's main interest is likely to be an editorial one, his job involves production problems too. As he knows the book in detail he can make the author's intentions clear to the designer and printer; and as he realizes the limitations within which the printer has to work, he can explain to the author why it may be impossible to carry out his wishes in exactly the ways he proposes. It is this joint role which gives the job its fascination.

2

Estimates and specimen pages

It may be necessary to obtain a printer's estimate, or to have specimen pages set, before (or while) the typescript is copy-edited; and, as I have mentioned before, the copy-editor can help brief the designer and estimator, and can also prepare for the copy-editing stage by diagnosing the general faults in the typescript and writing to the author about them. It may also be necessary to ask the author about any missing or unsatisfactory illustrations, captions or text.

If the typescript is a photocopy or carbon copy, find out whether this is in fact the copy that will be sent for setting, so as to avoid duplication of marking as far as possible. If it is proposed to use a photocopy or carbon copy for setting, check whether it will be clear enough for the printer, especially if there are unfamiliar names and words in it; it may be necessary to ask the author for the top copy or even to have the book retyped.

Before going any further I should explain the sense in which I shall use certain words:

folio: a sheet of typescript
page: a page of a proof or a finished book, for example p. 85 of this book
leaf: two pages which back on to one another – a 'recto' (right-hand page) and its 'verso' (left-hand page) – for example pp. 85–6 of this book

The distinction between 'page' and 'folio' is a useful one, because a page and a folio will contain a different amount of material: an index that is ten A4 folios long will (if it is typed double-spaced and single column as it should be) occupy only two or three pages when it is printed.

part: a group of related chapters with a part number or title or both

section: a subdivision of a chapter
subheading: a heading to a section of a chapter or of a bibliography

The other kinds of headings are called part headings, chapter headings, table headings and headlines. A headline – also called a running head or pagehead – is the heading that appears at the top of every page (with some exceptions) in most non-fiction books and some novels.

2.1 *Briefing the designer*

The designer needs two kinds of information: first the suggested page size and general appearance, the kind of reader for whom the book is intended, and the desired production cost or selling price; and secondly what the book consists of, which parts of it should be distinguished typographically, and so on – the individual items in the designer's specification (fig. 2.1). This section deals with the second kind.

Look at every folio of the typescript, to ensure that you see all the things you need to tell the designer: he will probably not have time to look at every folio himself, and might not notice an extra grade of subheading in chapter 10 or unusual characters wanted in chapter 2.

List factors that might affect the choice of typeface or setting method. It is not necessary to point out something that will be obvious to anyone glancing at the typescript, for example mathematics in a mathematics book, though it may be useful to point out that it contains a particular complication such as superscripts to superscripts. Mention things that occur occasionally, for example the use of bold type, phonetics, Hebrew, Greek, unusual accents, underlined letters that are not to be italic, or passages with a great deal of italic or capitals. Give folio references to examples. If the typescript contains a large number of cross-references to pages, which cannot be completed until the book is paged, give an approximate number.

If the book is to be set in the same style as an earlier one, warn the designer of any differences that will affect his typographical specification (see fig. 2.1). The new book might be more complicated and include one or two of the following: an extra grade of subheading, tables, bibliography, appendixes, the contributor's name below each chapter title; bold, Greek or mathematical characters in text or headings. It might have much longer or much shorter headings. It might be less complicated and might not need headlines; or for economy one might decide against separate leaves for part titles.

Special sorts

The term 'special sort' is used in more than one sense. I use it here to mean the characters that a printer would have to obtain specially for the book; but you may also hear it used to mean either a character not in the standard fount of type, or a character that has to be set by hand because the typesetting machine has room for only a certain number of matrices (the metal moulds, film negatives, etc., used to create the individual characters) in its matrix case, grid or disc (see, for example, appendix 8).

Only the printer knows what unusual characters he already has, but you should give a warning if the book contains letters that are outside the usual range of alphabets, for example consonants with dots below them. If the author has not written the special characters clearly, ask him now to tell you exactly what they should be, so that the printer does not order the wrong ones. Try to persuade the author out of using very unusual characters, for example in mathematics or in transliterating oriental languages; he may not realize that he is asking for something difficult. If unusual characters are used in long quotations or in appendixes as well as in the text, tell the designer; he may decide to set all quotations and appendixes in text type, in order to avoid the expense of purchasing special sorts in an extra size.

Even if the printer has all the characters the author wants to use, he may have to insert some of them by hand. It is therefore very useful if you can say whether each unusual one is used a great deal throughout the book, or only a few times, or in only one chapter.

If you are planning to use something not yet marked on the typescript (for example bold italic for vectors, or bold for volume numbers), say so now, so that the printer can include this in his estimate with a warning if he would have difficulty in setting all the necessary characters on his standard machine.

Headings

Say whether parts are to have half-titles (see p. 29).

Try to limit subheadings in the text to three grades. This should be ample except in a reference book, and it is difficult for the designer to specify more than three kinds that will be sufficiently distinct from one another and from table headings, headlines, etc.

7

PUBLISHING DIVISION
CAMBRIDGE UNIVERSITY PRESS

Typesetter — C.U.P.   Printer —   Litho/Letterpress   Sub-ed

Author/Editor — Melissa Meriam BULLARD
Title — Filippo Strozzi and the Medici
Series — C. Studies in Early Modern History

Trimmed size — 228 x 152 mm   Margins (trimmed): Head 3½ picas   Back (single) 3½ picas
Type area (picas) — 27   (measure) x 42   text lines plus running head & folio
Text type: (Mono/AUP/Linotron/Laser/IBM) Ehrhardt 453-11/12   No of lines on chapter opening page 33
Extracts (Ext) — 453-10/11, unaltered, full measure   turnovers
Poetry (P) — 453-10/11, unaltered, centred — indent? / pm most   turnovers
lsm (t)   turnovers

Footnote (FN) — 453-8/9   note no. flush left indented + em (cleared for 10/409) then en # to 1st word
    turnovers aligned on first word/flush-left
    note no. flush left (cleared for 10/409)
    turnovers aligned on first word

Table type   (see separate specification)
Running heads — 453-12 ital u/lc centred   (see section, see title/page instion, old title)
Left (verso) — book title
Right (recto) — chapter title   Drop folio at foot — 453-10 space above   6pt
Folio at head   figure style — old-style   word spacing close
Para indent — 1 em   453-10/11   Indent turnovers 2 ems, new title by same author 1 mm
Bibliography (Bib) — 453-10/11   turnovers
Appendices (App)
Reference (Ref)
Index — probably 453-8/9, 2 cols x 13 picas, unjust(h/ref)   6 pages allowed
    11A 453-12 small caps, 10½ units letter-spaced, centred

SUB-HEADINGS
    turnovers centred/flush-left
    space above 1½ lines   space below   next line flush left
(X) 453-10/11 small caps, 10/96 units l.#. centred
in Bibliography   space above 1t lines   space below ½ line   next line fl.left
    turnovers centred/flush-left
(X) 453-10/11 italic u/lc, centred
    space above 1½ lines   space below ½ line   next line fl.left
    turnovers centred/flush left
    space above   space below   next line

PART TITLES   starts new page / recto / flush / over / above chapter head
Part Number (PN)
Part Title (PT)   turnovers
Part Quotations (PQ)

CHAPTER starts new page (recto/verso/run-on)
Chapter Number (CN) — 453-14 o.s. arabic fig., centred, on base of 2nd text line
Chapter Title (CT) — 453-18/20 rom. u/lc, centred, on base of 5th line   turnovers centred
Author (CA)
Author Affiliation (CAA)
Chapter Quotation (CQ)
Chapter text begins — 453-11/12 mm. u/lc, flush left, on 10th text line
Breaks in text — 1 line #   next line flush left
SORTS — French, German, Italian
(or see attached list)
ILLUSTRATIONS — 1 line

Captions (Cap) to line and tone illustrations — 453-9/10   turnovers

ADDITIONAL SPECIFICATION

SPECIAL INSTRUCTIONS

PRELIMS allow 12 pages; Index allow 6 pages
Other copy to follow: allow — pages for
SIGNED for estimate John Trevitt   Date 7 December 1978
    for setting JT   Date 1 February 1979

Fig. 2.1 Designer's typographical specification.

the transfer of church funds destined for Rome. His bank in Seville handled the shipment of revenues from Spain which it passed on to Rome via the Lyons branch.[55] His company in Florence received and disbursed many of the large subsidies sent from Rome through the Depository General to the papal armies in the north. And when the Depository General was assigned the income of the *decima* exacted in the Kingdom of Naples, Filippo's bank in Naples received the commission to manage it.[56] Filippo's bank used the Depository to engage surplus funds and to increase the circulation of capital through letters of exchange with branch companies in other cities. Since most of the Depository's payments were made at the end of the month, he could arrange to have his capital (*mobile*) from Lyons sent via Florence to Rome through several profitable exchanges and still have time to meet payments. With so many of the smaller payments, especially of stipends, in silver coins, his bank also engaged in money-changing and speculation on the fluctuations in the value of petty coins in relation to gold.[57]

The primary advantage of the Depository General, however, for Filippo was the entrée it provided into other lucrative areas of papal finance, an advantage that Benedetto Buondelmonti had been quick to point out back in May 1515 when he wrote Filippo: 'I see this [the Depository General] to be the ladder enabling you in time to enter into many different areas of church affairs.'[58] Filippo's status at the curia afforded him unparalleled opportunity to employ his manifold talents as a businessman on the highest levels of international finance. In 1515 when he assumed the responsibilities of the Depository General he had reached a major juncture in his life. His new company in Rome together with his connections at the papal court which he began to exploit and expand were the keys to his future. They transformed him from just a rich Florentine aristocrat, the brother-in-law of Lorenzo de'Medici, into a highly privileged *parente* of the pope and high-powered international financier.

55 *Ibid.*, vol. 1208, fols. 84, 109, 127, 144.   56 A.V., Div. Cam., vol. 60, fols. 5-6.
57 Filippo explained the procedures in a letter to Francesco del Nero, C.S., Ser. III, 110, fol. 148.
58 M.A.P., vol. 108, fol. 148.

6

War finance and Florentine public funds

Before considering papal war finances and Filippo's role in them as conduit between the Florence and Rome depositories, we must first turn our attention to the broader context of papal banking and the financial predicament which engulfed the Medicean papacy. The papacy in the early sixteenth century faced the same fiscal problems we have already encountered in the Depository General, only on a much larger scale. Although the popes had regular sources of income from taxes on ecclesiastical possessions in all parts of the Christian world, substantial revenues from the Papal States, and income from the sale of offices and indulgences, these monies arrived at Rome too slowly and unpredictably to alleviate immediate needs for cash. The *Introitus* accounts illustrate how annates or common services and *decima* payments dribbled in often months late. The distance some monies had to travel whether as a cash shipment or in a letter of exchange added to the delays. Once the papal collector in Spain had managed to force payment which was sometimes years in arrears, it still took over four months to transfer the money from Seville through Lyons to Rome. Spanish monies collected by Giovanni Poggio from September 1532 through December 1533 were not receipted in Rome until the end of May 1534.[1] Even the sale of benefices and offices, which became an increasingly productive source of revenue, was sporadic and sometimes at a standstill. A lack of vacancies such as that which occurred in August 1514 when money was in severe shortage in Rome caused Baldassarre da Pescia to write Lorenzo de'Medici in Florence the following observation: 'In fact here there is not a *quattrino*. The *datario* has debts of 8,000 to 10,000 ducats with Bernardo Bini [depositor of the Datary] and there are no vacant offices.'[2]

We have already noticed this chronic lack of cash at papal Rome in the records of the Depository General where it showed up in the continual deficits carried on the depositor's books. Filippo frequently made mention of *strettezza*, or shortages of money, as in August 1514. This shortage had apparently occurred for no other reason than that the pope had spent what

1 A.V., Div. Cam., vol. 95, fols. 170-172.   2 M.A.P., 107, fol. 57.

The headings should be coded in pencil in the margin, by a letter or number in a square, according to their place in the hierarchy (see section 9.3). If you know which passages are to be set in smaller type, code those headings differently from the ones in text type, because the designer's specification will give the size as well as the style appropriate for each code letter. Tell the designer how many grades there are in the text and endmatter, and how they are coded: for example 'three grades in the text, labelled A, B, C; one grade in the bibliography, labelled X'. Mention any factors that might affect the typographical style, for example that the headings are extremely long or short or include numerals or italic or Greek; or that grade A appears only in chapter 5.

If headings or notes must appear in the margin, point this out, as it may affect the printing method.

Footnotes and endnotes (see section 9.4)

Tell the designer whether the notes are to be footnotes or endnotes; whether any footnotes should be keyed by number or symbol, and, if by number, whether the numbering must start afresh on each page or may continue through each chapter.

There may be some very long footnotes which would be better taken into the text or moved to an appendix.

Cross-references

Cross-references to pages in the text may entail resetting every line involved when the page number is known, and references to chapters and sections should be substituted where possible. If cross-referencing by page cannot be avoided, draw it to the designer's attention.

Passages to be distinguished typographically

Say whether it is necessary to distinguish long quotations (see section 11.1), exercises, etc., typographically from the main text, leaving it to the designer to decide whether small type or indention – or perhaps italic – should be used to distinguish them. If there is a particular advantage or disadvantage in using text type, small type or italic, say so; one might want to use text type because the quotations or exercises contain the same unusual characters as the text. Give folio references to isolated or particularly complicated examples.

'Small type' is the size between text type and footnote type. The use of an intermediate size of type is partly an editorial decision, but it also depends on the setting method and the need for economy. In Monotype and slugsetting, for example, different sizes have to be set separately and assembled later: this means a double extra expense, which should be avoided if it is not essential. It may not be worth using an extra size of type if there are only half a dozen long quotations; but if a book contains endnotes, which are usually set larger than footnotes, one could use the endnote size for quotations in the text, with only the additional expense of assembling the different sizes of type.

Appendixes are usually set in small type, but may be in text type for one of the following reasons: to save an extra size of type; because of the need to distinguish long quotations within them by the use of small type; because they have footnotes or contain special sorts which do not occur in any other passages set in small type; or because the book is very short and you wish to make it longer. Point out any relevant factors.

Tables

Tables may be set in small type or in footnote type, or the type size may vary according to the size of the table. Give folio references for any complicated tables, and say whether very large ones may be split or turned to read up the page to avoid having a pullout.

Illustrations (see chapter 4)

It is helpful if you can at this early stage provide the following information: which illustrations must be reproduced same-size or at a particular reduction; which illustrations must be reduced by the same amount as one another or reproduced at the same scale; which drawings or photographs have been borrowed and must not be lettered; whether any coloured originals are to be reproduced in colour or black and white.

Half-tones: say how many there are. If they are not to be printed in the text, say whether they are to be grouped, scattered or pasted in individually to face the relevant page of text; the last option is much more expensive, and may have to be vetoed on grounds of cost. If you already know that the half-tones cannot be trimmed without losing some essential detail (and therefore cannot be bled), or that there are editorial factors affecting sizing, say so. If you do not yet know which of the photographs will be used, or whether each will occupy a whole page or half a page, make this clear and provide a simple hypothetical basis for the estimate.

11

Line drawings: say how many there are; mention any points about style and size (maps and large diagrams may sometimes affect page size). Count numbered figures as one each, even if some are made up of more than one part.

Possible pullouts: say whether they are to pull clear, and whether they must face a particular page or may be bound in at a place that is more convenient for the binder (e.g. between two folded sheets – 'signatures'– of the text). Give figure numbers and ask the designer whether he can suggest a cheaper way of dealing with the material.

Possible artwork needed for things, other than illustrations, which may require artwork as well as typesetting, for example genealogical tables with many rules (lines), music, chemical formulae containing diagonal lines, crossed-out letters, tables with complex ruling, etc. Give folio references unless they occur throughout the book.

Illustrations not yet available: give as much information as possible. Printers can estimate the cost of printing a half-page or whole-page illustration; but it is impossible to estimate for drawing without knowing how complex the illustration is likely to be. If necessary give hypothetical details, so that some estimate of cost can be made.

2.2 *Marking the typescript for an estimate*

See that the typescript is complete: check the folio numbering and also any other numbering schemes such as sections, tables, equations, figures and plates. The folios should be numbered in one sequence (see p. 28), though the preliminary pages may be numbered separately. As you will have to provide complete copy for the preliminary pages at some stage, it is probably worth doing so now (see chapter 7).

Write 'fresh page' or 'right-hand page' at the top of the appropriate folios, including those for preliminary matter, bibliography, etc. Write 'verso blank' on half-titles to parts.

Code the subheadings (see above and section 9.3). If the author wants space left between sections that have no headings, mark these 'space' or use a space mark (see p. 68).

If passages such as long quotations, which are to be distinguished typographically in the printed book, are not clearly distinguished in the typescript, identify them by a pencil line in the margin, so that the printer can estimate the cost accurately.

If the tables are not typed on separate sheets, it may be helpful to identify them and their notes (see p. 158).

Footnotes need not be marked if they are clear in the typescript. See that the endnotes are conveniently placed for the reader (see p. 156).

Illustrations (see chapter 4)

Originals for line drawings. The illustrations should be separated from the text, by photocopying if necessary, though it is not worth copying folios containing things that may not need artwork. If the author's roughs will not be clear enough for a draughtsman to follow, ask for better ones. See that the figures are identified by author's name, short book title and figure number; unnumbered figures can be identified by the folio number, plus 'top', 'middle', etc., if necessary. Give some information about the length of the captions if a list is not yet available. Mark the approximate position of the illustrations in the margin of the typescript, if you can do this without first reading the text; if you cannot, say which chapter the figures belong to. If the author is likely to need more than a few days to check the artwork, warn the production department.

Originals for half-tones. It is essential that photographs are treated with the utmost care, as any marks may reproduce. They should be handled as little as possible and never folded; keep them between pieces of stiff card a little larger than the prints, so that the corners do not become dog-eared. Do not use paperclips or mark the face of the prints; any marking on the back should be done very lightly, with a soft pencil or china marker.

Each print should be labelled with the author's name, short book title, and illustration number. This information is best typed or written on a slip of paper which is then attached to the back of the photograph with a little rubber solution (e.g. Cow gum) – not paste, which may cause the illustration to buckle. The top of the picture should be identified if there is any possibility of confusion, as there may be with aerial photographs or electron micrographs.

Give some information about the length of the captions if a list is not yet available. Unless the half-tones are to be printed separately, mark their approximate position in the margin of the typescript, if you can do this without reading the text.

Revised estimate

If the typescript is returned to the printer for a revised estimate (e.g. on

13

a different format or pattern) and you can definitely say that the copy has not changed since the last estimate, or alternatively how it has changed, it will save the printer's estimator from having to go through the whole typescript in detail again.

2.3 *Specimen pages*

Specimen pages are intended to show solutions to all the general typographical problems that the printers will meet in the book. They may consist of as little as one page to show small, recurring problems such as those in a dictionary, or as many as eight for an exceptionally varied and complicated book. Four pages should usually be enough, because parts of two or more folios may be combined on one page.

The specimen should show a full page including headline and page number, a chapter opening, all the grades of subheading, footnotes or endnotes, and long quotations (or other passages distinguished from the main text). Do not include a table unless they are an important feature of the book or unless the specimen is to be used as a guide for authors. There is no need to show a problem that occurs only once; this, with its folio reference, can be mentioned to the designer, who can mark up the relevant part of the typescript accordingly.

Choose folios which show the recurrent problems, and flag or photocopy them, listing the items to be included on each specimen page, and giving the wording for the headline and the page number to be set. (It is quite convenient to use the folio number, changing it to odd or even as necessary to make it suitable for a right-hand or left-hand page, so that one can easily refer back to that folio.) As a rough guide, allow two folios of double-spaced quarto or A4 typescript for each page of the specimen, unless you are compressing an extravagant typescript layout, perhaps into double-column small type.

On the chosen folios mark up spelling, capitalization, punctuation, abbreviations, etc., in the editorial style you propose to follow in the book.

Illustrations are not often included in specimen pages; but if there is some problem of sizing or of style (say the use of a second colour) it is worth a delay at this stage in order to save time and money later.

Incomplete typescripts. Specimens based on small parts of the book may turn out to be unsatisfactory unless they are well planned and prepared early enough to be used as a model by the author: a sample, particularly of a multi-author work, is often not typical, and illustrations that are not yet available may have some influence on the page size. Find out whether there are likely to be more kinds of subheading, more complicated mathematics, etc., in the rest of the book, and what the illustrations will be like. The more the designer can see the better, so three sample chapters and a few illustrations are better than one of each; and give what information you can about what is still to come.

Specimen for a series. Find out how typical the present book is: whether others are likely to contain more mathematics, subheadings, Greek, complicated tables, diacritical marks, etc., and pass this information on to the designer.

When the specimen is set, and you have discussed it with the designer, send the author his copy of the specimen, explaining any specific problems, and the reason for any departure from his own layout. If there are small amendments to the specimen, it is sufficient to mark these on your own reference copy and on the copy that will go to the printer with the copy-edited typescript. If larger amendments are needed, a revised specimen will probably be necessary.

15

3
Preparing the typescript for setting

If a typographical specification has not yet been written, you may need to brief the designer (section 2.1). See that the specification covers all the material that needs to be distinguished typographically. It will say what setting method is to be used, and the production department will be able to tell you of any consequent limitations. For example, unless the book is being set in Monotype, footnotes should be numbered in one sequence through each chapter. Similarly if it is to be typewriter-set, there will be no small capitals and it may be expensive to use italic.

If the book has already been sent to a printer for estimate, and he has provided a list of special sorts, look through it before he is given permission to order the sorts, to see that he has interpreted the author's intentions correctly. If the list includes some characters that you think could be avoided, ask the author as soon as possible. The sorts may take several weeks to obtain, and may delay the book if not ordered before the book is sent for setting.

If the book needs retyping, consider whether this should be done before or after copy-editing. Some marking (e.g. of small capitals) will have to be done after the retyping; but if the typescript is poorly written or inconsistent, the necessary changes would obviously be better carried out before the book is retyped. If the typing is to be done first, the typist may be able to carry out some straightforward, recurrent changes without your marking them: she could, for example, change double to single quotes or punctuate the bibliographical references according to your house style. When the typing has been done, send the author a copy to check.

3.1 *Writing to the author*

When the typescript first reaches you – perhaps before it is sent to a printer for an estimate – you should look for general points to raise with the author. These may include points where your own house style differs from the author's, or a suggested system to replace his own inconsistent practice. Not all authors want to be bothered with such things as -ize or -ise spellings; but even authors who are very inconsistent in their typescripts may care a good deal about such things as capitalization; and minimal punctuation may be just as intentional as punctuation according to the rules. If authors are not consulted about changes at typescript stage, they are likely to object when they see them in the proof, and to insist that their original system should be reinstated.

Write as early as you can about general points, so that you may receive the author's reply before you start going through the typescript in detail. The kinds of thing you may decide to mention are:

parts and chapters: no separate leaf for part headings; renumbering chapters in arabic

subheadings, if the system is overcomplicated or confusing

headlines: what is to be used (e.g. chapter title on the left, section title on the right); ask the author for shortened forms if necessary

notes: whether the footnotes are to be numbered through each chapter or afresh on each page; the fact that the notes will be endnotes, not footnotes; the position of endnotes if the author has placed them where the reader will not be able to turn to them easily

quotations: the use of single quotes; whether (and how) long quotations will be distinguished; the use of square brackets and three-point ellipses (see section 11.1)

tables: the need to number long ones because they will not be placed exactly where they are in the typescript (see section 9.5)

illustrations: where any half-tones will be placed

bibliographical references: the content and form of references in the text or notes; the organization of the bibliography

cross-references, if the author has too many or uses forms such as *v. inf.*

spelling, capitalization, accents, hyphens, form of possessive (see section 6.12)

italic

numbers: use of words or figures; elision of pairs; comma or space for thousands

dates

abbreviations: inclusion of full points

scientific nomenclature and terminology, displayed formulae, etc.

You may have a printed sheet which outlines your house style.

Explain why you have had to depart from the author's own system; and avoid the use of jargon such as 'copy', or abbreviations such as 'a/w', 'p/up', 's/s', or 'ts'.

As you go through the typescript in detail you will find small points not covered in your general letter. It is not necessary to tell the author about every change you make, but you should give him one or two examples of every *kind* of change, so that he can ask to see the typescript after copy-editing if he is uneasy. Warn him that when he receives proofs he should not alter anything except printer's errors, and ask him to let you have any late corrections of his own now.

If you send the typescript to the author after it has been copy-edited, ask him to mark small alterations in a distinctive colour, to retype large ones and list the folios affected, so that you can easily check the new material for consistency with the rest.

Record any decisions or agreements with the author on general points. Someone else may need this information when you are on holiday or ill, and it will be difficult for him if most of the information is in your head, or if any letters have not been filed. Similarly record anything received from or sent to the author. Remember too that other departments may need a note of the author's changes of address.

3.2 *How much copy-editing to do*

You may not yourself be responsible for the general content, organization and style of the book; for picking up any errors of fact or potentially libellous passages; or for obtaining permission to reproduce quotations, illustrations, etc. However, even if all this should have been done by the time you receive the typescript, it is worth looking out for these things yourself, for out-of-date material, parochialisms and problems of safety (see sections 6.10 and 6.15). Your role is to try to ensure that neither author nor publisher has second thoughts at proof stage.

How far one should correct an author's style is a matter of judgement: it will depend on the author's reactions to one's proposals, and on the level at which the book is written, though of course one must always change misleading, ambiguous or obscure English and the misuse of words.

As the copy-editing problems vary from book to book, it is impossible to list all the things you should do. A checklist of the most obvious things appears as appendix 1, but you will want to modify the list to suit the kinds of book you work on. To avoid too much repetition, the present chapter contains only brief references to things treated in more detail elsewhere in the book.

You must provide copy that the printer can follow without misunderstanding or delay. The typescript must therefore be complete, legible and unambiguous; passages to be distinguished typographically must be identified, and all subheadings coded; fresh pages and rectos, and the position of all text illustrations (and tables where necessary), must be marked; roughs for any line drawings must be intelligible to the draughtsman; and so on. All these things must always be done, however rushed the book is. See section 3.4.

For the reader's sake you should see that the book is well organized, clear and consistent (see section 3.5). How much you do will depend on the length of time available, the level at which the book is written, and whether your firm has a house style which is implemented in every book. Having such a style means fewer decisions for the individual copy-editor. However, the more marking there is to do, the more likelihood there is that something will be missed and that the book will be inconsistent; and there is nothing that annoys an author more than having an inconsistent system substituted for his own – whether his own was inconsistent or not. If your firm does not have a rigid house style, it is usually easier and safer to implement consistently the author's own conventions.

What can be left to the printer's copy-preparer

The copy-preparer's job is to translate the designer's typographical specification into instructions written throughout the typescript. He, or the publisher's designer, will mark the layout of individual tables and other displayed material; but it is for you to ensure that the author's meaning is clear, for example which columns in a table should share a joint heading.

The printer may also be able to do some copy-editing: that is, to impose a predetermined style on such things as spelling, capitalization, abbreviations and contractions, dates, numerals and italicization, and to

19

correct straightforward errors in syntax and punctuation. The tasks should usually be limited to the fairly obvious and mechanical because of the way in which many printers' copy-preparers have to work.

They will almost certainly have to pass part of the typescript on before they have been through the whole of it; and because different sizes of type have to be set separately, they may well have to pass on the footnotes or endnotes before they have looked at the text; so they cannot be expected to devise suitable conventions for the book. If your house rules do not cover all the points that need marking, give specific instructions. A printer's copy-preparer may well be preparing small batches of three or four typescripts in the same day, in order to keep three or four keyboard operators busy; so he cannot be expected to remember everything that has gone before, or to implement a system of capitalization that depends on the sense in which the author uses a particular word. He is not in contact with the author, and if he has to ask questions the book may be delayed; so you must be sure the typescript is unambiguous and complete, for example that all the notes have indicators in the text and that all the bibliographical references are complete and consistent in content.

It is a waste of time and money for the publisher and printer to do the same work; so the publisher must make it clear how much he wants the printer to do. Some publishers send their printers three clearly identified categories of typescript: fully copy-edited; partially copy-edited and accompanied by a list of specific instructions as to what still remains to be done; not copy-edited and to be prepared by the printer's copy-preparer in accordance with the publisher's house style.

Even if you do not want the printer to do any copy-editing, his readers in particular will find it useful to have a note of any particular style points for that book, especially if you have decided to retain some unusual conventions. Fig. 3.1 shows a sample style sheet.

3.3 *The typescript and how to mark it*

If the keyboard operator is to work quickly and economically, he must be able to read straight down each sheet of typescript: flaps of paper will hide what is underneath; additions written up the margin or on the back will mean that he has to turn the sheet to read them; instructions

STYLE CHECKLIST

N.B. This is designed to summarise how the subeditor <u>has marked up</u> the typescript, and is for the reader's reference only. Any <u>instructions</u> will be headed 'Instructions for printer' and listed on the back of this sheet or on a separate attached sheet.

<u>Author and title</u>: White, Euripides

<u>Spelling</u> (notes on spelling, possessives etc. do not apply to quoted matter):

 English/~~American~~, ~~ise~~/ize, ~~connection~~/connexion, ~~inquiry~~/enquiry, judgement/~~judgment~~, ~~co-ordinate~~/coordinate, focused/~~focussed~~, ~~elite/élite~~, role/~~rôle~~, regime/~~régime~~, ~~artefact/artifact, disc/disk, formulae/formulas~~, ~~naive~~/naïve, ~~premiss/premise~~

<u>Accents</u>/~~no accents~~ on capitals. ~~Ligatures~~/no ~~æ~~, œ ligatures in French

<u>Possessives</u>: Menelaus' Euripides' but Zeus's Paris's

<u>Abbreviations</u>: per cent/~~%~~ U.S.A. etc. full/~~small~~ caps with/~~without~~ points

<u>Inverted commas</u>: single used except for extracts set in small type (which have none) and quotations within 'single-quoted' passages (which have double). Punctuation follows closing inverted comma except for question mark or exclamation mark belonging to the quotation, or a full stop if the quotation is or ends with a grammatically complete sentence beginning with a capital.

<u>Dates</u>: 1 May 1968; 1860s; nineteenth century, nineteenth-century (adj.), thirties

<u>Cross-references</u> to specific figs, plates, chapters, tables, sections, equations: (e.g. Fig. 1. §5.2) Chapter 5, pages 1-6

<u>Numbers</u>: Pairs of numbers (but not units) elided e.g. 300-1 but 310-11

<u>Thousands</u>: ~~1200~~/1,200, ~~12 000~~/12,000 ~~Decimal point: low/raised~~

~~Footnotes: keyed by superscript figure/symbol: to be numbered by chapter/page~~

<u>Endnotes</u> (at end of text/~~each chapter~~) keyed by superscript figure, numbered by chapter

<u>Bibliographical references</u>: (e.g. use of vol., p., arabic/roman small caps for vol. nos.)
Homer, Iliad XXIV.17   Thucydides III.7-11   Poetics 54a16
Kitto, Greek Tragedy (Methuen 1950) 230
Smith, 'The ironic structure of Alcestis', Phoenix XIV (1960) 127-45
NB Play titles: The Women of Troy but in precise refs Women of Troy 640
Any peculiarities of <u>capitalisation, hyphenation, italics</u>, etc. ~~are listed on attached sheet or back of this sheet.~~
Caps. for characters' titles: Messenger, Slave, Nurse

<u>Subeditor's name</u>   <u>date</u>

Fig. 3.1 Style sheet.

for transposing paragraphs on different folios will also delay him. It is well worth spending some time retyping where necessary, and re-assembling the text in the right order. An occasional addition is acceptable when headed 'Insert at X on fo. 000', typed on a *full-size* sheet following the relevant folio and keyed into the text by a marginal note 'X insert from fo. 000a'; if the author has used some half sheets, paste them on to full-size sheets, or they may be overlooked. If you need to fasten some new material over the lines it replaces, it is best to use paste or sticky tape, rather than pins or staples. However, it is difficult to write on most kinds of sticky tape, so do not cover any wording with it.

The printer will not read the back of any sheet unless instructed to.

See that all handwritten material – especially proper names, un-familiar words and potentially ambiguous letters – is legible. Identify l and 1, capital O and zero, k and kappa, minus, en rule and em rule, x and multiplication sign, multiplication point and decimal point, etc. Typists sometimes use '11' to mean 'lines', 'eleven' or even 'roman two'. See section 13.2 for possible ambiguities in mathematics and science books.

How to mark the typescript

Whatever you decide to mark must be marked throughout. It is not enough to mark the first few instances, because the book may be set by more than one keyboard operator, and the footnotes and small type may be set before the text type. Nor should your marking be spasmodic (as a reminder): if it is, the printer will not know whether you intend a distinction between the cases you have marked and those you have not, and he may follow copy.

Use the signs in British Standard 5261, *Copy preparation and proof correction*. Some of these are given on pp. 66–9.

The following should be marked in the left-hand margin:

'fresh page' or 'right-hand page'

pencil letters in squares, to code subheadings

any vertical lines to indicate passages to be set in a different type size; see that the beginning and end of such passages are absolutely clear, for example if a long quotation begins or ends in the middle of a line in the typescript

22

35

unfamiliar words and potentially ambiguous letters is legible.
ldentify 1 and l, capital O and zero. k and kappa, minus, en rule
and em rule, x and multiplication sign, multiplication point and
decimal point, etc.   Typists sometimes use '11' to mean 'lines',
'eleven' or even 'roman two'.   See section 13.2 for possible
ambiguities in mathematics and science books.

B How to mark the typescript

Whatever you decide to mark must be marked throughout.   It
is not enough to mark the first few instances, because the book
may be set by more than one keyboard operator, and the footnotes
and small type may be set before the text type.   Nor should your
marking be spasmodic (as a reminder): if it is, the printer will
not know whether you intend a distinction between the cases you
have marked and those you have not, and he may follow copy.

Use the signs in British standard 1219, Proof correction
and copy preparation.   Some of these are given on p. 5.4.
5261, Copy preparation and Proof correction, pp. 000-00.

The following should be marked in the left-hand margin:
'fresh page' or 'right-hand page'
ringed pencil letters or numbers used to code subheadings in squares,
any vertical lines to indicate passages to be set in a
different type size; see that the beginning and end of
such passages are absolutely clear, for example if a long
quotation to be set in small type begins or ends in the
middle of the line in the typescript
instructions for the placing of text illustrations (and
tables where necessary) and indication of space before an
unheaded section.

All instructions should be ringed to show that the words

Fig. 3.2   Page of corrected typescript.

23

instructions for the placing of text illustrations (and tables where necessary) and indication of space before an unheaded section. All instructions should be ringed, to show that the words are not to be set

the identification of an ambiguous letter (capital O/zero, en rule/em rule/minus/hyphen, multiplication/decimal point, etc.) if there is no room to do so clearly above the letter, or if the identification applies throughout the folio

'n.p.' to indicate a new paragraph where this is not clear in the typescript.

All other marks should be between the lines of the typescript if there is room to make them clearly. Unlike the compositor making the proof corrections, who needs to have his attention drawn to any change, the keyboard operator is going to read every word of the typescript; and if a correction is marked in the margin of a typescript he is going to have to look at the word concerned, then at the margin and then back to the word, which will slow him down.

Every note written on the typescript will be read by everyone who handles it, so keep instructions to a minimum, and erase or cross out any comments that the printer need not read. If you have to leave queries for the author on the typescript, head them 'Author' and ring them.

The following do not need a marginal instruction:

deletion: just delete the letter or word, but make sure it is clear exactly how much is to be deleted. Use a vertical line to delete a single letter; use a horizontal line to delete something longer, with a vertical line at each end if there is likely to be any doubt whether, for example, the punctuation at either end is to be deleted:

the world, ~~however~~ if

If you wish to retain the punctuation that follows a deleted phrase, rewrite it immediately after the word it should follow; otherwise the keyboard operator will have tapped a word space before he sees it (see Fig. 3.2). If you delete a hyphen in the middle of a word, make it clear whether you want the word to be closed up or printed as two words.

transposition: use ⊔⊓

italic: use a single underline

bold: use a wavy underline

capital: use a treble underline

small capital: use a double underline

lower-case letter: put a diagonal line through the top of the capital letter. If several letters or words are to be made lower-case ring them and write 'l.c.' by the ring

cancellation of underlining: whiting-out is the clearest way

a stet mark below an unusual spelling or an end-of-line hyphen

ae, oe ligatures: put ⌒ over the pair of letters

close up: use ⊃

no space between paragraphs, where an extra line has (occasionally) been left in the typescript: use vertical 'close-up' mark

no space to be left where there is extra space in typescript: use wavy horizontal line to fill up a line, a vertical or diagonal line to fill up a page

not fresh line, not new paragraph: use ⌒ . If several lines are to be run on, or there is very little space between the lines, you may omit the horizontal line joining the curve at either end:

England,⌒
⌐Ireland,⌐
⌐Scotland

space, e.g. in those items listed on p. 87: if they are closed up in the typescript, put Y where the space is to be inserted

en rules: write 'en' or 'N' above the dash; if the rule is to be spaced (as for a parenthetical dash) put Y either side if the dash is closed up in the typescript; if the dash is to be unspaced, use 'close-up' mark if spaced in the typescript. Similarly for em rules.

For the marking of mathematics see section 13.2.

Make sure that your marking is unambiguous. When changing double to single quotes, use a *vertical* line; a diagonal one may touch the other inverted comma and lead the keyboard operator to think you are deleting the quotes altogether. If you want to cancel an underlining for italic, white it out, or put two or three short lines through it, not a wavy line which may look like an instruction for bold. If you do want to change a straight underlining to a wavy one, do not put a wavy line above or below the straight one, or it will look as though you want bold italic; white-out or cancel the straight one.

When you white something out, be careful not to obliterate descenders

25

in the line above; if you leave the patch to dry, do remember to complete it. Always reread any sentence you have altered, to make sure that the right amount has been deleted or added and that it is correctly punctuated.

There is one exception to the rule that the typescript should be marked throughout: it is helpful to the keyboard operator if you put a stet mark below the first occurrence (in each type size and in the preliminary pages) of an alternative spelling, to show that this is the one you are using. For the same reason, stet American and all unusual spellings that are to be retained. In a book that contains unusual spellings, tell the printer to follow copy, and make sure you have corrected typing errors (if you yourself can distinguish them).

If you add letters between two foreign words, make it clear whether the added letters are a separate word or should be joined to the preceding or following word, by using close-up or space marks.

parcere subjectis et bellare superbos

Where two additions or substitutions fall close together, with only a word or two unchanged between them, it is easier for the keyboard operator if the whole thing is written above the line so that he does not have to look down to the line to see the unchanged words and then up again.

For good typesetters it is enough to stet the end-of-line hyphens that are to be retained even when the word is not broken; for other type-setters it would be wise to mark each hyphen to be retained or to be deleted and closed up.

En rules should be identified where a hyphen is not an acceptable alternative.

Marking up photocopies of printed material
There is less room between the lines, so you may need to use more marginal marks, but keep them to a minimum. The main differences from marking typescript are:

roman: ring the italic word and write 'rom' in margin

italic: if the word is already in italic, do not mark it; if it is not, under-line it

bold: as for italic

delete the original headlines and page numbers unless they are to be reproduced exactly as they are

3.4 *Complete, self-explanatory copy for the printer*

If there is time, wait to start detailed copy-editing until the typescript is complete. A missing chapter often arrives much later than the promised date, so that the copy-editor has to refresh his memory as to detailed points of style; and if the bibliography has not yet arrived, the bibliographical references in the text or notes cannot easily be checked.

Similarly, the printer can work more quickly and efficiently if he receives the whole book at once. He should at the very least receive everything that will appear in the text from the beginning of the first chapter to the end of the last one, and preferably also any appendixes and bibliography. If some preliminary matter, such as a foreword, cannot be provided before the book goes for setting, and its exact length is not known, warn the production department and list that item as 'to come'.

Line drawings may reach the printer later if they are being drawn by a freelance draughtsman. Send the figures for drawing before you finish the text, if you can; and warn the production department if the author is likely to take more than a few days to check the drawings. Half-tones may, if it is unavoidable, be sent later.

Any list containing a large number of page references – an index, a table of cases or a list of references doubling as an author index – should not be sent for setting until the author has added the final page numbers; if the author sends such lists with his typescript, return them to him when you have finished copy-editing. On the other hand, an index which refers to item numbers rather than page numbers should be sent for setting with the text.

Checking for completeness

You may be the first person to look at the typescript and illustrations closely enough to make sure that nothing is missing. Check the folio numbering and also any other numbering schemes such as sections, tables, equations, text figures and plates: gaps in the sequence are a warning that part of the typescript may be missing, or that the author has cut the text and has not tidied up afterwards. You should provide those things that the author may not have thought of: *complete* copy for the preliminary pages including half-title and verso of the title page, lists of captions for the illustrations, and a list of headlines if short forms are to be used.

Numbering systems

The folios should be numbered in one sequence, not by chapter, so that the printer can see at once where a folio belongs, though the preliminary pages may be lettered or numbered in roman. If a folio is added after 166, 166 should become 166a and 165 should carry a note '166a–b follow'; if 165–6 have been replaced by a single folio, this should be numbered 165–6, so that it will be obvious whether or not a folio is missing. If there are many inserted folios, or if the chapters or papers are numbered separately, it is best to renumber the whole typescript.

Avoid the use of roman numerals as far as possible, except where an author has used them for volume numbers in references to other books and journals. If you renumber chapters etc. in arabic, remember to change the numbers not only in the headings but in the contents list and in cross-references.

Chapters are better numbered in one sequence rather than separately in each part, so that cross-references can consist of a chapter number only. Section numbers may include the chapter number:

> chapter 6
> section 6.1 (first section in chapter 6)
> subsection 6.1.3 (third subsection in section 6.1)

Some authors number introductory sections 0, so that the introductory section in chapter 6 would be 6.0. If sections are distinguished from sub-sections by their number, it is not necessary to distinguish their headings typographically. If there are many cross-references to section numbers, the chapter and section numbers should be included in the headlines.

If an author numbers (or letters) the points in his argument and refers to them, make sure he refers to them by the right number and that there are no intervening numbered sequences that might be confused with them. If he does not refer to the points often, you may want to persuade him to remove the numbers: they may just be remains of the scaffolding on which he constructed the book.

See that numbered paragraphs are laid out consistently, for example with normal paragraph indention or hanging indention (first line full out, turnover lines indented, as on p. 187 of this book). If some of the numbers cover more than one paragraph, and it is essential to show where the last numbered point ends, hanging indention is the only clear way.

Preliminary pages (see chapter 7)

Provide the complete wording, including that for the half-title and title-page verso. Check the contents list against the text and see that any material not yet available, such as an index, is included in the list. Check any lists of illustrations or tables against the captions or headings respectively.

Headlines (see section 9.2)

If short forms are to be used, provide a typewritten list giving the wording for each headline, with the correct capitalization, spelling and punctuation; make sure that the headline is short enough to fit across the top of the page. The list should be headed by the author's name and short book title, and may be divided into columns. For example:

left-hand	*right-hand*
title of part 1	title of chapter 1
	title of chapter 2
title of part 2	title of chapter 3 (first chapter in part 2)

If you do not provide a list, tell the printer whether upper- and lower-case headlines should have an initial capital for all main words or only for the first word and any proper names.

Fresh pages

Put 'fresh page' or 'right-hand page' (or 'fresh recto') at the top of folios where appropriate, including those for preliminary matter, bibliography, etc. A general note saying whether chapters start fresh pages or fresh rectos, or run on, is also useful to the printer.

Parts. The chapters may be grouped into parts. Each part may have a half-title, that is, a right-hand page containing just the part number and title, and usually backed by a blank left-hand page; the first chapter heading in that part is placed at the head of the next right-hand page. There is occasionally an introductory note, which may be placed immediately below the part heading or on the verso; or a map may be placed on the verso; but the first chapter should not start there. If the part heading is to occupy a separate leaf, it should be on a separate folio in the typescript, included in the folio numbering and marked 'right-hand page', with 'verso blank' at the foot.

If the parts have half-titles, the appendixes should have one too, to show that they are not just appendixes to the final part; but there is no need for a joint or separate half-title for the bibliography and index – or to mention them on the half-title to the appendixes – because there is no risk that the reader will think that they do not refer to the whole book.

To save space, the part may just start on a fresh page, with the first chapter starting lower down the same page. See that the wording for the part heading is written above the chapter heading; or, if it is given on a separate folio, make clear to the printer that it is not to occupy a separate page. The folio should be labelled 'fresh page' (or 'right-hand page' if it is decided to start all parts on a right-hand page).

Chapters. The first chapter (or introduction) always starts on a right-hand page. Later chapters may start on a fresh page, or may run on, separated from the preceding chapter only by a space. If there are to be off-prints of individual chapters, the chapters may start on a right-hand page.

Appendixes. The first appendix to a book always starts on a fresh page; the others may run on from the first or start on fresh pages; it depends on their length and importance. Appendixes to chapters run on at the end of the chapter.

Subheadings

Subheadings should be coded to show their place in the hierarchy (see section 9.3). Do not code merely by the way the subheadings are typed; see that the system works logically.

Spaces

The designer or the printer's copy-preparer will, where necessary, mark the space wanted above and below headings, tables and other displayed material, but if you want the printer to leave space elsewhere you must make this clear.

Space between unheaded sections. Some typists are erratic about the amount of space they leave between paragraphs, and the printer may not know whether the extra space is intentional. If the author wants extra space, write 'space' or put a space sign in the margin. Some publishers place an asterisk in the space: this shows up more clearly than space alone if the section ends at the foot of the page or if the page already has spaces above and below displayed quotations, tables or illustrations.

Similarly a retyped passage may end half-way down the folio; and the printer needs to know that this space does not indicate the end of a section and therefore extra space: draw a vertical or diagonal line across the empty space to show the printer that the space has no significance; but do not do this at the end of a chapter if chapters start fresh pages.

Space within paragraphs. Some authors white-out unwanted words on a master copy of the typescript, and then photocopy it; and on the photocopy the reason for the blanks is not apparent. If the author's revision has resulted in large blank patches, put a pencil line through these so that the printer does not think that they have been left for extra material to be inserted at proof stage.

Footnotes and endnotes (see section 9.4)

See that every note has an indicator in the text, and vice versa. It is very important that this should be got right at the typescript stage, and essential if the first proof is to be paged or if the notes are numbered in one series through each chapter. If the printer finds that a note or its indicator is missing when he is dividing the book into pages, he will have to stop work and wait until you can tell him the correct position for the text indicator or obtain the missing footnote from the author. Alternatively the printer can guess where to put the indicator or how much space to leave for the footnote; but guessing can lead to expensive re-paging at proof stage.

If the notes are to be numbered in a continuous sequence through each chapter, see that there are no gaps or additions (such as 10a) in the numbering.

Move note indicators to follow punctuation, and preferably to the end of the sentence or a break in the sense, unless the reference is to a specific word. See whether very long footnotes, or parts of them, could be incorporated in the text or an appendix.

It helps the printer if you tell him, on the first folio of the typescript, where footnotes can be found, unless, of course, they are typed at the foot of the relevant folio of text. Some authors put them at the end of each chapter, some at the end of the typescript; if they are at the end of each chapter, give the folio number for the relevant notes on the first folio of each chapter.

Tables (see section 9.5)

If the tables are on separate sheets, mark their position in the margin of the text; if they are not on separate sheets it may be helpful to show their exact extent (see p. 158); and those over four or five lines should probably be numbered. See that the structure of each table is clear.

Other passages to be distinguished typographically

See that all such passages in the text and appendixes are clearly identified, and that it is obvious whether the sentence immediately following should start at the margin or be indented. If whole passages such as long quotations are to be indented, make sure this is clear in the typescript.

If definitions, proofs, etc., are not to be distinguished by being set in small type or italic, the end of each one should be indicated in some way; consult the designer about a suitable device. Space before and after each definition etc. may break up the text too much.

Cross-references (see section 6.3)

Check all cross-references to illustrations, sections, tables and equations, etc. If the author has given folio numbers in his cross-references to other pages, change the digits to zeros, to remind him to fill in the page number at proof stage. Although you cannot tell exactly how many digits will be needed, try to see that a reasonable amount of space will be left by the printer; for example 'see pp. oo' implies more than one page, in which case 'see pp. ooo–oo' would be better.

3.5 *A well organized and consistent book for the reader*

Look at the general organization. Are subheadings and numbered paragraphs used with restraint? If there are too many they will confuse instead of helping. Are some of the illustrations unnecessary; would a map or glossary be helpful? Would tabulated material be better in the form of a graph, or vice versa; would certain passages of running text be better tabulated, or vice versa? Would a particular section of the text be better as an appendix, or vice versa? In a book containing two or more interrelated parts, such as a catalogue with a separate section of illustrations, see that the system of cross-references is adequate.

All abbreviations that may not be familiar to the reader should be explained in a list in the preliminary pages or the first time they occur; a list is more helpful if the abbreviations appear only in footnotes or only rarely in the text.

Bibliographical references in the text and notes should be consistent and full enough to lead the reader unerringly to the right item in the bibliography; if there are many references in the text or notes, the bibliography should not be broken up into several sections through which the reader will have to search to find the book he is looking for. See chapter 10.

Consistency

If the author is inconsistent in matters of detail, the reader or reviewer may begin to doubt the facts he gives and the inferences he draws. In some cases inconsistency may lead to ambiguity: if the author capitalizes a word inconsistently the reader may think some distinction is intended. Watch out for names as well as other words, especially those that have alternative spellings, e.g. Ann(e), Mackintosh or McIntosh. Novelists sometimes change the names of their characters and do not notice the one or two instances they have left unchanged; in a published novel I read recently, the author had given the two boys names very similar to her own sons' names, and in one case her son's own name appeared. Colour of hair and eyes, ages and time spans, also need checking in novels; for example:

At ten, Anne was a quiet child, whose brown eyes looked at you thoughtfully.
   She first caught sight of Neil seven years later...
   There was a faraway look in Ann's blue eyes. She was thinking of herself at sixteen, watching Neil as he...

Few readers notice whether dates are written '10th August, 1974' or '10 August 1974', but inconsistency in style will distract their attention from what the author is saying – even though they may not be conscious of what has distracted them.

The easiest way to ensure consistency is to make a list, as you go through the typescript, of the author's general style – spelling, capitalization, hyphens, italic – and unusual proper names, with the folio number of first occurrence (or every occurrence if you think you may need to change the style later).

Remember that quotations and book or article titles should *not* be made consistent in spelling etc. with the rest of the book.

The things which should be consistent are:

spelling (see section 6.13): watch out particularly for alternative spellings such as -ize or -ise, Basel and Basle; also anglicization of personal and place names

accents, particularly on semi-anglicized words such as regime, role, elite, and on transliterated words

hyphenation/one word/two words, not only in ordinary words but also
in such place names as Hong Kong, Cape Town

capitalization (see section 6.2)

italic, especially for semi-anglicized words or those very familiar to the
author, e.g. Indian terms in a book on India. See section 6.6

abbreviations, particularly the use of full points in groups of capitals
(see section 6.1)

dates (see section 6.4)

units of measurement (see sections 6.7 and 13.3)

numbers, especially elision of pairs of numbers, and the use of words or
figures (see section 6.9)

single (or double) quotes (see section 11.1)

bibliographical references (see chapter 10)

cross-references (see section 6.3)

singular or plural verb after group nouns such as 'government'

'it'/'she' referring to countries

Some publishers have a house style for all these things; others follow
the author's own system, provided it is sensible and consistent. Even
the latter group are likely to have a preferred style for some or all of the
following; in each case I think the simplest form is the best:

dates: 1 May 1973, 1970s (see section 6.4)

elision of pairs of numbers (see section 6.9)

omission of points after contractions containing the last letter of the
singular (e.g. Dr, St, Ltd) and after abbreviated units of measurement (e.g. mm, lb). Note that the plural of these units is the same as
the singular, viz. 5 mm, not 5 mms

single quotes, except in books where a distinction between single and
double is needed (see section 11.1)

placing of punctuation in relation to closing quotes (see section 11.1)

three-point ellipses to indicate an omission (see section 11.1)

low decimal point (as recommended by the Royal Society)

SI units in science and mathematics books

thousands indicated either by space in numbers over 9999 (in science and
mathematics books) or by comma in numbers over 999 (or over 9999)

Apart from consistency of convention within the text, you should see

34

that the following are consistent. The contents list, lists of figures, plates, tables, etc., must tally in wording, numbering (preferably arabic), spelling, capitalization and hyphenation with the chapter headings, sub-headings, captions, etc., that they refer to, though they may be given in a shorter form. The list of abbreviations should tally with the text, for example in capitalization, italicization, and inclusion of points.

You should check quotations repeated within the book (e.g. in comments on phrases from a longer quotation) and spot-check other quotations if the source is available.

You should also check the alphabetical order of the list of abbreviations, bibliography, glossary, etc.

3.6 *Copyright permissions and acknowledgements*

Under his contract, the author is usually required to obtain permission for the use of any copyright material in his work and to pay for it. In complex cases such as an anthology, however, the publisher often does this work for the author; and in any event the publisher should see to it that this often rather onerous work is done properly: that there is a proper clearance of the desired rights, enshrined in a businesslike way in an exchange of letters. All permissions correspondence should be lodged with the publisher, so that, when you are going through the typescript and illustrations, you can make sure that all permissions have been cleared and that acknowledgements are in the form required by the copyright owner.

What requires permission

In the United Kingdom, if a work is published during the author's lifetime, copyright subsists until fifty years from the end of the calendar year of the author's death. If a work is not published during the author's lifetime, copyright subsists until fifty years from the end of the calendar year in which it was first published. If a work is never published, it remains in copyright. Under the old US Copyright Act, US works were in copyright for a period of 28 years, renewable for a further 28 years. It is not always the case that a US copyright was renewed at the end of its first 28-year period, and it may be necessary to check this. The new US Copyright Act of 1976, which covers all works created on or after the beginning of 1978, gives protection until fifty years after the death of the (last) author. Other countries have different copyright periods: a useful guide to these will be found in *Copinger and Skone James on Copyright* (12th edn, London, Sweet and Maxwell, 1980).

Extracts. Both British and US law allow free use of copyright material in certain situations. In particular, UK law provides for such use where the material is not 'substantial', where one or other of the 'fair dealing' provisions apply, or where the material is of some brevity and to be included in a 'collection intended for the use of schools'. US law provides for free use in the case of what is called 'fair use'.

It is necessary to decide in each case whether or not permission need be gained. Sometimes the answer is clear, at least to the experienced eye. Often, the case is borderline, or may seem to be so because of some basic misapprehension of the nature of fair dealing. See Christopher Scarles's booklet *Copyright* (Cambridge University Press, 1980) for fuller treatment of this subject; but the following points should be made here.

In British law:

1. A *non-substantial part* of a work may be used without permission, but it must be said that in practice this freedom seems to be very rarely exercised owing to the general vagueness of the phrase ('substantiality' in this context meaning importance more than length).
2. The full wording of the fair dealing provision most directly relevant to publishing runs:

> No fair dealing with a literary, dramatic or musical work shall constitute an infringement of the copyright in the work if it is for purposes of criticism or review, whether of that work or of another work

and is thus limited in its application but not necessarily on length of quotation (as is often thought to be the case).

3. The full wording of the exception for collections for the use of schools is to be found in the UK Copyright Act (1956) and should be studied carefully by anyone involved in such works.

The fair use provision in the new US Copyright Act is wider in its scope than any exception in the UK Act, and again it is suggested that a copy of the Act be obtained and studied.

For anthologies, books of readings and other books that rely heavily on copyright material, permission has to be obtained for *all* material used (assuming it is still in copyright), however short the passage.

Music. A musical composition is protected in the same way as a literary work, and one would normally expect to have to ask for permission for any quotation from a score in copyright, no matter how small. Sometimes there are two copyrights involved – in the melody and the arrangement – so the fact that its composer has long been dead, or that it is from a traditional folk melody, does not necessarily mean that a quotation is out of copyright. Sometimes there are three copyrights: in the melody, in the arrangement and in the words.

Illustrations and tables. If drawings or photographs have not been made by the author or specially commissioned, and they are still in copyright, permission must be obtained unless they fall within the scope of the agreement between publishers belonging to the International Group of Scientific, Technical and Medical Publishers (STM). If an illustration is used on the cover, permission for that purpose is necessary even if permission has already been obtained for its use in the book.

If the basis of a map or table is a map or table originally appearing elsewhere, then permission should usually be sought, whatever the degree of modification. But clearly this rule needs a sensible interpretation in the case of maps: there is a great difference between copying the outline of South America from an atlas and using, in a modified form, somebody else's map of possible Roman settlements in Norfolk.

Crowd scenes excepted, if the author wishes to use a photograph of a living person (other than a photograph of a public figure used for its news or historical value), he should obtain that person's permission. In some photographs – for example those used in medical books – the person's identity should be disguised by a patch covering his eyes.

Acknowledgements

The sources of all in-copyright quotations (words or music), tables and illustrations should be given, whether or not it was necessary to obtain permission for their use. The law requires one to make 'sufficient acknowledgement' by giving author (composer etc.) and title.

In the normal run of events, fuller acknowledgement is given using any special wording provided by the copyright holder, so check the correspondence carefully; in some cases this correspondence may continue after the typescript has been sent to the printer, so check again at proof stage to see that no additions or changes are needed. Do not try to make the wording of American credit lines consistent: under earlier US law copyright can be lost entirely if the acknowledgement is not given correctly. If you do have to depart from the wording laid down by the American publisher, tell him why and give him the wording you propose to use: if you do not tell him, he may think that you are wilfully disregarding what he said, and he may be reluctant to grant you permission to use other copyright material in the future.

The acknowledgement must also be made *in the place* required by the copyright holder: he may say that the acknowledgement should be made immediately below the quotation or illustration, or on the copyright page (verso of the title page). This can sometimes cause difficulty if the instruction about wording and placing is not received until the book is in page proof; again, tell the copyright holder as soon as possible if you cannot do as he asks.

Unless all the acknowledgements are given in the text or on the copyright page, it is useful for the reader to have a complete list in the preliminary pages or at the end of the book, even if this means that some sources are given twice. Acknowledgements lists may be in alphabetical order of copyright owner or in numerical order of first (or each) illustration or page number for each copyright holder. If illustrations are identified by page number, a descriptive phrase will of course be needed as well if all the illustrations on one page were not obtained from one copyright holder; also such a list cannot be completed and sent for setting until the page numbers are known.

If the illustrations are the only copyright material, the acknowledgements may be included at the end of the relevant items in the list of illustrations – if there is one – instead.

In collections of papers acknowledgements may be in the first footnote of the appropriate paper, or in a small separate section at the end of it, so that they are included in offprints.

In science books acknowledgements for illustrations are given at the end of the caption, usually in the form of a short reference to the source – 'From Smith, 1960', or 'After Wilkins & Mayo, 1968' if the illustration is modified or adapted – provided that the full reference is given in the list of references *and the copyright holder has not asked for other wording*.

Other points

If the permission covers only one edition or only one printing, note this information where it will receive the attention of anyone dealing with a new edition or reprint of the book. The correspondence with the copyright holders should be kept where it can be consulted by the department dealing with permissions and foreign rights.

4

Illustrations

Printed illustrations are of two kinds: line and half-tone.

A *line* illustration is drawn in solid black ink, and can be included at any point in the text, whatever the printing method, subject only to the exigencies of page make-up. Line illustrations, and hence artwork, may be needed for some things that are not pictures, that is for things that cannot easily be set in type. These may include ringed or crossed-out letters or numbers, chemical formulae with rings or diagonals, structural diagrams in linguistics books, non-roman characters and genealogical tables. The ease with which such things can be typeset (or assembled from film) depends on the printing method and the printer's facilities; and it is essential to point them out to the designer at the earliest possible stage.

Half-tone reproduction is needed for illustrations such as photographs and wash drawings, which contain gradations of tone between black and white. This kind of illustration is photographed through a screen ruled with a fine grid that breaks the illustration into tiny black dots of various diameters to simulate the strength of tone. (An examination of a newspaper photograph through a magnifying glass will show this clearly.) There is inevitably some loss of definition, and an inadequate half-tone may not make a point as clearly as a diagram would.

As well as ordinary half-tones (with various screens) there are two other kinds which are more expensive but useful in certain cases. Cut-out half-tones may be made from photographs of objects such as statues, if the background is obtrusive; a cut-out effect is usually obtained by painting out the background on the negative. Combined line and half-tone may be used for a photograph that needs some lettering or a scale; this is usually done by stripping a line negative into a half-tone negative.

Half-tones may be printed by lithography on the same paper as the text, but letterpress printing may necessitate the use of coated ('art') paper, which is expensive and often too shiny for the text of the book.

If the half-tones are to be printed separately from the text, it is most economical to print them in multiples of four pages, with, say, two horizontal or one upright illustration on each page. Each four-page unit can be either wrapped round a section of text pages (usually 16 or 32 pages), 'insetted' in the middle of it or inserted inside the last fold of the sheet (see fig. 5.4, p. 78); this costs less than pasting-in single leaves. In a book with a large number of half-tones, these may be grouped into a section or sections of 16 pages, for economy and for ease of reference. For restrictions on the placing of such groups see section 5.6.

Reductions

Although you are unlikely to be responsible for sizing the illustrations, you should know a little about it.

Reductions are linear: that is, 2 = 1 means that the final version will be half as wide but have only a quarter of the original area. Reductions may be expressed as percentages, but this is potentially ambiguous unless expressed as 'reduce to 60%' to show that the illustration should not be reduced *by* 60%. Reductions, especially for half-tones, are often expressed in the form of a final width when the illustration is reduced. See fig. 4.1, which also shows how to calculate the final height.

Line drawings. Reduction tends to improve final quality, provided the line thicknesses are suitable and any shading or lettering is sufficiently open: reduction minimizes slight irregularities by decreasing the thickness of the lines, but it also decreases the distance between them, with the result that closely spaced lines may close up.

The use of the same reduction for all the figures means that the same size of lettering can be used throughout and that the blockmaker or printer will be able to photograph several pieces of artwork at a time and will not need to keep resetting his camera – which takes time and is therefore expensive. A reduction of 3 = 2 or 2 = 1 may be most convenient for typeset lettering. Maps cannot always easily be drawn for uniform reduction, as the draughtsman may find it more convenient to draw them the same size as the relevant maps in the atlas he is following.

If the author provides finished drawings requiring various reductions, it can be expensive to achieve the same final size for all the lettering: typeset lettering is available only in certain sizes. Very large originals may contain more details than can be shown on a page, and are difficult to handle; they may therefore have to be redrawn. If the final size will

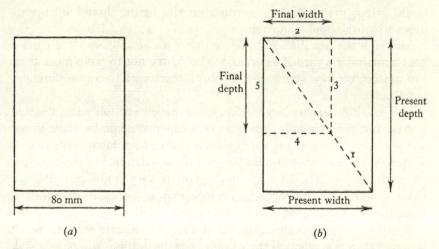

(a)   (b)

Fig. 4.1   (a) How the final size of an illustration may be marked. The vertical lines by the arrowheads show the exact width to be reduced and therefore the exact reduction. (b) If you wish to know what the final height will be, draw a rectangle the same size as the illustration, omitting any areas to be masked off; and rule a diagonal line from corner to corner (1). Mark off the final width on the top line of the rectangle (2) and draw a vertical line to meet the diagonal (3). The vertical line will be the final height; and a rectangle the final size may be obtained by drawing a horizontal line from the point where the vertical and diagonal meet (4). A similar method (but with steps 2–5 in the reverse order) can be used if you know the final height and want to know the final width.

be much smaller than the originals, warn the author; it may be as well to have one original reduced to the final size, to show the effect.

Half-tones. Here again some reduction tends to improve final quality. If an author provides a half-tone that contains fine detail likely to disappear after reduction and screening, ask him whether some of the photograph may be omitted.

Large illustrations

Illustrations that are turned on the page. Illustrations that are to be compared with one another should be printed the same way up. If some half-tones in a group have to be turned, try to place them together, so that the reader does not have to keep turning the book.

The bottom of turned illustrations should be at the right-hand side of the page; preferably no wording on the figure should be upside down when the book is upright.

Although the headline and page number are usually omitted from a page containing a turned figure, one should try not to have more than two consecutive pages without a number if there are any cross-references or an index.

Pullouts. Pullouts are large sheets which have to be folded and pasted into the book individually. They are very expensive, cumbersome to use and apt to tear along the folds, especially if they fold downwards as well as sideways. They should only be used if the relationship between the parts of a large detailed map or diagram is very important. Pullout half-tones are rare, but occasionally one may be necessary in order to reproduce an old map at a reasonable size.

If there is to be a pullout, tell the production department whether it is to pull clear (i.e. whether the whole of the illustration, when unfolded, should be visible even if the book is not open at that page). If the pullout is referred to often, it should pull clear. See section 5.6 for the best position for a pullout.

If there is no list of illustrations, the pullout should have '*facing p. 000*' printed at the foot, so that the binder knows where to insert it.

Double-page spreads. A double-page illustration will have to be printed in two separate halves unless it is in the middle of a signature; so it is not suitable for an illustration with important wording right in the centre. Double-page illustrations are usually split into two equal parts, but they may be better split to one side of the centre, to avoid a break at a critical point.

Endpapers. If an illustration printed on the endpapers is referred to in the text, it should be repeated in the body of the book, as the endpapers will disappear if the book is rebound by libraries.

4.1 *What needs to be done*

Separate the illustrations from the text, because they will go through different processes before they are brought together again at proof stage. See that all the illustrations are available; identify each one and mark up any lettering for such things as capitalization and italic; and give any instructions about scale, consistency, masking and so on. Check all the illustrations against the text, and provide a typed list of captions, also checked against the content of the illustration and against the text. The list should be typed double-spaced, with the author's name and short book title at the top of the first folio; keep a copy in case the top copy goes astray, especially if you have had to compile the captions yourself. Make sure someone tells the printer whether each caption is to be the same width as the illustration (in which case the appropriate width should be written beside each caption) or text measure, and also whether turnover lines should start flush left or be indented or centred.

You may need to provide a list of illustrations for the preliminary pages.

See that permission has been obtained to reproduce all borrowed illustrations, and include the necessary acknowledgements in the caption or in the list of illustrations or a separate note. (See section 3.6.)

I treat half-tones and line illustrations separately in this chapter, although this entails some repetition, because they need different treatment to a large extent, and because many books contain only half-tones or only line drawings. Special points about maps and graphs are dealt with separately, after the general section on line drawings.

4.2 *Line drawings*

If the author's sketches have to be redrawn and checked before they are incorporated in the proof, they may delay the book. So, if you can, send the roughs for drawing before you have finished work on the typescript: you should not send them before you have checked them against the text and captions, and marked up any lettering; but the text may be held up, perhaps while you wait for the author to answer queries, or while you work through the footnotes, and there is no need for the drawings to wait too. If some of the illustrations are likely to occupy a whole page, send a copy of the captions too, as the person sizing the illustrations will need to know how much space to leave for the captions.

Separating the originals from the text
If the author has drawn the illustrations on folios that also include text, photocopy the folios if you can, and put the photocopy in the text so as to give the draughtsman the best possible original. On the photocopy, ring the figure and caption and write 'artwork', so that the keyboard operator knows that these are being dealt with separately and that he

need not set any of the wording with the text. (The captions are set separately, from the list you provide.) On the copy to be used by the draughtsman, ring everything that is not to be included in the artwork, for example lettering that will be incorporated in the caption.

It is important to leave a copy of the folio in the text if there is anything at all on it other than the illustration and the caption: if artwork is needed for a genealogical table, the heading and any notes may be set with the rest of the text and if so should not be ringed. If in doubt ask the designer.

You may not be sure whether certain things, such as benzene rings, will have to be artwork, because this depends on the printer's facilities; again, ask the designer.

Numbering

Each original should be clearly identified by author's name, short book title and figure number.

Diagrams that are referred to in the text should usually be numbered in the finished book, and referred to by number in the text, because the printer may not be able to place them in exactly the right position: there may not be room at the foot of the page, or the publisher may have a rule that all illustrations should be placed at the top of a page. While you are going through the text, change 'is as follows': to 'is shown in fig. 10'. If the figure is in the middle of a paragraph in the typescript, and is followed by a new sentence, mark the new sentence to run on.

If there is some reason why the figure numbers should not be printed, the illustrations should still be numbered (or lettered) for identification.

Small pieces of artwork occupying less than four or five lines of text are not difficult to place exactly where they occur in the typescript; and if they are not really 'figures' they need not be numbered but may be identified for the printer by the folio number with, if necessary, 'top', 'middle', 'bottom'.

Figures may be numbered in one sequence through the book, or by chapter (fig. 6.1 being the first figure in chapter 6). In symposia or other collections of papers, they may have to be numbered afresh in each paper, in which case each original will have to carry the contributor's name as well as the general identification for the book. Where possible, avoid having more than one sequence of numbers for text illustrations; for example, graphs are usually numbered in the same sequence as other diagrams. If, however, the book contains some diagrams relevant only to the immediate context, and also some maps to which the reader may wish to refer several times – and which should therefore be listed in the preliminary pages – they may be numbered separately; but make sure that you always refer to them as 'fig. 1' or 'map 1', so that neither the reader nor the printer has any doubt as to which one is meant. If half-tones are to be printed in the text, they should be numbered in one sequence with the line illustrations, though maps may again be numbered separately. Frontispieces are not usually numbered.

Position

See that the place for each figure is given in the margin of the text: the best position is usually near the first or most detailed reference to the illustration. If you think the order of the figures should be altered, suggest this to the author, and if necessary renumber the relevant figures – and of course the captions and any cross-references. The marginal note should be in the form 'Fig. 6 near here' and ringed. It is easy to omit a marginal reference to a figure, so check that every figure has been mentioned in the margin, and that if there are two series of numbers (e.g. of diagrams and maps) it is clear whether fig. 6 or map 6 is referred to.

Content and captions

The copy-editor is the last person to see the text and illustrations together while they can both be changed without difficulty and expense. So it is extremely important to check the one against the other.

See that drawings are complete (for example that both axes of graphs are labelled and that the scales are unambiguous), and that symbols and conventions are used consistently in all the figures, as well as in the captions and text. This check is particularly necessary when an author uses someone else's illustrations which may employ a different set of conventions.

See that each figure tallies with its description in the caption and text; it often happens that an author changes his text slightly but forgets to change the relevant diagrams. Check particularly the style for abbreviations and the spelling of proper names.

Any identification letters or unusual symbols or abbreviations should be explained in a key or in the caption or text.

Remove as much lettering as possible from the drawing into the caption; this leaves the illustration uncluttered, and has the incidental advantage in letterpress books that some corrections can be made without the cost of a new block. However, any magnification or reduction (' × 1000' or 'half actual size') given in the caption would have to be changed if the illustration was reduced for reproduction, so it is usually better to include a scale on the artwork.

Keys employing letters and numbers can always be part of the caption. Some common symbols, such as solid and outline squares, circles and triangles, can also be typeset: $+$ $\times$ $-$ $\cdot$ $\triangle$ $\triangledown$ $\square$ $\bigcirc$ $\blacktriangle$ $\blacktriangledown$ $\blacksquare$ $\bullet$ $\triangle$ $\triangledown$ $\boxdot$ $\odot$ $\oplus$ $\otimes$ $\ominus$ $\leftmoon$ $\rightmoon$. Ask the designer whether keys employing symbols should be included with the figure copy or the caption copy.

See that the caption contains all the necessary information, so that the figure is intelligible without reference to the text; but delete unnecessary wording such as 'Graph showing . . .' Figure captions usually start 'Fig. 1' or 'Map 1', though where there is only one sequence of illustrations in the book, and where the caption consists of more than just the number, 'Fig.' may be omitted. If the figure numbers are not to be printed, ring them on the list of captions. See that there consistently is or is not a point after the figure number and at the end of the caption.

In science books the source of the illustration is usually given at the end of the caption.

Shading

Shading is usually applied in the form of tints, which are ready-made patterns of dots, lines, etc., obtainable in various densities, that can be applied either by the draughtsman or by the blockmaker or printer. Their use permits the differentiation of several types of area.

Information for designer and draughtsman

If you wrote some notes for the designer in preparation for an estimate (see section 2.1), check what you wrote and tell him of any changes. Otherwise make a list of general points now.

If diagrams are to be reproduced in more, or fewer, colours than in the original, state any preference the author may have as to the use to be made of the extra colour, or the conventions to be used to replace colour (perhaps a solid bold line to replace red, and a dashed line to replace green). See that any illustration that must not be redrawn, or any original that has been borrowed and must not be relettered, is mentioned in the list. If graph grids are to be included, say so; if only some are to be included, make it clear which are to be retained.

Warn the designer if, for example, three figures must be fitted into one double-page spread for comparison, or if the drawings must be reduced either by the same amount or in proportion to the size of the objects they portray, or if they must be printed to a certain scale (say × 200 or 10 mm to a mile).

A typed list of the wording should be provided for figures such as genealogical tables and maps which contain a number of unfamiliar words or proper names that are handwritten on the rough.

Ensure that the author's intention for each illustration is clear and unambiguous; the draughtsman has no knowledge of the book and cannot without loss of time refer back to you over problems encountered once he has started drawing; so see that instructions and annotations are simple, legible and unambiguous. If the author's roughs are not accurate enough to be copied exactly, explanatory notes on individual figures may be needed, or a photocopy of a similar illustration from another book. The notes should include all the points that may not be apparent to anyone who has not read the book: for example, that the line AF in fig. 4 should be twice as long as the line AD in fig. 1, or that six lines which appear to meet at E actually do meet there. The notes should be written on the originals themselves, or firmly fastened to them by sticky tape or rubber solution so that they do not go astray.

If the figures are not to be redrawn, any marking-up of the lettering etc. should be on a photocopy or overlay. An overlay is a flap of tracing paper fastened to the back of the drawing and folded over to cover the front; take care that it is fastened and folded in such a way that it cannot slip out of position; if there is any chance of movement the correct position in relation to the drawing should be identified by corresponding marks on overlay and drawing. Any other instructions should be on a separate sheet attached to the original.

Some originals are more elaborate than they need be, because they have been taken from other publications. In that case tell the draughtsman, or draw a rough sketch to show him, what needs to be included.

Creative illustrations. The artist may need to be told about – or, better still, shown – appropriate geographical or historical details to be used in his drawings. See that the briefing provided is appropriate and adequate; it may take the form of detailed roughs, photographs of places or of objects in museums, or drawings and relevant text from other books. If the artist is to consult other books, it is not enough to quote author and title: an artist cannot be expected to have access to any but the standard works of reference; nor can he be expected to read through several books to find the information he needs. If source books have been recommended by anyone other than the author, make sure that he agrees with the choice: authorities often disagree, particularly about historical reconstructions.

The artist should also be given a duplicate typescript, or at least the relevant folios. Mark the text passages which describe the drawings.

Marking-up the lettering

If the figures are not to be redrawn, use a pale blue pencil, or mark up a photocopy. Ring any material that is not to be included in the drawing. See that lettering is legible; identify capital O/zero, Greek, subscripts, etc.; remove any unwanted full points after abbreviations; and mark capitals, italic, bold and so on, according to the usage in the text. Keep capitals to a minimum: only the first word of a label – if that – needs an initial capital.

Redrawn and lettered artwork

It is best to ask the author to check any redrawing, and any complicated lettering. Alterations to artwork are caused as often by authors' inadequate or incorrect roughs, or second thoughts, as they are by draughtsmen's mistakes.

As original artwork is extremely vulnerable in transit, send the author a photocopy instead if you can. Before sending it, check that no drawings are missing. See that each one is clearly and correctly identified, and, if there is time, check the drawings against the roughs.

If you send the author photocopies of the artwork, ask him to mark corrections in a colour that will show up, or to give some indication in the margin, to make sure that no small change is overlooked. If you have to send him the artwork itself, see that it is carefully packed; if possible, it should be packed flat with plenty of padding, and it should never be folded. Ask the author not to mark any corrections on it, as ballpoint – and sometimes even erased pencil – will be picked up by the camera. Pale blue crayon is satisfactory, but very few authors have a pale enough one, so it is best if your art department can cover each drawing with a transparent overlay, on which the author can mark his corrections, using a soft pencil or crayon in order to avoid damaging the artwork underneath.

Tell the author about any wording you have moved from the drawing to the caption, and explain that areas coloured (usually) blue on the artwork will be covered by a tint. Make it clear to him that this is the last stage at which corrections can be made without great expense, and ask him to check the drawings and lettering carefully. On the other hand he must confine himself to correction of actual errors: an alteration to typeset labelling, for example, could mean a delay while new wording was typeset.

When the author has checked the drawings, see that his corrections are clear and sensible, and that he has not departed from the agreed conventions. If he was sent the artwork, see that he has returned it all; there is, of course, no need for him to return photocopies that contain no corrections. He need not return the roughs unless they will explain a correction, or unless he wants to show that the draughtsman has not followed his rough.

If you did not have time to check the drawings before you sent them, have a general look at them now. If sans serif lettering is used, make sure that l, 1 and I are easily distinguishable. If a dot tint is already laid, see that it does not come too close to the lettering: if it does, it can make the letters look deformed. You need not worry about general technical aspects: the designer will ensure that the artwork will reduce and reproduce well; that its style harmonizes with the typographical style of the book; and that each illustration is properly sized.

Unless the corrections are very small, tell the designer or production department whether the changes should be charged to author, draughtsman or publisher.

If the book is already being made up into page (or if the author sends a substitute figure at proof stage), check that no change in size is likely, for example because the vertical axis of a graph has been extended or cut; if it is, consult the production department. If the compositor has already passed the relevant page, decide whether the author should be asked to alter the figure so that it can be reproduced the same size as before, or whether the printer should be asked to repage as far as the end of the chapter.

Separate the artwork that needs correction, and list those figures; then pass all the artwork to the designer or production department. Corrected artwork will probably be given to you to check; if the author particularly asks to see it, warn him if this will delay the book.

4.3 *Maps and graphs*

Maps

Maps should include all the places a reader is likely to look up, but should be free from unnecessary detail. Inexperienced authors may provide copies of printed maps which, through the use of more than one colour or a larger size, include more details than can be shown in a one-page black-and-white map. They may not have stopped to ask themselves: is all the information necessary for the readers of my book? Are the right places shown? Are boundaries or contours needed, and if so which? Should any mountains be shown; which seas, bays, etc., should be named, which rivers included? Are roads and railways necessary? Does the map need latitude and longitude lines, a north point, a scale (see below)?

I have already mentioned the disadvantages of pullouts, double-page spreads and endpaper illustrations. If a map is too crowded or covers too large an area to be fitted into one page, it can probably be split geographically or by subject – say physical features on one map and density of population on another – or even chronologically. The reader will probably find the maps easier to follow if each contains only the minimum of information. One can, if necessary, have an inset map, on a larger scale, covering a particularly crowded area.

If only one or two place names are outside the main area of a map, and it would mean making this main area very small if the places outside it were to be shown, it may be more sensible to omit the distant places or to indicate, by an arrow, the direction in which they lie.

Briefing for the draughtsman. The draughtsman will need photocopies of existing maps, or sketch maps; information about the inclusion of boundaries, contours etc. if this is not clear from the sketch maps; and a typed list showing the correct spelling of the names to be included in each map. See that the briefing is adequate, for example that it is clear exactly which areas should be shaded, how many kinds of shading are needed, whether one particular tint should be a combination of two of the others, or whether all the tints should be graded in density to show, say, different densities of population. See also that the draughtsman will know whether he is to follow the author's neat-looking, but possibly inaccurate, drawings for coastline and placing of towns or archaeological sites, etc. If the map is to show the position of ancient places that no longer exist, the draughtsman must be told exactly where to place them.

The list of names should have a column each for countries, provinces, towns, smaller villages or settlements, old sites, rivers and other natural features, ethnic groups, etc., because a different kind of lettering is likely to be used for each. If the lettering is to be typeset, add to this list all the other lettering needed on the map, for example the latitude and longitude numbers, the wording for the scale, key, etc. The designer will specify type size and the use of bold or italic, but you should tell him if any kind of name needs to be particularly prominent. Mark capitalization of things that are not proper names: for example, 'Railway station', 'Land above 1000 metres'.

As you go through the text, check place-name spellings against the list. See that all the necessary names are included, and that the spelling does not vary from map to map. The *Times atlas* and *Times index-gazetteer* are two standard authorities for place-name spelling, though some experts disagree with them.

Watch out for out-of-date names for, say, African states and towns.

Tell the designer which maps must be reproduced to a certain scale. Maps to be compared with one another should be reproduced to the same scale if this will not mean that maps of different areas vary greatly in final size. Ordnance Survey maps are often reproduced to the same scale as in the sheet from which they are taken; make sure that the whole of the required area will fit on to the page with grid numbers added at the edges if necessary (give instructions about this). In school books maps may be used as the basis for exercises in measuring distance, in which case they must be on a scale that can be measured in millimetres or inches.

Boundaries. Be careful about Indian boundaries. India will not import books unless the maps in them show Kashmir (and preferably Bhutan also) as part of India.

North points are usually unnecessary if north is at the top of the map. If maps are to be compared, north must be in the same direction and preferably at the top unless there is some particular reason for another orientation: for example a map may have the North Pole in the centre, in order to show the relationship of northern North America and northern USSR.

Scales should have both metric and imperial gradations, unless the book uses only metric measurements. One cannot have two sets of

51

contour lines, or two labels for each line; but, if land over a certain height is shaded, and the shading is explained in a key, the height can be given in both forms. Persuade the author to choose a height shown in an atlas, and if possible one that can be converted approximately to a round number.

Town plans, and maps of a district and of any country except the very biggest, should have scales, because many readers will not be familiar with the distances involved. For larger areas, such as continents and countries such as the USA and USSR, it will depend on the projection used: directions and distances may vary so much across the map as to rule out the use of scale and north point completely. If a north point cannot be used, orientation – and distances – can be made clear by having a marginal indication of latitude and longitude. Maps of a large area are usually drawn with an average north and south orientation on the page. If distances are more important than orientation, say so, so that the draughtsman can use the most helpful projection.

Keys. See that the key, or the caption, contains all the necessary information, and that the items in the key are in a sensible order.

Checking the artwork. Check the following for consistency from map to map: style of north point, scales, conventions to indicate sea and high ground, etc., comma or space in thousands, full points after abbreviations, capitalization, spelling, and so on.

See that the labelling does not obscure rivers, boundaries or small areas of shading, and that town names are if possible placed so that the relevant dot is near one end of the name. All names that must be nearly vertical, because they follow the course of a river or label a very narrow area, should read the same way.

See that there is sufficient distinction between the tints used, and that they are correctly coded in the key. See that dot tints do not come so close to lettering that they may make it look deformed when the map is reduced.

Graphs

It is easier for the draughtsman to follow a careful drawing than to make a graph from a list of numbers. The grid is not usually reproduced; tell the draughtsman whether it should be. If artwork for graphs is drawn on graph paper, it must be ruled in pure pale blue if the grid is not to be picked up by the camera. If a graph is to be used for actual measurements and the grid is not reproduced, it helps the reader if horizontal

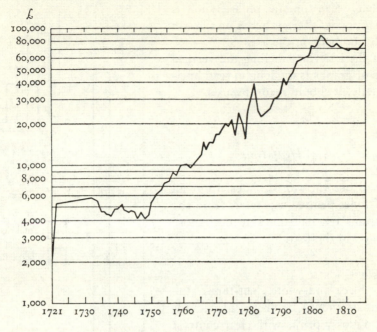

Fig. 4.2 Logarithmic graph.

and vertical axes are repeated at the top and right-hand side, respectively.

Graphs are sometimes drawn with one or both axes on a logarithmic rather than a linear scale. A logarithmic scale is one where, for example, the distance between 1 and 10 is the same as that between 10 and 100, 100 and 1000, and so on (see fig. 4.2). This means that a great range of values may be plotted, and also that small changes show up in the lower part of the range and only very big changes in the higher part.

A histogram is a graphical method of illustrating frequency distributions. The graph is normally made up of vertical columns, the heights of which are proportional to the number of observations occurring in the range that each covers; this range is indicated on the horizontal axis (see fig. 4.3). Each column may be divided to show constituents as well as total value.

The numbering on the axes of a graph may not start at zero; and O may mean origin rather than zero, in which case it should be marked to be an italic capital. *O* is usually to be found only in graphs showing positions relative to co-ordinate axes labelled, say, *x* and *y*, where the text probably also contains phrases such as 'the *Ox* axis'. Zero is better on a graph with numbers on the axes.

If the lettering labelling the vertical axes of graphs is too long to read horizontally, it should read upwards.

4.4 *Half-tones*

I shall use the word 'plates' to mean half-tones printed separately from the text, and 'text half-tones' to mean those printed in the text.

Originals

For black-and-white half-tones the originals should be sharp, black-and-white glossy prints with clear contrast in tonal values, detail visible in both highlights and shadows, and an un-cluttered background. Matt or 'pebble-dash' prints, photocopies or illustrations from other publications (which will already have a screen) will not re-produce well and should be avoided. Approximately 8 in × 6 in (200 mm × 150 mm) is the most suitable size for prints, because all illustrations are sharpened by subsequent reduction.

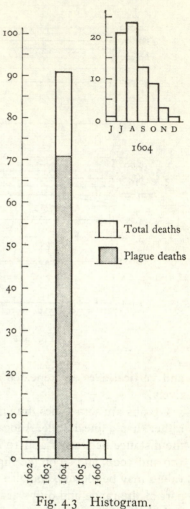

Fig. 4.3 Histogram.

As I have mentioned before, photographs should be handled as little as possible and should be kept between pieces of stiff card so that the corners do not become dog-eared. Do not use paperclips, which may scratch the surface and will almost certainly dent it; such dents tend to cast a minute shadow that has to be eliminated by the blockmaker or printer. For the same reason, do not mark the face of the prints, or mark them so heavily on the back as to dent them; any writing should be done very lightly, with a soft pencil.

Position

Text half-tones are placed in the text near the first or most detailed reference, and you should mark the approximate position in the margin of the typescript ('Fig. 79 near here').

Plates. The exact position cannot be decided until the book is in proof (see section 5.6), but the publisher will decide at typescript stage whether the plates are to be grouped, wrapped round signatures, inserted in the centre of signatures, or pasted in individually. The decision may depend on the desired selling price, and also on whether there are detailed references to the plates in the text. If there are, and it would be too expensive to paste each one in to face the relevant page, it is most convenient to the reader if they are grouped, because it is then easier to find a particular plate.

If there is no list of plates, each pasted-in plate, and the first and last page in each group should have '*facing p. oo*' (or '*frontispiece*') printed at the foot as a guide to the binder.

Numbering

Each print should be labelled with the author's name, abbreviated book title and illustration number. This information is best typed or written on a slip of paper which is then attached to the back of the photograph with a little rubber solution (e.g. Cow gum).

Although all half-tones must be numbered for identification, there is no need for them to be numbered in the finished book unless they are grouped or referred to in the text; in any case the frontispiece is not included in the numbering. Although the word 'plate' strictly means the whole page, it is more usual now to give each photograph a separate number, unless two or more are related, in which case they may be called 3(*a*), (*b*), etc.

Text half-tones are included in the figure numbering. Plates may be, but if there is to be any real point in this they must be bound in the correct position in the numerical sequence. If there are more figures than plates there are two snags: that most of the plates will have to be pasted in unbacked, which is expensive; and that the printers will have to avoid certain arrangements, for example placing figs. 5.4 and 5.6 on recto and verso respectively, because then fig. 5.5 cannot appear between them.

Instructions

See that the top of the photograph is indicated lightly on the back of the photograph if necessary.

Lettering. If a letter, arrow or scale is to be added to a half-tone it should be on a photocopy or overlay; see that the position for the letters or arrows is clear, and that the corners of the print are marked on the overlay if there is any likelihood that it may slip.

Masking. If the author has not already done so, mark on a photocopy (or lightly on an overlay) the area that must be included and anything that must be omitted, leaving the designer to decide the actual area as best suits the layout; but where an exact area is required this should be indicated. When photographs are intended to be bled (to run off the page) it is essential that significant details should not come too close to the edge of the print; so one that could only be trimmed on the left and at the top should appear at the top of a left-hand page, and so on. If a photograph can be trimmed to the same shape as the available space, it goes without saying that it will not have to be reduced as much, provided that the caption is not very long.

Retouching is very expensive if it is to be done well. Consult the designer if the author wants some retouching done; but the designer will in any case look out for any necessary retouching.

Sizing. Although detailed sizing is left to the designer, the sponsoring editor or copy-editor usually decides how many photographs will appear on a page (subject to later modification if the designer suggests it). Take possible masking and the length of the caption into account. If the author is worried about grouping and sizing, ask the designer to provide a layout; if necessary, this could include reduced photocopies of the photographs.

Avoid turning a half-tone on the page, if it can be reproduced upright without too great a reduction. If some half-tones in a group must be turned, try to place them together so that the reader does not have to keep turning the book. If the plate is turned, the foot should be at the right-hand edge of the page.

Tell the designer if the photographs are to be reproduced at a certain magnification or reduction in proportion to the original size of the objects shown.

Captions

Plate captions do not usually include the word 'Plate', but start immediately with the number (if any), or with 'Fig.' if they are included in the figure numbering. If the numbers are not to be printed ring them on the list of captions. See that there consistently is, or is not, a point after the number and at the end of the caption.

If the caption contains a magnification, this will have to be changed at proof stage if the half-tone is reduced for reproduction. For this reason it is better to include a drawn scale either on or below the half-tone.

Plate captions are usually kept short, so that the half-tones can be as large as possible; information about sources is normally given in the list of plates (if there is one), unless it will be of particular interest to someone looking at the photograph.

List of plates

See chapter 7.

Dispatching the plate material

Text half-tones for letterpress books must be sent with the typescript. If possible, plate material should be sent with the typescript, but it should not be sent until it is complete.

The caption copy should be sent with the photographs.

5

Proofs

Books set in metal type have proofs pulled direct from the type, on a letterpress proofing press; Fig. 5.1 shows the different types of proofs. Galley proofs get their name from the long tray or 'galley' used to hold the type. Page-on-galley proofs are often cut up into individual pages for ease of handling. Imposed proofs are printed on both sides of the paper, with the pages in their final position.

For filmset or typewriter-set books, proofs are produced by various forms of photocopying, often with an opening of two pages on one sheet. Where the filmset image has been produced on film, the proof is often reproduced in negative form. Some typesetting systems produce proofs in the form of a computer printout, but as these include typographical command codes, they are best restricted to the printer's reader, prior to preparing a photocopy proof of the actual typeface being used.

Setting and assembling a book is a complex process. It can be made up of some or all the following: two or three sizes of type for headings, text, displayed material such as tables or long quotations, and footnotes or endnotes; line illustrations, half-tone illustrations which may be placed in the text or printed separately; headlines and page numbers. These items have to be assembled, either by the printer or by the publisher; and some of them cannot be placed in their final position until the book is paged. Headings, text and quotations will be in the same sequence, however the pages fall; but the position marked for tables and illustrations may turn out to be so close to the foot of the page that there is not enough room, or the publisher may have a rule that they should usually be placed at the head or foot of the page. And headlines, page numbers and footnotes obviously cannot be placed in position until it is known how the pages fall.

How much of the material is assembled before the first proof depends on the typesetting process and on the publisher's and printer's preferred method of working. Galley proofs are preferable where there is likely to be heavy correction, and also for heavily illustrated books, but otherwise

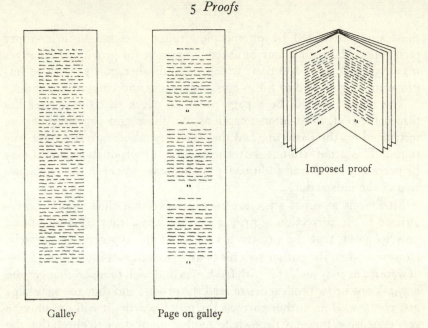

Galley   Page on galley

Imposed proof

Fig. 5.1   Galley proof, page-on-galley proof and imposed proof.

it is usually cheaper to proceed straight to page proof: the various sizes of type, which are set separately, have to be assembled so that the author can read the text, quotations, tables and footnotes together; and it is more economical to do this at the same time as dividing the book into pages, because, as I have already said, the final position of the footnotes and tables depends on how the pages fall. The other advantages of proceeding straight to page proof are that the author can make the index earlier, and that a second proof stage can often be avoided.

If the book contains line illustrations, the author should check the drawings before they are incorporated in the page proof, because any later alteration other than a simple deletion may be costly and delay the book.

If the book contains many illustrations, it will probably be paged by the publisher. The printer sends out galley proofs of the text only, and while the author is reading his set for printer's errors a designer pastes another set on to layout sheets (showing a page or pair of facing pages), incorporating the illustrations as he goes along. This paste-up is sent to the author so that he can see what size the illustrations will be and where they will be placed in relation to the text. In the paste-up the illustrations are represented by photocopies, rough sketches or just empty rectangles. The author may be asked to approve (or provide alternatives to) any deletions or additions which the publisher may suggest to improve the layout, and to fill in cross-references and compile the index.

The next stage will be a page proof, to check that the printer has placed the text, illustrations, captions, headlines and page numbers as instructed on the paste-up, and that the illustrations are the right way round. This proof will not show the quality of reproduction, and it may be necessary to have an additional proofing stage to check the reproduction of the illustrations.

Alterations at proof stage are so expensive that they should be restricted to the correction of printer's errors: the author receives a proof only to check that the printer has followed the typescript accurately. However, when the author sees his book again after an interval, and in a new form, he may look at it with fresh eyes and wish to make changes; he may ask one or two colleagues to read the proofs, and they too may suggest changes. If an author corrects the proof heavily, it will not only be very expensive, but may necessitate another proof stage to check that the corrections have been carried out properly, which will delay the book and may tempt the author to tinker further. So the publisher opts for the minimum number of proof stages appropriate to the complexity of the book and the production method; and at the editing stage he should stress to the author that all his second thoughts must be received before the typescript is sent to the printer.

The publisher also tells the author about the proofs he will receive, explaining that it is essential to compensate for an insertion (or deletion) by deleting (or inserting) the same number of characters in the same line or an adjacent one, asking him to correct legibly and in ink, and to use conventional signs and colours (see p. 73). The British Printing Industries Federation issues a booklet called *Authors' alterations cost money and cause delay*..., which explains, with photographs, why correction is expensive, and lists the proof correction signs.

When dates for the proof stages are known, they are sent to the author, so that he can keep them free or say straight away if they are inconvenient.

5.1 *First proof*

When the printer has set the type, and assembled the various items that will make up the first proof, a proof will be 'pulled'. Most printers employ proofreaders who check proofs against the typescript. This reading 'against copy' can be organized in various ways: a 'copy holder' may read the typescript aloud, mentioning punctuation, capital letters, italic, etc., to the proofreader who is checking the proof; the proofreader may himself read the typescript into a tape recorder and then play it back while he checks the proof; or he may compare the typescript with the proof a few words at a time; the last way is probably the most usual one. When the proofreader has compared some galleys or pages with the typescript, he reads them again straight through, to spot any errors of grammar or omissions that may have been copied from the typescript.

If there are many mistakes, the printer may correct them straight away and pull another proof to send out to the author: it is more expensive to correct at this stage instead of waiting to make all the corrections when the author's proof is returned by the publisher; but it is much more difficult for the author and any other proofreader to notice all the errors if the proof they read contains many mistakes. If the printer corrects the type and pulls another proof, his reader will check that the corrections have been made, and will transfer to the 'marked set' any queries for the author, before the proof is dispatched to the author, either direct or via the publisher.

The author is usually sent his typescript and two copies of the proof: the marked set and a duplicate for him to keep for reference or to use when compiling the index. It is best for the author to read the duplicate set, because he can annotate that set as he wishes. Then, when he has checked it, he can eliminate all but the essential corrections, and copy these legibly on to the marked set.

Some publishers transfer the printer's and their own queries to a duplicate set to send to the author, and retain the marked set to mark-up neatly themselves and colour-code when the author sends his corrections.

The author will be asked to return his proof to the publisher; many publishers also ask for the typescript, so that the allocation of correction charges can be checked. In some publishing firms the sponsoring editor or copy-editor reads a set of proofs; other firms employ freelance proofreaders, or rely on the author and printer. In any case it is essential for the copy-editor to go through the marked proof before it is returned to the printer, and the production department should allow a day or two for this in the schedule. The copy-editor not only makes sure that the author's corrections are clear and consistent in style, and that the printer's queries are answered; he can also save his firm money by persuading authors to cancel unnecessary corrections and to make others in a more economical way. In addition he sees that corrections are properly colour-coded, so that printer's errors are not charged to the publisher. I shall deal with these various functions later in this chapter, but I shall talk first about how to read proofs and the best way to express the corrections on the proof.

5.2 *How to read proofs*

As an ordinary reader one trains oneself to disregard spelling mistakes and to concentrate on the author's meaning; and quick readers take in a whole phrase at a time. To become a proofreader one needs to unlearn these habits. Train yourself to read slowly, so that you see every letter in each word and note the punctuation of each sentence. You may find it easier to notice errors if you place a strip of paper across the page, and move it down a line at a time, to isolate the line you are reading from those that follow. It is also sensible to reread any line in which you have found an error. Look particularly to see that no opening or closing quotes or parentheses (round brackets) are missing, as this is the sort of thing the author is likely to miss.

You will probably read a duplicate proof, not the marked set, but even so it is better to use pencil rather than ink for queries or other marks that may be cancelled later. If these can be rubbed out, leaving the proof uncluttered, there is no risk that essential corrections will be missed when they are transferred to the marked proof.

If you are asked to check the proof against the typescript, do this as a separate operation. Some proofreaders 'read against copy' first, and then read straight through for spelling, punctuation and missing words; others prefer to do the general reading first, so that the queries raised then can be checked when they compare the proof with the typescript.

One cannot rely on complete consistency in the book; so if you are proofreading a book that you did not copy-edit, and you have no list of the spellings, capitals and hyphenations, make one as you go along. I myself have found it useful to mark all such optional forms by a simple pencil marginal mark until I have discovered what the most usual form of each one is. It is much quicker to run through the proof afterwards, looking at each of these marks and making any necessary alterations, than to list all the page numbers for each, or, worse still, to realize half-way through that a spelling somewhere earlier in the book will have to be changed. Look out also for errors in foreign phrases, discrepancies in names, periods of time and ages, and in novels such things as colour of hair or eyes and inconsistent capitalization of such words as 'mother' in 'Yes, mother'.

Some dangers.

(1) If there is a glaring error, one's eye tends to leap over the intervening words; so, when you have marked the correction, read the whole line again.

(2) Whereas a word that is obviously misspelt is fairly easy to spot, a printer's error can change one word to another and this is more likely to slip through: for example, 'causal relationship' can become 'casual relationship', 'ingenuous' 'ingenious', 'unexceptionable' 'unexceptional', 'alternatively' 'alternately'. Watch out also for 'its' and 'it's'; and 'yours' and 'theirs' sometimes appear with apostrophes.

(3) On the other hand, the author may intentionally not use the obvious word but substitute something similar in look but different in meaning, just to give his readers a jolt; so one must not take it for granted that a slightly different word is necessarily wrong.

(4) If a printer is asked to retain American spellings, he may through habit spell some words in the British way. Watch for this specially, because otherwise the British spellings will not strike you as wrong.

(5) See that you do not alter inconsistent spelling, capitalization and punctuation in quotations.

You should check particularly the things that the author will take for granted: the preliminary pages, headings, headlines, and the numerical sequence of pages, notes (and their text indicators), sections, tables, illustrations, equations, etc. See that illustrations and tables are sensibly placed. Add the missing page numbers to the contents list and any lists of illustrations or tables, checking the titles against the captions or table headings at the same time. Missing cross-references to pages will probably have to be filled in by the author but all references to illustrations, tables, section and equation numbers should be checked.

Mark wrong founts (letters in the wrong type or size), unequal spacing between words or lines, and broken letters; but if a printing fault occurs throughout a page or throughout the book, make one general comment rather than marking each instance. Mark inconsistent indentions, for example after headings; and check that there consistently is, or is not, punctuation following a run-on heading.

At proof stage, word breaks should be left unaltered unless they are actually misleading or startlingly wrong. Misleading breaks are those which lead the reader to think that the word is a different one. This is largely a matter of pronunciation, because many readers 'pronounce' the first half of the word as it stands, even if they are reading quickly. For example, psycho- is a suitable place to break psychosomatic but not psychology, even though the root is the same in both cases; Christian should be broken after Chris-, not Christ-. Three classic examples of bad breaks are read-just, reap-pear and the-rapist. American typesetters follow Webster's dictionary, which approves word breaks frowned on in Britain. Correction of Webster-approved breaks must be paid for as an author's alteration. (For word breaks in foreign languages see Hart's *Rules*.)

If someone else will be collating your corrections with the author's, keep your queries to a minimum. If you do query something, show clearly what you are querying and say why: '? meaning', '? construction', '? see p. 314' (and mark the relevant part of p. 314). Similarly if you change something that is in itself correct, such as an optional spelling which is not on the agreed list of spellings, say why you are changing it, so that the person collating the proofs knows that the change is necessary for consistency and is not just a matter of your own preference. If something is inconsistent and you do not know which way to make it consistent, mark *all* the instances; no one else will have time to go through and look for them.

5.3 *How to mark corrections*

One corrects proofs differently from typescript, because the printer just runs his eye down the margin to see which lines contain corrections; a correction that is made only in the text will not be noticed. The correction should be written in the nearer margin and level with the error. If the line of text contains more than one mistake, the corrections in the margin should be written from left to right in the same order, separated by oblique strokes. Use the signs in the British Standard on proof correction; the most usual ones are given in fig. 5.2.

Keep the marginal corrections short and clear (see fig. 5.3): if only one letter is wrong, merely cross out that letter and put the correct letter, followed by an oblique stroke, in the margin. Some authors put a marginal deletion sign for deleting the wrong letter, and an insertion sign for inserting the right letter; do not follow their example, because the printer charges according to the time he takes, and the more he has to read, and the more unconventional the marginal marks, the slower he will be. The whole word should not be written in the margin unless there is more than one group of letters wrong in it, or unless the correct form is unusual. On the other hand, a whole phrase may have to be rewritten in the margin if there is a complicated change in word order; or one may need to show how a complicated piece of layout should look and what should line up with what. Anything other than the actual correction should be ringed.

Ring full stops and colons for clarity. Distinguish a closing quote from a comma (see p. 66), and distinguish superscripts and subscripts.

Except in typewriter setting and some forms of filmsetting, a letter with an accent is a single character, and so are the groups of letters called ligatures: ff, fi, fl, ffi, ffl. If part of one of these needs correction – if an accent must be added or deleted, or fl changed to ffl – the whole character must be crossed out and the correct form written in the margin.

If you delete a letter or letters, make it absolutely clear how much is to be deleted. A carelessly written diagonal stroke through one letter can pass through part of its two neighbours, and the printer may not be able to tell whether you are deleting one letter or three. Even horizontal deletion signs are clearer if they have a small vertical stroke at each end: for example, a horizontal line through a word may extend above a following comma, and it may not be clear whether the comma is to go or to stay.

Where there can be any doubt, make the word division clear by the use of 'space' or 'close-up' marks. For example, if a hyphen is deleted, make clear whether one word or two is wanted instead; if one or more letters are added between two foreign words, show whether the letters form a separate word or are to be added to the preceding or following word.

Instruction	Textual mark	Marginal mark
Leave unchanged	------ under characters	✓
Remove extraneous marks	Encircle marks to be removed	✕
Delete	/ through character(s) or ⊢——⊣ through words	♂
Delete and close up	⌠ through character(s) or ⊢═⊣	♂
Insert in text the matter indicated in the margin	⅄	New matter followed by ⅄
Substitute character or substitute part of one or more word(s)	/ through character or ⊢——⊣ through word(s)	New character or new word(s)
Substitute ligature e.g. ffi for separate letters	⊢——⊣ through characters affected	⌣ e.g. ffi
Substitute or insert full stop or decimal point	/ through character or ⅄	⊙
Substitute or insert comma, semi-colon, colon, etc.	/ through character or ⅄	,/ ;/ ⊙/ (/)/ [/]
Substitute or insert character in 'superior' position	/ through character or ⅄	⎤ under character e.g. ²⎤
Substitute or insert character in 'inferior' position	/ through character or ⅄	⎣ over character e.g. ⎣₂
Substitute or insert single or double quotation marks or apostrophe	/ through character or ⅄	⎡⎤ and/or ⎡⎤
Substitute or insert ellipsis	/ through character or ⅄	...
Substitute or insert hyphen	/ through character or ⅄	⊢─⊣
Substitute or insert rule	/ through character or ⅄	⊢──⊣ Give the size of the rule in the marginal mark e.g. ⊢1em⊣ ⊢4mm⊣
Substitute or insert oblique	/ through character or ⅄	⊘
Wrong fount. Replace by character(s) of correct fount	Encircle character(s)	⊗

Fig. 5.2 Proof correction symbols.

Instruction	Textual mark	Marginal mark
Change damaged character(s)	Encircle character(s)	✕
Set in or change to italic	——— under character(s) Where space does not permit textual marks encircle the affected area instead	⊔
Change italic to upright type	Encircle character(s)	�
Set in or change to capital letters	≡≡≡ under character(s)	≡
Set in or change to small capital letters	 ═══ under character(s)	═
Set in or change to bold type	∿∿∿ under character(s)	∿
Set in or change to bold italic type	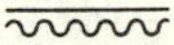 ∿∿∿ under character(s)	⊔∿
Change capital letters to lower-case letters	Encircle character(s)	≢
Change small capital letters to lower-case letters	Encircle character(s)	≠
Invert type	Encircle character	↻
Close up. Delete space between characters or words	linking ⌢ characters	⌒
Insert space between characters	| between characters	 Y Give the size of the space when necessary
Insert space between words	 Y between words	 Y Give the size of the space when necessary
Reduce space between characters	| between characters	 ⋀ Give the amount by which the space is to be reduced when necessary
Reduce space between words	 ⋀ between words	 ⋀ Give the amount by which the space is to be reduced when necessary

Fig. 5.2 (*cont.*)

67

Instruction	Textual mark	Marginal mark
Make space appear equal between characters or words	| between characters or words	Y
Close up to normal interline spacing	(each side of column) (linking lines)	
Insert space between lines or paragraphs	___ (or) _	Give the size of the space when necessary
Reduce space between lines or paragraphs	___) or ⊃	Give the amount by which the space is to be reduced when necessary
Start new paragraph	⌐	⌐
Run on (no new paragraph)	⌒	⌒
Transpose characters or words	⌐⌐ between characters or words, numbered when necessary	⌐⌐
Transpose lines	⊏	⊏
Transpose a number of lines	——— 3 ——— 2 ——— 1	Rules extend from the margin into the text with each line to be transposed numbered in the correct sequence
Centre	⌐enclosing matter to be⌐ ⌐centred	[ ]
Indent	⌐	⌐ Give the amount of the indent
Cancel indent	⊢⌐	⌐
Set line justified to specified measure*	⊢⌐ and/or ⌐⊣	⊢→⊣
Set column justified to specified measure*	⊢——→⊣	⊢→⊣

Fig. 5.2 (*cont.*)

Instruction	Textual mark	Marginal mark
Move matter specified distance to the right*	enclosing matter to be moved to the right	
Move matter specified distance to the left*	enclosing matter to be moved to the left	
Take over character(s), word(s) or line to next line, column or page		The textual mark surrounds the matter to be taken over and extends into the margin
Take back character(s), word(s) or line to previous line, column or page		The textual mark surrounds the matter to be taken back and extends into the margin
Raise matter*	over matter to be raised / under matter to be raised	
Lower matter*	over matter to be lowered / under matter to be lowered	
Move matter to position indicated*	Enclose matter to be moved and indicate new position	
Correct vertical alignment		
Correct horizontal alignment	Single line above and below misaligned matter	placed level with the head and foot of the relevant line

*Give the exact dimensions when necessary

Extracts from BS 5261 Part 2 1976 are reproduced by permission of the British Standards Institution, 2 Park Street, London W1A 2BS, from whom complete copies can be obtained.

Fig. 5.2 (*cont.*)

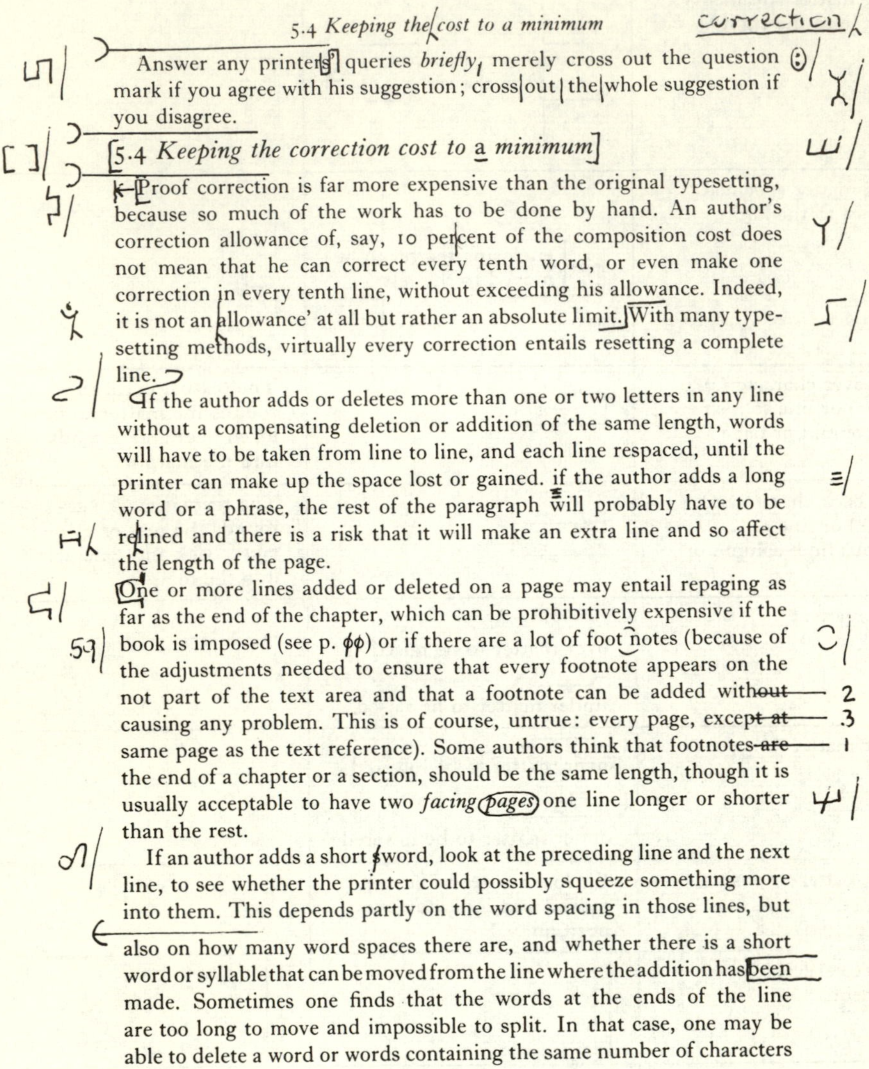

5.4 *Keeping the cost to a minimum*

Answer any printers queries *briefly*, merely cross out the question mark if you agree with his suggestion; cross out the whole suggestion if you disagree.

[5.4 *Keeping the correction cost to a minimum*]

Proof correction is far more expensive than the original typesetting, because so much of the work has to be done by hand. An author's correction allowance of, say, 10 percent of the composition cost does not mean that he can correct every tenth word, or even make one correction in every tenth line, without exceeding his allowance. Indeed, it is not an allowance' at all but rather an absolute limit. With many typesetting methods, virtually every correction entails resetting a complete line.

If the author adds or deletes more than one or two letters in any line without a compensating deletion or addition of the same length, words will have to be taken from line to line, and each line respaced, until the printer can make up the space lost or gained. if the author adds a long word or a phrase, the rest of the paragraph will probably have to be relined and there is a risk that it will make an extra line and so affect the length of the page.

One or more lines added or deleted on a page may entail repaging as far as the end of the chapter, which can be prohibitively expensive if the book is imposed (see p. ∅∅) or if there are a lot of foot notes (because of the adjustments needed to ensure that every footnote appears on the not part of the text area and that a footnote can be added without causing any problem. This is of course, untrue: every page, except at same page as the text reference). Some authors think that footnotes are the end of a chapter or a section, should be the same length, though it is usually acceptable to have two *facing pages* one line longer or shorter than the rest.

If an author adds a short word, look at the preceding line and the next line, to see whether the printer could possibly squeeze something more into them. This depends partly on the word spacing in those lines, but also on how many word spaces there are, and whether there is a short word or syllable that can be moved from the line where the addition has been made. Sometimes one finds that the words at the ends of the line are too long to move and impossible to split. In that case, one may be able to delete a word or words containing the same number of characters

Fig. 5.3   Page of corrected proof.

Answer any printer's queries *briefly*: merely cross out the question mark if you agree with his suggestion; cross out the whole suggestion if you disagree.

5.4 *Keeping the correction cost to a minimum*

Proof correction is far more expensive than the original typesetting, because so much of the work has to be done by hand. An author's correction allowance of, say, 10 per cent of the composition cost does not mean that he can correct every tenth word, or even make one correction in every tenth line, without exceeding his allowance. Indeed, it is not an 'allowance' at all but rather an absolute limit.

With many typesetting methods, virtually every correction entails re-setting a complete line. If the author adds or deletes more than one or two letters in any line without a compensating deletion or addition of the same length, words will have to be taken from line to line, and each line respaced, until the printer can make up the space lost or gained. If the author adds a long word or a phrase, the rest of the paragraph will probably have to be re-lined and there is a risk that it will make an extra line and so affect the length of the page.

One or more lines added or deleted on a page may entail repaging as far as the end of the chapter, which can be prohibitively expensive if the book is imposed (see p. 58) or if there are a lot of footnotes (because of the adjustments needed to ensure that every footnote appears on the same page as the text reference). Some authors think that footnotes are not part of the text area and that a footnote can be added without causing any problem. This is, of course, untrue: every page, except at the end of a chapter or a section, should be the same length, though it is usually acceptable to have two *facing* pages one line longer or shorter than the rest.

If an author adds a short word, look at the preceding line and the next line, to see whether the printer could possibly squeeze something more into them. This depends partly on the word spacing in those lines, but also on how many word spaces there are, and whether there is a short word or syllable that can be moved from the line where the addition has been made. Sometimes one finds that the words at the ends of the line are too long to move and impossible to split. In that case, one may be able to delete a word or words containing the same number of characters (letters and spaces), to make room for the addition. If you cannot do so in the same line as the addition, you may be able to in an adjacent line, but make sure that any word that must be moved from line to line will fit. If you are not sure whether a compensating deletion is necessary, ring a possible word and say in the margin 'delete if necessary'.

If you need to 'save a line', look for the paragraph with the shortest last line and see whether you can shorten the final sentence of that paragraph so as to take the last few words back to the preceding line. If you need to 'make a line', look for the paragraph with the longest last line and try to add a word or two in that line or the preceding one. It will sometimes be cheaper to make or save a line by cutting or adding a word or two on the next (or preceding) page rather than by extensive rewriting on the relevant page. However, there are some things to watch out for if one wants to move lines from page to page. See that the following are not split between two pages: a footnote and its indicator; a subheading and the text that follows it (if possible there should be at least two lines of text at the foot of the page); short entries in a bibliography or index. A page should not start with a 'widow', a short line which is the last line of a paragraph, if this can be avoided.

In some books it is difficult or impossible to delete anything, for example in a transcribed text or in a book written in note form, such as a dictionary. However, the printer may find the space for an extra line without deleting anything, by taking back a single word forming the last line of a paragraph. If a page contains a number of spaces above and below displayed material such as mathematics, quotations and tables, it may be possible to reduce each space very slightly to make room for one extra line of text or footnote. Two short footnotes may be 'doubled up' in one line, or a short one may be moved to the same line as the end of a long one; but a long footnote should not start in the middle of a line. If a new piece of research must be referred to, this can be done in the preface or at the end of the relevant chapter, if there is enough space.

If you are not sure what is the best way of compensating for a deletion or addition, ask the designer.

If possible, contact the author and explain the difficulties to him. If you cannot manage this before the proofs are due back with the printer, you may have to make a compensating alteration and write to the author and tell him what you have done – but of course it depends on the kind of book and author. If there is to be a revised proof, you could cancel the correction on the first proof and ask the author to reword the line when he receives the second one, in order to minimize the cost of the correction.

If correction is heavy, warn the author that he may exceed his correction allowance. If an extra proof of part or all the book will be necessary because of the amount of correction, warn the production department, etc., because the extra proof stage will mean delay and extra expense.

Even if it is a printer's error that has caused an expensive correction, try to compensate for it by a deletion or an addition, giving the printer the choice between paying for any necessary repaging or for your compensating alteration; such a case should be mentioned in a separate note to be sent to the printer with the proofs.

5.5 *Allocating the cost of corrections*

The printer will charge for all corrections which are not his own errors and colour-coded as such. The following is the standard system of colour-coding:

green: printer's own marks (corrections and queries)

red: author's or publisher's correction of printer's errors

blue or black: author's and publisher's own alterations (including any carried out in response to printer's queries), plus the following, which the printer should be asked to charge as part of the composition cost and not as author's corrections: insertion of cross-references and any headlines that cannot be written until proof stage

Some publishers ask authors to distinguish any publisher's errors (errors of omission or commission made during editing or copy-editing) by marking those in black. Printers will not separate the charges for blue and black corrections unless specifically asked to; but without this extra colour, authors may mark all errors by other people (printer or publisher) in red, and the copy-editor will have to see that the colour-coding is made fair to the printer.

The author's colour-coding will anyway need checking: one must see that the printer is not charged with things that are not his fault. If you distrust the author's coding entirely, you will have to check the corrections against the typescript. Some publishers do not ask authors to return their typescript with the proof, because of the high cost of all postage, particularly airmail; and in that case one must use intelligent guesswork in all but the extreme cases.

It is sometimes difficult to allocate errors fairly, and it is not worth spending hours worrying about the allocation of small corrections; it is probably cheaper to get them allocated as publisher's errors.

If the author has allocated the corrections fairly but in the wrong colours, it is a waste of time to rewrite or ring them all in the correct colour. Instead, explain the author's system on the first page of each batch of proof, or in a covering note with each batch.

If the author does send his typescript back with the first proof, and the printer does not need it, keep it until any query about correction costs has been settled, and then ask the author if he would like it back. Similarly, keep the marked first proof, if the author returns it.

5.6 *Other points*

Make sure that all queries have been answered, and that something has been done about any pages marked long or short.

See that all the author's corrections have a marginal mark and are legible and unambiguous. The extent of deletions must be made clear. Identify ambiguous characters; distinguish quotes from commas, and see that commas are not written so large that they look like parentheses. See that the author has used the correct underlining for capitals: some authors use two lines instead of three. If letters are added in non-English material, see that it is clear whether the addition is a separate word or is to be added to an existing one.

See that the corrections are consistent in spelling, capitalization and so on with the rest of the book.

Anything written on the proof will be read by everyone who handles it; so if the author has written an explanation as to why he has made a correction, or a long answer to a query raised by the printer's reader, ring it and put a line through it so that the printer knows he need not read it.

If lines of text are to be moved from one galley or page to another, do not cut up the marked proof. If the correction is very complicated you could cut up and rearrange a duplicate proof or photocopy and attach this to the marked proof.

If the author alters a heading, see that it is also altered in the contents list and headlines if necessary.

If someone other than the author is making the index, he will be working from an uncorrected proof, so make a note of any changes in the spelling of proper names, and incorporate them in the index type-script when you receive it. If some corrections may affect page references in the index – for example if a table has to be moved from page to page – ask the author to check the relevant page numbers when he receives the second proof, and to alter the index if necessary.

Only one copy of the proof – the marked set – should be returned to the printer, so if you have more than one corrected copy, see that the marked set contains all the essential corrections. Some publishers keep a fully corrected duplicate set in case of accidents.

Preliminary pages

Read the whole prelim proof, as authors tend not to read these pages carefully. Any late material, such as a foreword, list of plates or acknowledgements, should be sent for setting when the first proof is sent for revise.

Watch out particularly for any changes the author makes on the title page. If the title or the form of the author's name or his description is changed, see that the information reaches the people responsible for the cover, jacket and publicity; and be certain to check this on jacket, cover and Chemac proofs. If the title is changed, see that the half-title, and if necessary the headlines, are changed accordingly. If the book is mentioned in other books already in production, for example in a series list, see that its title is corrected there. Make sure that a translator or artist has been mentioned where appropriate.

Title-page verso. Are the publisher's addresses given correctly?

Is the copyright notice set out correctly? Is the date correct? Is the owner given correctly? Should there be a separate notice for the illustrations or translation? Should the notice be omitted or qualified? See p. 124.

Is the publication date correct?

Add or check the CIP data. Is the ISBN correct? Should there be more than one? (See pp. 125–7.)

Does the printer's address include the name of the country?

List of contents etc. Have all the page numbers been correctly filled in? Have the lists been changed in accordance with any changes made in headings and captions? Should the index start on a left-hand page, in order to make an even working?

Acknowledgements list. Should any changes or additions be made as a result of recent correspondence or any alteration in the numbering of the illustrations? If the illustrations are unnumbered, the list cannot be compiled until the page numbers are known: see the list is sent for setting.

Page numbers and headlines

It is sensible to check these, as the author is unlikely to. You will need, in any case, to check the page numbering to see that each batch of proofs is complete.

Page numbers should not appear on blank pages or on the half-title or its verso, the title page or its verso, the dedication and epigraph pages, or pages carrying only part titles. They may also be omitted on pages containing turned tables, turned illustrations, or illustrations extending into the margin where the page number would normally appear; but if there are references to these pages (in the preliminary pages, cross-references or the index), see that not more than two consecutive pages are without a number.

Discourage the author from any change that will affect the headlines. But if he does insist on such a change, see that all the relevant headlines (and the contents list) are altered.

Headlines are omitted above headings that intentionally start new pages (e.g. chapter or part headings); above all turned illustrations and tables; above text illustrations and tables which extend beyond the type area (except at the foot) and are not turned. Headlines are included above headings which *accidentally* occur at the heads of pages (including chapter headings in a book with run-on chapters); above text illustrations and tables which fall within the type area and are not turned.

Where section titles are used for headlines and a new section starts a page, the chapter title or an abbreviated form of the section title should be used for the headline, in order to avoid having identical headings one above the other. Where a new section starts below the top of the page, the title of the new section should be used as the headline.

See that the correct page numbers are inserted in the headlines for endnotes.

Footnotes and endnotes

Check the sequence of numbers if no one has already done so. See that footnotes are placed correctly on short pages, and that rules are included (if required) above the continuation of every footnote that runs on to another page.

Line illustrations

Check that any scale given in the form of a magnification or reduction in a caption has been altered if the illustration has been reduced for reproduction. See that the foot of any turned illustration is at the right-hand side.

If any corrections are essential, put a line through the relevant illustration on the proof and say 'Substitute corrected version' in the margin. Send the artwork with the proof, packing it carefully so that it cannot be folded or crumpled. Any instruction should be on a separate piece of paper attached to the artwork, and not included in any general note about that batch of proofs. If the proof is paged, make sure that any alterations will not increase or reduce the size of the illustration.

If the first proof is in galley and does not include the illustrations, make sure that their position is marked (unless this is done on a separate paste-up).

Half-tones

The proofs do not show the final quality of reproduction, and are intended only to show the layout and caption wording. Authors are often worried by the quality, and you may need to reassure them.

As with line illustrations, check magnifications and scales in captions, and see that the foot of turned illustrations is at the right-hand side. See that each half-tone is printed the right way round and has the right caption.

Plates. If the plates have not been proofed by the time the first proof of the text is returned to the printer, check with the production department, as plates sometimes get overlooked.

Once the book is paged, you should insert the 'facing page' numbers in the list of plates (if any). If there is no list of plates, any plates to be pasted in individually should have '*facing p. 000*' (or '*frontispiece*') printed at the foot of the page below the caption; and each group, wrap-round, etc., should have '*facing p. 000*' at the foot of the first and last page. This helps ensure that the plates are incorporated in the correct position when the sheets of the book are bound up.

Where to place the plates. Except in the few cases where plates are pasted in individually to face the relevant page of text, their position will depend on how the signatures fall, and that in turn will depend on the number of pages in each signature. The production department will be able to advise you about this, and will check that the page numbers you give are feasible.

There are some other limitations on the placing of plates:

(*a*) A group of plates between signatures of text should be placed at least twenty-four pages away from the centre of the book; during binding, the book may be lifted by a blunt blade inserted into the middle of the book, which might damage art paper. Also for technical reasons, a group of plates should not be placed between the first two signatures or the last two, or right at the end of the book. Nor should the plates divide a particularly complicated bit of text, or face an unconnected text illustration or the end of a chapter. Look for the most relevant suitable position, or a place where the prospective book-buyer is likely to notice them.

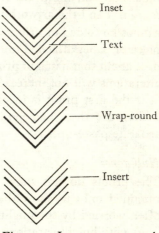

(*b*) A small group of pages may be sewn into the middle of a signature; such a group is called an 'inset' (see fig. 5.4). An 'insert' is a small group inserted so that half appears between pp. 4 and 5 of a sixteen-page signature, and the other half between pp. 12 and 13. A wrap-round

Fig. 5.4 Inset, wrap-round and insert.

is a small group wrapped round the outside of one signature; a frontispiece cannot be wrapped round if there is a half-title. A wrap-round should not begin or end between the first two signatures or the last two. A wrap-round or insert is often laid out in a different style from an inset, so if there is need to convert a wrap-round or insert into an inset, consult the designer.

(*c*) One backed plate is less expensive than two unbacked plates pasted in separately.

(*d*) Unbacked plates usually face left, to avoid blank right-hand pages; but if a plate is referred to in detail on a right-hand page it should face the description.

Pullouts

If a pullout refers to the whole of the book it may be best placed after the index (so that it can lie almost flat), pulling clear and folding out to the right. The end of the book is also the best position for a figure or table consisting of two or three pullouts, as the bulge they form is less unsightly there and they are easier to handle. If a pullout refers to only one section of the book it should either pull out left at the beginning of the section or pull out right at the end of it. Two large illustrations can be printed back to back on one pullout if they need not be compared. If there is no list of illustrations, see that each pullout has '*facing p. ooo*' at its foot.

Paste-up

If there is a paste-up, see that any corrections on the marked galley proof will not affect the layout, and that any corrections marked on the paste-up are incorporated in the marked galley proof.

Covering note

It may be necessary to send a covering note or notes, so that something important is not overlooked. Any comments or requests addressed only to the designer and production department should not be included in a note for the printer. A covering note might contain the following.

For the designer: points you think he should look at (with page references) and any queries.

For the designer, production department and printer: a list of illustrations for correction; a request for an extra revise because of heavy correction or new material.

For the printer: any large corrections for which you think he should pay. If the printer is going to read the proofs again, list any special points his proofreader should look for, such as a recurrent error which the author wants changed but which he may have missed in one or two places.

5.7 *Second proof*

If the first proof was in galley, the printer will divide the book into pages as he corrects, inserting headlines, page numbers ('folios' to the printer) and illustrations, and moving tables and footnotes to their final position. If the footnote numbering or symbols start afresh on each page, some numbers or symbols will have to be changed both in the text and at the beginning of the note. In order to avoid 'widow' lines – the short final line of a paragraph at the top of a page – he may respace the last few lines of a paragraph to make or save a line, and similar 'over-running' may be necessary to fit in tables, illustrations or footnotes.

When the compositor has finished his work, a fresh proof is pulled and the printer's reader reads the lines that have been affected by the corrections; if this is the first page proof, the reader will also check the headlines and page numbers, and the footnote numbering.

The author should use the second proof only to see that the alterations he marked on the first proof have been correctly made. He should be warned, though, that he needs to check the whole of every line affected, to make sure that new errors have not been introduced, and to read the lines immediately above and below the correction, to be sure that the corrected line has not been transposed to the wrong position on the page. He should also look for marks on the first proof indicating that the printer has reset lines which themselves contained no errors.

The author returns the proof to the publisher, who goes through it as before and gives the necessary instructions to the printer. The second proof is best returned to the printer in one batch, though the production department may ask you to return the preliminary pages and text before the index. Even if you are planning to keep the proof until it is complete, look at each batch as it arrives from the author, in case you need to get in touch with him about any of his corrections.

5.8 *Before passing the proof for press*

Read the correspondence file – or at any rate the correspondence since you sent the book for setting – in case any decisions have been taken that you did not know about.

All queries on the proof must be answered and all cross-references completed. See that proofs of the plates and pullouts are returned to the printer, and that their position is given either in the preliminary pages or on the plates or pullouts themselves.

It is worth checking the publication date, copyright notice, acknowledgements list and ISBN again. See that the correct page number is given in the contents list for the index.

5.9 *Jacket or cover proof*

Check the ISBN, book title, inclusion or omission of sub-title, author's name and appointment, etc., against the proof of the preliminary pages; make sure that any changes made on the title-page proof have been incorporated. See that the blurb tallies with the text in spelling and general style, and that any caption or acknowledgement for a jacket or cover picture or design has been included. The jacket carries only the ISBN for the hard-cover edition, and the paperback cover only the paperback ISBN; the jacket should contain the words 'Printed in [Great Britain]'.

5.10 *After passing the proofs for press*

When the press proof is returned to the printer, he will make the corrections and check them; but this may not be done until just before that part of the book is printed, when any delay would mean keeping a printing machine idle. If the author wants to check that the corrections marked on the press proof (the final proof) have been made, it will mean repeating the ordinary correction and reproofing procedures, and this will mean delay and additional expense.

If the author sends late corrections, ask the production department whether there is time for them to be made, and if so pass them on after making sure they are absolutely clear; they are best marked on a copy of the proof page. If they are too late, tell the author and put them in the corrections file for a reprint. Erratum slips are expensive to insert and may make a worse impression on reviewers and readers than the mistakes they refer to. If there is an erratum slip, put a copy in the corrections file, to make sure that the correction will be incorporated in the text when the book is reprinted.

An errata slip should be headed by the author's name, book title and ISBNs. Use italic for *for*, *read*, etc., so that inverted commas can be reserved for use within the quoted phrase if necessary. Spell out 'line' to avoid confusion with 1.

Smith, *Kafka*
ISBN 0 521 12345 6 hard covers
ISBN 0 521 65432 1 paperback

Errata
p. 112, line 1, *for* anonymity *read* 'ambiguity'
p. 121, fig. 5, *insert 2 beside the unlabelled circle*

6

House style

Some publishers have a fairly rigid house style covering spelling, abbreviations, etc.; others follow the author's own style in most things, if it is sensible and consistent. Each procedure has its advantages and disadvantages. If one is to follow the author's style one cannot always start the detailed marking straight away: one needs to discover what the style is, which may be difficult if the author is not entirely consistent or if the system is unconventional; and one then needs to evaluate the system. However, a rigid house style may mean altering a perfectly good system; and the more changes one makes the more likely one is to miss some instances and to present the author with an inconsistent version of a system he did not choose. If possible you should brief the author *before* he prepares his final typescript, to tell him about your firm's preferences, and to ask him above all to be consistent.

Even if you have a house style, it will not cover every spelling, hyphen or capital. So keep a note of the author's system as you go through the typescript, with the folio number of the first (or every) occurrence, so that you can easily find the earlier examples if the author changes to a different and better system later in the book. Some of the items in your list will be incorporated in the style sheet you send to the printer (see fig. 3.1, p. 21).

There are several books that give useful guidance on tricky spellings, hyphenation, capitalization, punctuation and so on, and I list some of them here. I shall myself just mention the points that seem to cause particular difficulty.

British Standard 5261: *Copy preparation and proof correction.* Part 1: 1975 *Recommendations for preparation of typescript copy for printing.* Part 2: 1976 *Specification for typographic requirements, marks for copy preparation and proof correction, proofing procedure.* Gives the standard signs meaning 'transpose', 'close up', 'space', etc.

83

Hart's rules for compositors and readers at the University Press, Oxford, 38th
  edn, Oxford University Press, 1978
Manual of style, 12th edn, University of Chicago Press, 1969
MHRA style book, 2nd edn, London, Modern Humanities Research Associ-
  ation, 1978
MLA handbook for writers of research papers, theses and dissertations, New
  York, Modern Language Association of America, 1977
Oxford dictionary for writers and editors, Oxford, Clarendon Press, 1981. A
  successor to the eleven editions of Collins, *Authors' and printers' dictionary*
  and very useful for tricky spellings and printing terms.
Rees, H. *Rules of printed English*, London, Darton, Longman and Todd, 1970

For punctuation and style see:

Carey, G. V. *Mind the stop*, 2nd edn, Cambridge University Press, 1958;
  now a Penguin Reference book
Fowler, H. W. *A dictionary of modern English usage*, 2nd edn, revised by
  Sir Ernest Gowers, Oxford University Press, 1965
Gowers, Sir Ernest. *The complete plain words*, 2nd edn, revised by Sir Bruce
  Fraser, London, HMSO, 1973; now also a Pelican

6.1 *Abbreviations*

Avoid unnecessary abbreviations, and see that any unfamiliar ones are
explained at their first occurrence or in a list. Make sure that the
abbreviations used are not ambiguous: for example spell out 'verse' if
v. could be confused with a roman number; spell out 'lines' if the book
will have lining figures and ll. could look like 11; try to avoid the
use of ff to mean both 'folios' (fos. is better) and 'following'.

Use English rather than Latin, where possible: for example 'see
above' rather than '*v. supra*'.

Omission of full points. There should be no full point after per cent or
abbreviated units of measurement such as mm, lb, though 'in' may have
one to avoid ambiguity. Note that the plural of abbreviated units is
the same as the singular: 65 lb not 65 lbs. (Now that most of them take
no s in the plural, it does not seem worth retaining the s in hrs, qrs and
yds, as recommended in Hart's *Rules*.) Do not use ' and " to mean feet
and inches.

Most publishers omit the full point after contractions – abbreviations
including the first and last letter of the singular – for example Mr, Dr,
St, Ltd. The fact that a plural abbreviation, such as Pss. for Psalms,

includes the last letter of the full plural form, does not turn it into a contraction; it keeps the full point of the singular. The only common exception to the rule is 'no.' (number, from *numero*).

Some publishers also omit full points after abbreviations such as n ('note') and f, ff ('following'), which are unambiguous and appear in heavily punctuated passages such as bibliographical references and indexes.

Sets of initials. One can punctuate all, none, or those that consist of lower-case letters; or one can distinguish those which are pronounced as a word (e.g. NATO, UNESCO, which can also be in the form Nato, Unesco). Abbreviations consisting of initials should usually have a point after each initial, or no points at all, for example p.p.m. or ppm, but not ppm. with a single point.

Small capitals may be used in place of full capitals unless the book is to be typewriter-set or the abbreviations appear in passages or headings to be set in sans serif, bold or italic. However, if there are a number of capitalized words in the text or lining figures are used, the abbreviations may look incongruous and too insignificant, for example US Library of Congress, AD 1692.

Avoid the use of an apostrophe in the plural: NCOs is better than NCO's. However, some people think an apostrophe is needed with lower-case letters: e.m.f.s or e.m.f.'s.

Use lower-case for a.m. and p.m.

In translated matter see that the abbreviations are altered where appropriate, for example that EEC is substituted for EWG.

Punctuation after abbreviations. Where an abbreviation that takes a full point comes at the end of a sentence, do not add another full point to end the sentence. One point performs both functions.

See also under 'e.g.' and 'ibid.' below.

Italic. Italic abbreviations should be used for italic words such as book and journal names. If the author has used roman throughout it may not be worth changing them if there is no ambiguity, but it is, for example, worth using italic in classical references if the author's name is abbreviated too. In any case the abbreviations in the list of abbreviations should be in the same form as in the text. Common Latin abbreviations such as e.g. are roman.

Capitalization at the beginning of a footnote. A few authors and publishers prefer *c.*, e.g., i.e., l., ll., p., pp. to be lower-case at the beginning of a footnote, and Hart recommends this; others treat cf., *ibid.*, *op. cit.* and *loc. cit.* in the same way. If you decide to retain the lower-case forms, and the printer is not familiar with this style in your books, explain the system on your style sheet.

Superscripts. If the author quotes a passage which has abbreviations with superscripts, for example M^r, N^o, try to persuade him to lower the superscripts, because they can be expensive, especially if there is punctuation under the superscript letter.

Notes on individual abbreviations

AD, BC: see section 6.4

&: an ampersand is often used in the author–date system of bibliographical references (see p. 186). Elsewhere spell out & except in names of firms, statute references, and where the author is using it to make a distinction

&c. should become 'etc.' except where a document is being transcribed exactly

c., *ca*, approx.: use one of these consistently, rather than a mixture. *c.* is to be preferred to *ca*; both are usually italic

e.g., etc., i.e., viz. are set in roman. In the past, publishers expanded them unless the text was in note form; but the author may want his own usage to be followed, so ask before spelling them out. See that the author is consistent in his use (or omission) of commas before and after these abbreviations

et al.: see p. 186

f, ff, *et seq.*: 'pp. 95f' means p. 95 and the following page; 'pp. 95ff' or 'pp. 95 *et seq.*' means p. 95 and an unspecified number of following pages; so do not make f and ff 'consistent'. ff is preferable to *et seq.*, but a pair of page numbers is better. Remember that in all these cases one should use pp., not p.

ibid., *op. cit.*, *loc. cit.*, *idem*: all except *ibid.* are best avoided. They may be either roman or italic, but they should all be treated in the same way. The comma is often omitted after the first three, to avoid the spotted appearance given by double punctuation

v.: in references to legal cases v. is roman and the names of the parties are italicized (see section 14.2)

is commonly used by Americans to mean 'number'; but as readers outside the USA may not be familiar with the sign, it is best to substitute 'no.' The sign is also used as a symbol in linguistics books.

In the past it was the standard proof correction symbol for space, so warn the printer that the symbol is to be set, and remember to do this at proof stage too, if the symbol appears in a correction

Generic names: see section 13.5

Spacing

For copy-editors who mark the spacing of abbreviations table 6.1 lists some common ones.

Table 6.1 *The spacing of abbreviations*

Closed up

B.Chir.	6ff	a.c.	e.c.g.	kHz	μF
D.Phil.	6p	b.p.	ECG	kV	μg
e.g.	6% (but 6	Btu	e.m.f.	kVA	o.d.
i.e.	per cent)	°C	°F	kW	pdl
Ph.D.	16n	c.g.	ft/s	mA	pF
q.v.	1970a	c.g.s.	GMT	mCi	pH
	1s, 2s, 3p	c.n.s.	Hb	Mc/s	ppm
	(quantum	CoA	h.f.	mmHg	RNA
	states)	c/s	h.p.	m.p.	r.m.s.
		dB	i.u.	m/s	s.w.g.
		d.c.	°K	mV	VA
		DNA	kcal	μA	v.p.

Spaced

at. wt	initials, e.g. D. H.	20000
c. 1800	Lawrence	3:8 (ratio: equal space
cos ϕ	*loc. cit.*	either side of colon)
et al.	mol. wt	9 ft/s
et seq.	*op. cit.*	5 mm
fig. 23	p. 22	16 n. 5 (but 16 n5)
fl. oz	6 per cent (but 6%)	56vff (v = verso;
ft lbf	sp. gr.	space about one-ninth
	vol. 2	of an em in both places)

Mixture

AD 1605	25 °C	16 n5 (but 16 n. 5)
8 a.m.	$f: X \rightarrow Y$	16 nn1&2

List of abbreviations

See that the list contains all the unfamiliar abbreviations, that the abbreviations tally with the usage in the text, and that they are in alphabetical order. If the abbreviations are used in both text and footnotes, the most useful place for the list is at the end of the preliminary pages; but some authors prefer to list bibliographical abbreviations at the beginning of the bibliography.

6.2 *Capitalization*

Many authors have strong feelings about capitalization, so follow their system if they have a sensible one, and tell them what you propose to do if they have not. If you introduce a system yourself, do not carry logic too far, or you will find yourself with too many capitals or too few. If the system is an unusual one, outline it on your style sheet.

Titles and ranks

Titles and ranks are nearly always capitalized when they accompany a personal name, e.g. 'King John'; they may or may not be capitalized when they are used in place of a personal name, e.g. 'the king'; they are rarely capitalized when they refer to the rank and not to a particular person, and then only if they are preceded by 'the', e.g. 'all kings', 'a king', but 'the King would be bound by the laws of...'.

Administrative posts can be tricky, though in context no one is likely to be confused by 'the foreign secretary', 'the first secretary'.

Institutions, movements, denominations, political parties

Church used to be capitalized unless it referred to a building. Now it is often lower-case except when part of a title such as Roman Catholic Church. Similarly 'state' is now usually lower-case except in books on political theory.

Parliament is often lower-case, but Commons, Lords and House are capitalized to avoid ambiguity.

Protestant, Catholic, etc., are usually capitalized. Radical/radical, Liberal/liberal, etc., can be a problem, as it may not be easy to tell which meaning the author intends; it is probably best to tell him that you will follow his usage; then, if he intended no distinction, he may say so.

Periods, events, etc.
The names of periods (e.g. Carboniferous, Iron Age, Dark Ages) and wars are usually capitalized.

Peoples, races, genera and species
Negro should have a capital but black does not. Generic names have an initial capital, but species names do not, e.g. *Viola tricolor*; however, common names of species may be capitalized.

Geographical names
North, south, etc., are capitalized if they are part of the title of an area or a political division, e.g. South West Africa, Western Australia, the West, but not if they are descriptions in general terms, e.g. southern Scotland, the south of Scotland.

Astronomical names
In science books sun, moon and earth may be capitalized.

Theological terms
Personal pronouns referring to God are often lower-case; relative pronouns (who, whom, whose) should always be lower-case. Watch for the author's system for such words as Passion, Crucifixion, Resurrection, the Temptation, the Messiah, Messianic, etc.

Trade names
Makes of car etc. are capitalized, e.g. a Cortina, a Spitfire. Even though some trade names are now used as common nouns, proprietors insist on a capital for their product, e.g. Formica, Perspex, Pyrex, Thermos, Vaseline; common proprietary names are identified in dictionaries. Watch out for proprietary names of drugs. It is not necessary to put such names in inverted commas.

Book, journal and article titles
See pp. 171–2.

Cross-references
Be consistent in your use of capital or lower-case for 'plate' etc.

Use of small capitals

Small capitals are used for AD, BC, AH, except with lining figures; for quoted words originally in capitals; and for most capitalized roman numbers, e.g. vol. XII, though full capitals are used in titles such as Henry VII and for LXX (Septuagint). Some authors type lower-case roman numbers to indicate small capitals rather than full capitals; ask the author if you are in doubt as to what he intends.

Small capitals are not usually available for italic, bold, sans serif or typewriter setting so do not mark them in these cases. Warn the designer if italic or bold letters or words must be included in headings and headlines which he may want to set in small capitals.

Although subscript capitals are small, they should be marked as full capitals not small capitals.

6.3 *Cross-references*

'Fig.' is usually abbreviated, even in the text; 'plate' is often abbreviated in references in parentheses and footnotes, and spelt out in the text; 'chapter' and 'appendix' are usually abbreviated only in footnotes; 'section' may be replaced by a section mark (§) and equations may be referred to either in full or as '(6.3.3)', the parentheses distinguishing it from a section number; 'table' is never abbreviated. Be consistent in using a lower-case (or capital) initial for *all* these words.

Use pp., ff, not p., f, if more than one page is referred to (see p. 86). Where there are also references to pages of other books, it may be clearer for the reader if internal cross-references are followed by 'above' or 'below'.

Unless the cross-reference is to a whole section, a page number is more useful to the reader than a section number. However, the page number would have to be inserted at proof stage, which is expensive, whatever the setting method; if the book contains a large number of cross-references, consult the production department as to the best setting method; and see that the insertion of the cross-references is not charged against the author's correction allowance. It may save a little money if you can leave space for approximately the right number of digits, changing 'pp. ooo' to 'pp. ooo–oo'. If the author has given folio numbers in the cross-references, change the digits to zeros, as a reminder to him to fill in the page numbers on the proof.

Try to check that the author uses 'see' and 'cf.' (compare) correctly; many people use 'cf.' when they really mean 'see'.

Footnotes. If there are many cross-references to notes, it is best to number the notes by chapter rather than by page; if they are to be numbered by page, change 'see n. 75' to 'see p. 000, n. 0'.

Headlines. If the typescript contains a great many cross-references to section numbers, the section number should appear in the headline. (See section 9.2 for headlines to endnotes.)

6.4 *Dates and time*

Dates

In non-fiction keep dates simple: 1 May, 1 May 1975, May 1975. The American style is May 1, 1975, with or without a comma after the year. You may wish to persuade American authors out of using a comma in 'May, 1975', but some of them feel strongly about this. If you do change 'May 15, 1975,' or 'May, 1975,' to the British style, see whether the comma after the year is needed to punctuate the sentence, and leave or delete it accordingly.

If several dates within one month are given, so that it would be clumsy to give the month each time, say 'on the 12th'.

Decades are best expressed as 1860s (not 1860's or '60s) or thirties (not 'thirties). Century numbers are usually spelt out; fourteenth century (adjective fourteenth-century). Some authors prefer to hyphenate 'mid-fourteenth' in the noun 'mid fourteenth century', even though there is no such century; others prefer to omit the first hyphen in the adjective 'early-fourteenth-century'.

Pairs of dates are usually elided to the shortest pronounceable form – 1971–4, 1970–5 (or 1970–75), but 1914–18, 1798–1810 – with the following exceptions. BC dates cannot usually be elided, because 25–1 BC means something different from 25–21 BC, though a year of office may be given in the form 49/8 BC. Pairs of dates are usually left in full in the book title (the titles of other books should not be altered, of course), so as to provide a balanced title page; and the same may apply to chapter headings. If an author consistently elides to the last two digits (1974–76) you may decide to retain his system.

Where a single year, such as a financial year, comprises parts of two calendar years, an oblique stroke is used (1971/2 or 1971/72). This leaves the en rule to indicate a period covering more than one year: 'the years 1945/6–1968/9'.

When talking of a stretch of time between two years, say 'from 1924 to 1928' or '1924–8', not 'from 1924–8'; similarly say 'between 1914 and 1918', not 'between 1914–18'. 'To' may also be better than an en rule if each date contains more than one element:

| 18 September to 19 January | *rather than* | 18 September–19 January |
| c. 1215 to c. 1260 | | c. 1215–c. 1260 |

or a spaced rule may be used if there are no parenthetical dashes.

One should try to avoid starting a sentence with a figure, especially if it is a non-lining figure and so resembles a lower-case letter; one may have to turn the sentence round, for example change '1971 was an important year' to 'The year 1971 was [an] important [one]'.

Months may be abbreviated in tables and footnotes, but use names rather than numbers because 5.4.75 means 5 April in Britain, 4 May in the USA. The International Organization for Standardization's standard for the numerical writing of dates lays down that if numbers only are used, they should be in the order year, month, day; for example 12 January 1975 would be written 1975–01–12, with hyphens or en rules between the numbers.

AD and BC need be used only where there is any likelihood of confusion. AD and AH (*anno Hegirae*, used in Islamic dates) precede the year number, though when used loosely, as in 'fifth century AD', they follow the date. BC, BP (before the present = 1950), CE (Christian era) follow the date. (For the use of small capitals see p. 85.) Lower-case bp, bc or ad is used to indicate a radiocarbon date that has not been recalibrated. Though there are usually no commas in dates, BP dates do have a comma or space when they consist of five or more digits, e.g. 13,500 BP.

In England until 1752 the legal year began on 25 March, so the year 1673 comprised what we would now call 25 March 1673 to 24 March 1674. The dates between 1 January and 24 March are therefore often given in the form 23 March 1673/4. If the author gives only one year number he should make it clear whether he is following the contemporary system or the modern one.

The Gregorian calendar was introduced in 1582, but the Julian calendar remained in use in England until 1752. The Gregorian (New

Style) calendar was ten days ahead of the Julian (Old Style) calendar from 1582 to 1600, eleven days ahead from 1601 to 1699 and twelve days ahead from 1700 to 1752. The author should say in a note whether he is using New Style or Old Style dates, or should identify them 'NS' or 'OS', or give both, e.g. 11/21 October 1599, 25 October/6 November 1709. In Russia the Gregorian calendar did not come into use until 1918 (1 February 1918, Old Style, became 14 February, New Style).

In books dealing with Islam consider whether the book should give Islamic as well as Christian dates, and which should be given first; the two dates usually have an oblique stroke between them. Similarly with books on Judaism.

In works on astronomy or geophysics, dates are given in the order: year, month, day, for example 1971 March 15.

Time

Time is treated in the same way as other quantities: words are used for periods of time such as 'it took him six months', figures for exact measurements and for series of numbers. Use figures in 8.0 a.m., words in eight o'clock, no hyphen in half past eight. With the 24-hour clock use 19.45. A hyphen is usual in 'a five-minute start', an apostrophe in 'five minutes' start'. Apostrophes of this kind are often omitted from proper names such as Hundred Years War, but they should be retained elsewhere.

The Royal Astronomical Society's preferred style for the time is $12^h 09^m 12^s.7$ or $13^d.8675$; note the position of the decimal point with respect to the superior letter.

6.5 *Foreign languages*

Hart's *Rules* are a good guide on difficult points, and the Chicago *Manual of style* also has a useful chapter on foreign languages. This section merely warns you of some common pitfalls.

Foreign-language material falls into three categories:

(1) Texts for people who know or are learning the language. Such material will be in the original characters, or, if transliterated, will usually contain all diacritical marks. Foreign conventions such as *guillemets* are likely to be retained except in elementary books.

(2) Foreign proper names and technical terms in a book to be read

by people who may not know the language. Words from non-Roman alphabets will usually be transliterated; and some or all diacritical marks may be omitted from languages other than French, German and Italian. Foreign words in an English sentence should be in the nominative form. In German words, ü etc. is preferred to ue etc. where appropriate, and German nouns should retain their initial capital if they are italicized. For the use of italic, and of English plural forms, see section 6.6.

(3) Tables, figures, maps, etc., borrowed by an author from books or journal articles in another language. Not only should the wording be translated, but such conventions as *guillemets* and decimal commas should be anglicized.

Alphabetical order. See section 8.2.

Marking the typescript. All the desired accents and ligatures must be shown in the typescript. Remember that accented capitals are not available in typewriter setting, and that such accents would have to be added by hand; so avoid accented capitals if possible.

When the Scandinavian ø or the Polish ł are required, make it clear that these are letters with strokes across them and are not deleted.

Arabic

In transliterated Arabic the author may represent both 'ain and *hamza* by a typewritten single quote, but the printer *must* be told which is which. In type the 'ain may be represented by an opening quote or a Greek rough breathing, the *hamza* by a closing quote or smooth breathing. Because of this use of single quotes, double quotes should be used for quotations in books containing much transliterated Arabic.

Chinese

Many westerners have now adopted the Pinyin system of romanization in place of the Wade–Giles system; but the old spelling of some familiar names is usually retained, particularly where the Pinyin version gives a very different pronunciation, e.g. Beijing for Peking. Ask the editor whether Chinese words are, or should be, romanized according to the Pinyin system.

French

Accents may be omitted from capitals and small capitals, provided the author approves and the book is consistent. Some printers prefer not to accent capital A even if other capitals have accents. Accents and ligatures were not always used in medieval texts.

For capitalization of book titles see p. 177 below.

In personal and place names 'Saint' and 'Sainte' are normally spelt out and followed by a hyphen.

German

All nouns have capitals, and words are sometimes letterspaced for emphasis. If the author wishes ß (called *Eszett*) to be used for ss he must mark every occurrence, because not every ss becomes ß. In capitals or small capitals ß always becomes SS. For ligatures see Hart's *Rules* (38th edn, p. 108).

In pre-1900 works one may meet ue, oe, Th (for T) and variations in capitalization.

There are various ways of indicating quotations. If *guillemets* are used, they usually point inwards.

Greek
See section 14.1.

Latin
See section 14.1.

Russian
The Russian alphabet can be found in appendix 5. Consult the author as to whether any sloping Cyrillic is to be used; if so see that it is clearly marked on the typescript.

Turkish
Note that Turkish employs an undotted i as well as a dotted one.

6.6 *Italic*

Italic is used for:

titles of published books, except for the Bible, the Koran and books of the Bible, which are roman unquoted. Titles of chapters, articles, short stories and unpublished theses are roman in quotes. 'Preface' etc. are roman unquoted titles of periodicals; but article titles are roman and usually in quotes except in the author–date system (see p. 189). For use of roman 'the' or italic '*The*' in periodical titles see pp. 173–4

titles of long poems which are virtually books in themselves, e.g. *Paradise Lost*; but titles of short poems are roman in quotes

titles of plays and films, radio and television programmes

titles of major musical works such as operas, oratorios, ballets and song cycles given descriptive titles by the composer; but roman in quotes for nicknames given by other people, e.g. Beethoven's 'Pastoral' Symphony, and for the titles of songs. Roman without quotes for titles such as Symphony no. 5 in C Minor

titles of paintings and sculptures

names of ships, apart from such prefixes as HMS (HMS *Repulse*); but types of ship, aircraft and car are roman (a Spitfire, a Rolls-Royce)

genera, species and varieties; but orders, families, etc., are roman

mathematical variables (including geometrical 'points' and generalized constants such as constants of integration); but operators and chemical elements are roman

foreign phrases, not yet naturalized, in an English sentence; but roman for proper names such as institutions and streets, and roman in quotes for foreign quotations

names of parties in legal cases (see section 14.2), but v. between them is roman

directions to the reader, e.g. *see also* in an index, or *above* in a caption; also stage directions in plays

identification of letters or words referred to, e.g. 'the letter *h*'; alternatively roman, with or without quotes, may be used

emphasis, but it should be used sparingly. Authors of textbooks may italicize a phrase near the beginning of a paragraph, as a kind of sub-heading. Or they may italicize technical terms when they are first used; if so, they should not use italic for other kinds of emphasis too

Italic should not be used for the names of Acts of Parliament, for hotels, theatres, pubs, etc., or for possessive s following an italic word, e.g. 'the *Discovery*'s home port'.

Foreign words and phrases

Italic is used for foreign words (except the names of persons, institutions, places, etc.) in an English sentence, but not usually for foreign quotations. Some authors italicize foreign words only the first time they occur; this is an acceptable system, provided there are no foreign words that may be momentarily mistaken for an English one, e.g. *place* (French 'square'), *Land* (German 'region') or *man* (a measurement used in Iran). Of course, if the author is using italic for another purpose, say to indicate words of linguistic interest, other foreign words should not be italicized.

It is sometimes difficult to know where to draw the line between italic and roman: for example, if *louis d'or* is italic and franc is not (because it is now part of the English language) the author may complain of inconsistency. Most authors follow the general usage in their subject; some follow the *Concise Oxford dictionary*. I think *The Oxford dictionary for writers and editors* is a better guide.

If a foreign word is italicized, it should have the correct accents; it should probably be in the feminine form, where appropriate, but it should be in the nominative form unless it is quoted. If it is roman it does not matter whether it has an accent or not (or whether it agrees in gender), provided the author is consistent; but if he uses accents he must use them correctly, e.g. protégé, not protegé. It is usual to include the accents where they help to show the pronunciation, as in the third syllable of protégé.

Roman is now used for i.e. and e.g., and sometimes for ibid. and op. cit. In sums of money s and d (where they survive) are now often in roman (without points), following the pattern of p.

Plurals. Look at the author's use of native or English plurals for foreign words used in an English sentence: the plural form in some languages looks like a different word from the singular, and in such cases it would be better to use the English plural ending. Plural s is usually italic even if it is not strictly the plural form of the foreign word, e.g. *qanats*.

Explanation of foreign words. If the author uses a lot of foreign words, for example Indian terms for castes, ceremonies, etc., a glossary may be needed.

In headings

Where headings or headlines are in small capitals or italic, foreign words and titles of books etc. – which would normally be in italic – are sometimes put in quotes. This tends to give foreign words a self-conscious look; and it may be better to omit the quotes even though the word is italic in the text. Scientific words which are normally italic are not usually distinguished from the other words in italic headings.

Italic punctuation

Italic punctuation should be used only within an italic phrase, not before or after it:

In *Copy-editing: the Cambridge handbook*, one finds...
The best-known case, *Smith* v. *Jones*, raises an interesting point of law

6.7 *Measurements*

In science and mathematics books SI (Système International d'Unités) units are now normally used (see section 13.3). The basic SI units are:

Physical quantity	Name of SI unit	Symbol
length	metre	m
mass	kilogram	kg
time	second	s
electric current	ampere	A
thermodynamic temperature	kelvin	K
luminous intensity	candela	cd
amount of substance	mole	mol

In other books metric measurements should be added to or substituted for imperial ones. It may be necessary to ask the author how accurate his measurements are: for example, must 100 yards have an exact equivalent or an approximate round number?

Remember that abbreviated units of measurement, whether metric or imperial, have no full point and take no s in the plural, e.g. 52 kg.

6.8 *Money*

If whole pounds or dollars appear in the same context as fractional amounts, they should be treated in a similar way, e.g. '£6.00, £5.25 and £0.25', not '£6, £5.25 and 25p'. Do not use £ and p in the same expression.

Indian rupees can be given either in millions (Rs. 1,000,000) or in lakhs (Rs. 100,000 written Rs. 1,00,000) and crores (Rs. 10,000,000 written Rs. 1,00,00,000). If the editor wishes to retain lakhs and crores, see that the notation is explained in the preliminary pages; and warn the printer on your style sheet.

Where sums of money are tabulated, it is best to put the units in the column heading rather than beside each item.

6.9 *Numbers*

For science and mathematics books see chapter 13.

'*Numeral*' and '*figure*'

The British Standard on typeface nomenclature (BS 2961:1967) recommends that all numbers expressed in figures, whether arabic or roman, should be called numerals; but to some printers 'numeral' means a roman numeral. They use 'figure' to mean what the British Standards Institution would call an arabic numeral. To avoid possible misunderstanding, it is best not to use 'numeral' on its own where you are referring to a number to be set in arabic.

Old style (*non-lining*) and lining figures

Old style or non-lining figures have ascenders and descenders and look well with small capitals. They are easier to read in large groups

1 2 3 4 5 6 7 8 9

(for example in tables); but they have the disadvantage that the 'one' in most typefaces looks like a small capital roman 'one'. This can be confusing in bibliographical references, where arabic eleven (11) and roman two (II) may be confused. Another complication is that most mathematical superiors and inferiors are lining, and authors of books that contain them feel that it is a bad thing to use two 'ones' that look so different. Also non-lining figures next to capitals can look at first glance like subscripts: 3T3.

Lining figures are usually the same height as capitals and so align well with them.

1 2 3 4 5 6 7 8 9

Only one kind of figure is used in a book, with a few exceptions: as

99

I have just mentioned, superiors and inferiors in mathematics are nearly always lining figures; also the designer will ask for lining figures to be used in headings set in capitals, and for non-lining figures to be used in headings set in small capitals. Tell him if headings and headlines contain arabic figures, and if you notice other potential problems.

Ambiguous numbers

Distinguish capital O and zero, l and 1, roman and arabic one. Avoid the abbreviation ll. (lines) if lining figures are to be used. See that any handwritten figures are legible and unambiguous; for example the Continental 1 can be read as a 7, and some American 4s can be read as 7s. The word 'billion' should be avoided; if the author does use it he should make it clear whether he is talking of British billions (million millions) or US billions (thousand millions).

Words or figures

Most publishers use words for small numbers (usually those below 10, 12, or 100), except for exact measurements, cross-references and series of quantities. Round numbers above the chosen figure may be expressed in words when they are not part of a series. Where there is a series of round millions 2m is often used; with a pound or dollar sign, 2 million may also be used.

Where two series of quantities are being discussed, e.g. numbers of wards and numbers of beds, it may be clearer if words are used for one series of quantities: 'ten wards held 16 beds each, but fifteen others contained as many as 40'.

Spelt-out numbers such as twenty-one are hyphenated. Use figures to avoid a hyphen in an already hyphenated compound: '62-year-old man', not 'sixty-two-year-old man'.

One should try to avoid starting a sentence with figures, especially if they are non-lining and so resemble lower-case letters. If the number cannot be spelt out one may have to turn the sentence round.

Figures must be used before abbreviations: 5 kg, 6%.

Commas in thousands

In science and mathematics books there is usually no comma in thousands. Numbers with five or more digits either side of the decimal point have a space: 8478 but 84782, 782.68952. However, in a table containing both four-figure and five-figure numbers, the four-figure numbers must be spaced too, in order to align.

Authors of general books usually include a comma in numbers with four or more (or five or more) digits. See that four-figure numbers are treated consistently.

Commas and spaces are not used in dates (except for BP dates), in line numbers or in many reference numbers, where one should follow the usage of the issuing authority.

Decimal points

Say whether decimal points should be low or medial. The low point is now used in science and mathematics books. Where the author has borrowed, say, a French or German table, change the decimal commas to points.

The decimal point must always be preceded by a digit; add a zero where the author has no digit before the point.

Percentages

Percentages are usually given in figures, whether per cent or % is used; but if the percentages are not exact ones they may be spelt out if followed by per cent. In some cases per cent is used in the main text, and % in tables and footnotes (or in tables only). Although per cent is an abbreviation, it takes no full point; it should be roman, not italic; and for Americans it is one word.

Make sure that percentages are distinguished from actual numbers in tables. Do not worry if percentages do not add up to exactly 100; the individual percentages are usually rounded up or down, and the total should fall between 99 and 101, though given as 100.

Elision of pairs of numbers

Page numbers are elided as far as possible except for 11 to 19 in each hundred, which retain the 'tens' figures: 21–4, 130–5, but 211–15. Some publishers prefer to repeat the 'tens' if the first number ends in zero: 130–35.

Measurements, such as length, temperature, wavelength, latitude and longitude, percentages, should not be elided, because it is possible to use a descending scale as well as an ascending one: 21–2 might mean 21 to 22 or 21 to 2. Where an author consistently elides such pairs of numbers it will probably not be worth changing them unless elision really does lead to ambiguity.

Figures interspersed with letters cannot be elided, for example folio numbers which are followed by 'verso' or 'recto' (fos. 22v–24r) or numbers preceded by '*circa*' (*c.* 1215 to *c.* 1260).

Roman numbers should not be elided.

Other numbers, such as population, amounts of money, etc., are probably best treated according to the author's system. See that the author does not say 2–3,000 if he means 2,000–3,000 and there is any chance of ambiguity.

En rule between numbers

See section 6.12.

Roman numbers

Full capitals are used for titles such as Henry VII and for LXX (Septuagint); such numbers should not be followed by a full point (except of course at the end of a sentence). Small capitals (if available) are used for most other capitalized roman numbers, for example volume numbers, unless these occur in combination with lining figures. Lower-case is used for preliminary page numbers and such things as scene numbers in references which contain two roman numbers that need to be distinguished. Some authors type lower-case roman numbers to indicate small capitals rather than full capitals; ask the author if you are not sure what he intends.

Numbered items within paragraphs

Use (1) rather than 1).

Numbers and letters

Combinations of figures and letters (except units of measurement) are often unspaced: 2a, 17ff, 8n. See Table 6.1 on p. 87.

6.10 *Parochialisms and stereotypes*

Parochialisms

Alter 'this country' to 'Britain', 'our' (where appropriate) to 'British', 'the Great War' to 'the First World War', 'the [last] war' to 'the Second World War', 'in the last few years' or 'recently' to 'the early 1980s' or whatever is appropriate.

Spell American proper names correctly, e.g. Pearl Harbor, Lincoln Center.

If textbooks, particularly school books, contain many references to cricket, petrol, British money, radio and television programmes, etc., consider whether they should be changed to make the book more suitable for use overseas; educational authorities, naturally enough, prefer books that are related to the children's everyday life. Similarly references in prefaces to sixth forms, GCE, A level, etc., may need to be amplified to show that the book will fit into other educational systems, and how it will do so.

In other books American or British terms may be kept unless they may cause confusion. Leave American turns of phrase, for example the use of 'one thinks *he* can' in place of the English 'one thinks *one* can'. The American symbol # (=number) is not widely known in Britain and should be changed to 'no.' unless it is being used purely as a symbol.

Avoid abbreviations or slang which may be meaningless outside the United Kingdom: it is easy to notice unfamiliar or unintelligible terms and abbreviations from other countries, but you will need to think whether such terms as LSE or 'tube' will be clear to overseas readers.

Stereotypes

Sex stereotypes. In my view 'mankind', 'chairman', 'spokesman' are neutral and not sexist, because there have been female spokesmen and even chairmen for a very long time; and I much prefer them to 'spokesperson' etc. It is more important to look for underlying stereotypes in such things as sample sentences which may show women only as mothers, wives and secretaries, most other jobs being done by men.

There is no neutral personal pronoun yet; but 'he' has been used as one for so long that it is still understood by most people to refer to women as well as men, girls as well as boys. Here too the cure may be worse than the disease. Some authors say 'he or she' every time, which is clumsy; some use 'he' in odd-numbered chapters and 'she' in even-numbered or alternate the two pronouns, which can be disconcerting; others use 'their', even when referring to a single person.

There are other stereotypes about races, nationalities, classes; and one should look out for bias in the same way as one does when the author is writing about an individual.

6.11 *Proper names*

The names of foreign persons, places, institutions, etc., should not be italicized (except in a heading).

Consistent forms – native or anglicized

If the author uses foreign names in the text or as places of publication, check that he consistently uses either the anglicized form (if any) or the native form of each. It is easy to miss forenames that are inconsistently anglicized.

In books intended for readers who do not know the original language, some or all diacritical marks may be omitted from native forms if there is no anglicized form. As French, German, and Italian are widely known, accents are usually retained; for books about other countries, ask the author to add accents to proper names if necessary.

There may be more than one correct form of a place name, e.g. Basle, Bâle, Basel. *The Oxford dictionary for writers and editors* gives preferred forms of a number of these; but if an author consistently uses one of the other forms (e.g. Roumania rather than Romania), ask him before changing the spelling. Another authority is the *Times index-gazetteer*, though this is not altogether consistent with the *Times atlas*.

Rees, *Rules of printed English*, 256, gives a list of geographical names showing their forms in various languages.

Specific forms

Use United States rather than America(n), wherever there is any possibility of ambiguity. Similarly England, Great Britain (England, Scotland and Wales), the United Kingdom (Great Britain and Northern Ireland), the British Isles (United Kingdom plus the Irish Republic) should be used accurately.

Note that Holland is, strictly speaking, only the name of two provinces of the Netherlands: Noord-Holland and Zuid-Holland.

Up-to-date forms

Watch for out-of-date forms, particularly for newly independent countries, though of course one should normally use contemporary rather than modern names in historical works, for example St Petersburg rather than Leningrad in a book about nineteenth-century Russia.

If, say, African place names have to be brought up to date, ask the author to do it, for it is not only the names of countries that have been changed (see appendix 3); some towns and natural features have different names as well, and it is more difficult to find out the up-to-date forms.

Some common mistakes

Use	Habsburg	*not*	Hapsburg
	Hong Kong		Hongkong
	Cape Town		Capetown
	Nuremberg		Nuremburg
	The Johns Hopkins University		John Hopkins University

See Rees, *Rules of printed English*, 303, for some personal titles which differ slightly in spelling from place names.

Don't be misled by the stressed syllable into misspelling

Apennines   Caribbean   Philippines

Prefixes such as de, von, van

Except in anglicized names such prefixes are usually lower-case (except, of course, at the beginning of a sentence).

French names

Do not abbreviate Saint and Sainte in personal and place names. They should be hyphenated to the following element: Sainte-Beuve.

Dutch names

's (abbreviated from 'des') and 't (abbreviated from 'het') should usually be preceded and followed by a space, though in names of towns such as 's-Gravenhage there is a hyphen; ij is treated as a compound letter and so both should be capitalized at the beginning of a proper noun.

Names of companies

Retain the ampersand where the author has it in his typescript. Stet it so that the printer knows it is not to be spelt out.

Inverted forms for bibliographies etc.

If you are inverting names to bring the surname to the beginning of the entry, there are one or two pitfalls. For example, unwesternized Japanese and Chinese names already have the surname first, and in Spanish and Portuguese names it may be the penultimate element that should come first, e.g. Federico Gutierrez Granier should be under Gutierrez not Granier. An invaluable guide is *Names of persons: national usages for entry in catalogues*, definitive edition edited by A. H. Chaplin and Dorothy Anderson (International Federation of Library Associations, 1967).

6.12 *Punctuation*

Follow the author's system; if he has none, use the minimum punctuation necessary to clarify what would otherwise be ambiguous or misleading. This section does not deal with general rules of punctuation (for those consult Carey, *Mind the stop*). It attempts to cover points which may cause difficulty for new copy-editors; and as en rules cause most difficulty, it deals with those first.

En rules

An en rule is longer than a hyphen, and can be used either as a parenthetical dash or to convey a distinction in sense. Write 'en' or 'N' above it, and make clear whether it is to be spaced or closed up: en rules for parenthetical dashes are always spaced, en rules for sense are usually closed up.

To convey a distinction in sense. En rules are used when the first part of a compound does not modify the meaning of the second part. They can usually be thought of as standing for 'and' or 'to'.

En rules are used to mean 'and' in such phrases as:

Ali–Frazier fight
Labour–Liberal alliance
oil–water interface
gas–liquid chromatography
theocratic–military site
Urdu–Hindi issue
red–green colourblind (but hyphen in blue-green if it means bluish green)

Although 'Sino-Japanese' and 'Chinese–Japanese' mean the same thing, it is usual to have a hyphen in the first (i.e. where the first part of the word is a prefix that cannot stand on its own) and an en rule in the second. Hyphens are also used in such compounds as 1-chloro-3,6-dimethylnaphthalene. Some people prefer an oblique stroke (solidus) in terms such as 'oil/water interface' or where one or more elements consists of more than one word, e.g. electron/neutral particle collisions.

The en rule should not replace 'and' if the word 'between' is used: say 'the period between 1920 and 1930', not 'the period between 1920–30'.

En rules are used to mean 'to' in such phrases as:

1914–18 war
pp. 1–20
London–Glasgow railway
input–output ratio

The en rule should not replace 'to' if the word 'from' is used: say 'from 1970 to 1976' not 'from 1970–6'.

It may be better to substitute 'to' for the rule if there are also hyphens in the compound: one could have '5–10 day interval', but if one wanted to hyphenate '10-day' it would be better to have '5- to 10-day interval'; similarly '10- to 14-year-olds' is better than '10–14-year-olds'.

En rules meaning 'to' and 'and' are usually unspaced; theocratic–military, chapters 8–9, 101–50. However, spaced en rules may be used between groups of numbers and words to avoid implying a closer relationship between the words or numbers next to the en rule than between each of these and the rest of its group:

6. 6–8	*but*	6. 6 – 7. 8
September–January		18 September – 19 January
1215–1260		*c.* 1215 – *c.* 1260

But these spaced en rules should be used cautiously, especially if there are also parenthetical dashes, as the reader may not be able to tell one from the other; and it may be better to substitute 'to' in such cases.

Parenthetical dashes. Spaced en rules are now most often used. If the dashes are unspaced in the typescript, pencil a vertical line either side of each one, but there is no need to put a space sign.

Other uses. An en rule with a space before it can be used to indicate that a speech breaks off abruptly (an ellipsis in such cases suggests that the speaker paused, not that he was interrupted).

Use a hyphen rather than an en rule when the author is talking about parts of words, as in 'the prefixes pre- and post-'. Opinion is divided as to whether an en rule or a hyphen is a better way of symbolizing a missing letter in a word (if the author uses dashes rather than points).

Em rules

Em rules are sometimes used to introduce lines of dialogue, for example in James Joyce's stories and in some foreign texts; in such a system there is no sign to show where the speech ends, and it may be sensible to substitute inverted commas in a foreign-language reader for schools, to help the pupil.

Em rules may be used to indicate the omission of a word or part of a word:

She was said to have had an affair with — that season.
Would Mr T— consider taking responsibility?

In indexes and bibliographies em rules may stand for a repeated entry heading or author's name (two rules being used for entry heading plus sub-entry heading, or for joint authors' names respectively), though many publishers prefer to use indention. If you use rules in an index, see that it will be clear to the reader exactly how much is represented by the rule.

Em rules are also used in tables (see p. 164).

Hyphens

Some subjects have a conventional usage, and some authors have strong views, so ask them before imposing your own system. Introduce hyphens only to avoid ambiguity:

best known example	best-known example
deep blue sea	deep-blue sea
four year-old children	four-year-old children
little frequented place	little-frequented place

and do not carry logic too far; Hart gives lists that you may find helpful. American authors tend to use fewer hyphens than the British do. They may also write hyphens as double dashes like equals signs; warn the printer if you think he is likely to be confused.

Look at the hyphens at the ends of lines in the typescript, and stet those that are to be retained if the lines are broken in different places.

Floating hyphens as in 'sixteenth- and seventeenth-century architecture', 'pre- and postwar', may be avoided by rewording. If rewriting would lead to a clumsier sentence, see how many hyphens are in fact necessary. Sometimes the sense will be clear if the first hyphen is omitted: but in 'phosphorus- or sulphur-containing compounds' the sense would change. Sometimes a hyphen will have to be added to the second compound: 'pre- and postwar' is clear, but does 'nitro-' in 'nitro- or chlorophenylnaphthalene' mean nitrophenylnaphthalene or nitronaphthalene?

If you can, avoid ex- (formerly) qualifying more than one word, as in 'ex-public schoolboy'.

Brackets

To a printer the word 'brackets' signifies square brackets; round brackets are called 'parentheses' or 'parens'. The curly brackets that group items in a table are called 'braces'. For the conventional order of brackets in mathematics see p. 231.

Square brackets. Square brackets should be used to indicate words interpolated in quotations; the material within the square brackets does not affect the punctuation of the outer sentence. In editions of texts both square and angle brackets may be used (see section 11.5).

Square brackets may be used in bibliographies to enclose an author's name, publication place or date that does not appear in the publication cited. In such a case the entry may be punctuated as though the square brackets were not there:

Geddes, D. *St Michael's Church, Amberley*. Arundel, Blathwayt Press, [1871].

If square brackets are used for interpolations, they should not also be used to replace parentheses within parentheses: use double parentheses.

Apostrophes

Possessives. The inclusion or omission of the possessive s should be decided on the grounds of euphony; this means that some possessives will have an s and some will not, but there should be some system. Hart's *Rules* (38th edn, p. 31) recommend that (except in ancient names) 's should be used in all monosyllables and disyllables, and in longer words accented on the penultimate syllable. Another rule is that 's should be used except when the last syllable of the name is pronounced *iz*: Bridges', Moses', but James's, Thomas's.

Watch out for the incorrect apostrophe in its, yours, ours, theirs, hers.

Plurals. Apostrophes should not usually be used to indicate plurals:

the Joneses	*not*	the Jones's
1960s		1960's
NCOs		NCO's

109

However, some people prefer to use apostrophes after lower-case letters:

> e.m.f.s   *or*   e.m.f.'s
>
> dotting his *is*   dotting his *i*'s

Omissions. An apostrophe is not needed in commonly used abbreviations such as:

> thirties (= 1930s)   flu
>
> bus   phone

Commas

In lists of three or more items, a comma should be consistently omitted or included before the final 'and': red, white and blue; red, white, and blue.

Common faults of punctuation

There are some mechanical things that authors' typists very often forget.

(1) There should not be a comma before an opening parenthesis, except in an index where sub-entries are in parentheses.

(2) A full point should come before the closing parenthesis if the whole sentence is in parentheses; otherwise after the closing parenthesis:

> He wore a hat. (The sun was very strong.)
>
> He wore a hat (the sun was very strong).

(3) There is no need for double punctuation at the end of a sentence, either after an abbreviation or after a punctuation mark in inverted commas or a book or article title, e.g.

> The article was called 'Ruins in Malmesbury, Wilts.'
>
> He was editor of *Which?*
>
> He was awarded the D.S.O.

The exception is if the abbreviation or mark of punctuation is within parentheses inside the sentence.

> He edited a magazine (*Which?*).

(4) Nowadays parenthetical dashes usually stand on their own, without commas; but some authors insist on retaining the comma in certain cases:

The family consists of Mohammad Musa – my 31-year-old host, – his mother, his 17-year-old wife…

(5) There should be no full point at the end of items in a list of plates, figures, etc., or at the end of broken-off headings.

(6) Commas should be consistently included or omitted after 'that is' or 'i.e.'

(7) 'For example' and 'e.g.' are used in two ways:
(*a*) they may form the whole of the parenthetical phrase.

it was, for example, his habit to...

(*b*) they may introduce an example:

...superstitions, for example the belief...

In type (*b*) the comma should be consistently omitted or included after 'for example' or 'e.g.'

(8) A colon introducing a list or other displayed material should not be followed by a dash.

(9) Semi-colons or full points, *not* commas, should be used to separate main clauses that have different subjects and are not introduced by a conjunction.

6.13 *Spelling*

The spelling of book and article titles should not be made consistent with the rest of the book; and in scholarly works the spelling of quoted material is usually left unchanged (see section 11.5). Otherwise follow your house style or the author's system. Watch out for words with alternative spellings: the fact that both spellings are in common use makes it easy to miss inconsistencies.

acknowledgement	acknowledgment
ageing	aging
appendixes	appendices
biased	biassed
by-law	bye-law
centring	centering
connection	connexion
dispatch	despatch
encyclopedia	encyclopaedia
focused	focussed
gipsy	gypsy
gram	gramme

guerrilla	guerilla
inflection	inflexion (use 'inflexion' in maths)
inquiry	enquiry
-ise	-ize (but see below for words that must be spelt -ise)
judgement	judgment (use 'judgment' in legal works)
medieval	mediaeval
movable (but 'moveable' in legal works)	
premiss	premise
programme, *but* computer program ('programmer' has two *m*s in both cases)	
reflection	reflexion
storey	story
wagon	waggon

Even if the author is using the -ize spelling, the following words must be spelt -ise:

advertise	disfranchise	misprise
advise	disguise	mortise
affranchise	emprise	practise
apprise (inform)	enfranchise	precise
arise	enterprise	premise
braise	excise	prise (open)
chastise	exercise	reprise
circumcise	expertise	revise
comprise	franchise	seise (legal term)
compromise	guise	supervise
concise	improvise	surmise
demise	incise	surprise
despise	merchandise	televise
devise	misadvise	treatise

The following should be spelt -yse, not -yze (except in American spelling):

analyse	dialyse	hydrolyse
catalyse	electrolyse	paralyse

Watch out, too, for the inclusion or omission of accents on such words as 'elite', 'regime', 'role', and for the spelling of proper names; and also, of course, for hyphens.

112

Distinguish between:

dependant (noun)	*and*	dependent (adj.)
forbear (abstain)		forebear (ancestor)
forgo (do without)		forego (precede)
principal (chief)		principle (rule)

Note the following differences in spelling:

siege	*but*	seize
unmistakable		unshakeable

Watch out for the following words, which are often misspelt:

accommodate	millennium
analogous	sacrilegious
battalion	superseded
desiccation	trade union
harass	(*but* Trades Union Congress)
idiosyncrasies	

Ligatures (combinations of two or more letters) are not used for ae, oe in anglicized words such as manoeuvre, Oedipus; but they are used in Old English and usually in modern French. Mark them by putting a 'close-up' mark above them, and mention them on your style sheet. You don't need to mark the ligatures which printers use for roman and italic ff, fi, fl, ffi, ffl, etc.

American (US) spelling

If you are retaining American spelling, keep an American dictionary, such as the *American college dictionary* (Random House), beside you. A list of some common differences is given below, but Americans may use the 'British' spelling of some of these words, as they are alternatives. Also the changes listed do not apply to all words: for example en- is not always replaced by in-.

-am (not -amme), e.g. gram, program
-ay (not -ey), e.g. gray
-ck- (not -que-), e.g. check, checkered
-ce (not -se), e.g. practice (verb as well as noun)
-e- (not -ae-), e.g. anemia, archeology, esthetic
-e- (not -oe-), e.g. fetal (sometimes used in English spelling too)

113

-er (not -re), e.g. caliber, center, liter, somber, theater
-et (not -ette), e.g. buret
-eu- (not -oeu-), e.g. maneuver
f- (for ph-), e.g. sulfur
im-, in- (for em-, en-), e.g. imbed, inclose, insure (=ensure)
-ing (not -eing), e.g. aging, eying
judgment
-l- (not -ll-), e.g. marvelous, woolen
-ler, -led (not -ll-), e.g. traveler, traveled, *but* controller, controlled
-ll- (not -l-), e.g. fulfill, installment, skillful, willful
-og (not -ogue), e.g. catalog
-ol- (not -oul-), e.g. mold, smolder
-or (not -our), e.g. honor, labor
-ow (not -ough), e.g. plow
-per, -ped (not -pp-), e.g. worshiper, worshiped, *but* shipper, shipped
-se (not -ce), e.g. defense, license (noun as well as verb), offense, pretense
sk- (not sc-), e.g. skeptical
tire (noun), not tyre
toward, as well as towards
un- (not in-), e.g. undefinable
-z- (not -s-), e.g. analyze, cozy, paralyze

6.14 *Miscellaneous points*

This section contains a few extra points of style and syntax that tend to cause trouble. One aims throughout at clarity, simplicity and consistency, but without pedantry; and Fowler's *Modern English usage* (2nd edn, revised by Sir Ernest Gowers, 1965) is an invaluable guide. One must at least retain useful distinctions in meaning, by discouraging authors from using words incorrectly; the following are common solecisms: 'infer' to mean 'imply', 'disinterested' to mean 'uninterested', 'protagonist' to mean someone who supports a theory.

I, we, the present writer
'I think' is preferable to 'in the present writer's opinion' or 'we think', though an impersonal form may be necessary in a multi-author work.

One
American writers use 'he' to refer back to the impersonal pronoun, 'one': 'If one fell, he would hurt himself badly.'

A or an

Some authors still write 'an historical', 'an hotel'; publishers usually retain this where the author has it, but do not introduce it yourself.

With abbreviations it is sometimes difficult to know whether to use 'a' or 'an'; abbreviations can be pronounced as though they were spelt out (a Mr Brown), or as a word (a NATO base), or as separate letters (an MP): and there are borderline cases.

It or she

Countries should consistently be described as either it or she; similarly ships, railway locomotives and aeroplanes, which are normally referred to as she.

Singular or plural verb

See that the author treats each group noun such as 'government' as consistently singular or plural. It is very easy to be inconsistent about this, according to the context: 'The Labour Government was forced into a corner; after some weeks of tension they agreed among themselves...' (see Fowler, pp. 402–3).

'None' may be followed by a plural verb, but 'neither' as an adjective or pronoun should be followed by a singular verb; for number after 'neither...nor' see Fowler, pp. 386–7.

'A number of...are/is'. I suggest you follow Fowler, p. 403, in using 'The number...is' and 'A number...are'.

'Data', 'errata', 'media' and 'strata' are plural nouns and should normally be treated as such; but in data-processing 'data' is now treated as a singular collective noun.

Position of 'neither' and 'both'

See that these are correctly placed, e.g. 'which neither suits him nor me' should be 'which suits neither him nor me'; 'which both suited him and me' should be 'which suited both him and me'. Watch out for 'neither... or': authors slip up, especially where there is a long clause between 'neither' and 'nor'.

Position of 'only'

If there is any possibility of ambiguity, 'only' must be placed in the correct position; otherwise place it in the most natural-sounding position (see Fowler, pp. 418–19). Does:

Carpets only cleaned on Saturdays

115

mean

> Only carpets are cleaned on Saturdays
> Carpets are cleaned, but not dyed, on Saturdays
> Carpets are cleaned on Saturdays only

'*Owing to*' and '*due to*'

'Due to' is often used when there is no noun for it to refer back to:

> Due to bad weather, the outing was cancelled

Perhaps this is a lost cause (see Fowler, p. 141).

'*That*' and '*which*'

Fowler recommends that 'that' should be used for defining clauses and 'which' for non-defining:

> He stopped the second car that was driven by a woman
> He stopped the second car, which was driven by a woman

Note that although defining clauses often have 'which', non-defining clauses should always be preceded (and followed) by a comma. See Fowler, pp. 625–8.

'*Of which*' and '*whose*'

Some purists say that 'whose' should be used only when it refers to a person, but the use of 'whose' instead of 'of which' can save a very clumsy sentence (see Fowler, p. 712). To cite one of his examples:

The civilians managed to retain their practice in Courts the jurisdiction of which was not based on the Common Law

is not as clear as

The civilians managed to retain their practice in Courts whose jurisdiction was not based on the Common Law

Position of descriptive phrase

Such a phrase at the beginning of a sentence continues in force until the subject changes or is restated. In the sentence: 'In 1672 he went to Mantua and married a dressmaker in 1678', the date 1672 applies to both verbs, and the sentence should be turned round to read 'He went to Mantua in 1672 and...'. Or one could say 'In 1672 he went to Mantua, and he married...'.

Unattached participles
Watch out for these, and reword them (see Fowler, pp. 659–61).

Having pitched the tents, the horses were fed and watered

Split infinitives
Avoid them if you can do so without distorting the sentence (see Fowler, pp. 579–82); but sometimes a split infinitive is the lesser of two evils:

She put out a finger to almost touch a petal

A few verbs appear to marginally permit pronominal indirect objects

Very honourable exceptions were Italian restaurants, said positively to like children, and Chinese ones, said positively to love them ['positively' really belongs to 'like' and 'love', not to 'said']

Subjunctive
If the author uses the subjunctive, see that he uses it correctly (see Fowler, pp. 595–8); do not introduce it yourself.

Adjectival nouns
To avoid headline language, keep adjectival nouns to a minimum, preferably not more than two in a row, e.g. *not* 'Water resources development plan board meeting'.

Ditto marks
Ditto marks, 'ditto' and 'do' should be avoided in printed matter, except in a quotation. Sometimes it is possible to tabulate the material so that no repetition is necessary; otherwise the word or phrase should be repeated.

6.15 *Safety*

Safety is extremely important: if you are copy-editing a cookery book, chemistry textbook or book with practical instructions, ask the author to check that the materials are correctly named, that the quantities are correct, that diagrams (such as wiring diagrams) are accurate and that any safety measures such as protective clothing or adequate ventilation are mentioned early enough. For example, in cookery books translated from French, bay leaves (*laurier*) have been translated as laurel leaves, which are poisonous; and in a chemistry textbook an extra zero made a mixture in a recommended experiment dangerously explosive.

7

Preliminary pages

The preliminary pages may consist of any or all of the following items:

half-title or bastard title
list of series editors
list of other books in the same series or by the same author
frontispiece
title page
publication date, publisher's and printer's names and addresses, copyright notice, International Standard Book Number, etc. (See chapter 15 for reprints and new editions.)
dedication
epigraph
contents list
lists of plates, figures, maps and tables (usually in that order)
list of contributors
foreword
preface
acknowledgements
list of abbreviations
general map(s) relevant to the whole book

usually in that order. At one time it was thought that the foreword and preface should precede the contents list; but the general view nowadays is that the contents list should be as easy as possible to find, and so should be as near to the beginning of the book as possible.

The preliminary or front matter can be any length unless it is to be printed separately from the text, in which case it should be a multiple of eight pages (plus an extra four if this is unavoidable).

If your firm has imposed proofs (see p. 58), tell the production department if there is some reason why the preliminary pages should be imposed separately (or not imposed until after the proofs are passed

119

for press): for example, you may not know the length of a foreword to come at proof stage.

Preliminary pages in complex books are usually numbered in lower-case roman, so that extra material can, if necessary, be added at proof stage or for a new edition. The numbering starts with the half-title, but no number will be printed on the pages that contain the first eight items in the list at the beginning of this chapter, or on any blank pages, so the first page number to be printed will probably be v or vii. The arabic page numbering should always start at 1.

One should look for ways of keeping the number of preliminary pages to a minimum, but there are certain conventions. The verso of the half-title is used only for certain things (see below). The contents list, the foreword or preface, and anything of more than one page usually starts on a right-hand page; anything shorter may be on a left-hand page or even fitted on to the last page of the contents list or preface. A dedication or epigraph is usually on the right-hand page following the title page, with a blank verso, if two pages can be spared.

Provide all the wording for the preliminary pages; the man who sets the type may not be familiar with things that seem obvious to you, such as your firm's address. The sheets of typescript should be numbered, so that the printer can see at a glance whether a folio is missing. If the author's numbering does not start until, say, the preface, identify the earlier folios by letter (A, B, etc.) and say 'fo. 1 follows' on the last lettered folio. If the numbers on the first of the author's numbered folios have to be changed to letters because they are followed by an item not included in his numbering, it is important to say 'fo. 3 follows' on the last lettered folio so that the printer does not think that fos. 1 and 2 are missing.

Half-title

Prepare a sheet for the half-title showing the wording, which is usually just the book title, series title, the names of the series editors and the volume number, but may also include a blurb or information about the author. The sub-title is usually omitted from the half-title; but include it if you think the main title is not sufficiently meaningful on its own. (If it is not, perhaps you should suggest a better main title, because the main title is all that will appear in many bibliographies.)

If the preliminary pages are complicated, and contain items, such as a dedication or epigraph, which are not mentioned in the contents list, the printer will find it helpful if you list the preliminary material on the half-title, giving the printed page numbers where possible (not the folio numbers) and making it clear what should start a fresh page or a right-hand page. If some material is not yet available, include it in the list, followed by 'to come' and the number of printed pages it is expected to occupy; and put a folio in the preliminary material headed 'Preface: copy to follow, approx. 2 pp.' However, there is no need to include blank folios in the typescript to represent blank pages. Say both on the half-title and on the appropriate folio where the arabic pagination is to begin. In the following example I have given the folio letters in square brackets, but they should not be included in the list.

[A]	p. i	half-title
—	ii	blank
[B]	iii	title page
[C]	iv	imprints
[D]	v	dedication
—	vi	blank
[E–I]	vii	contents list
[J]	recto	preface – to come, approx. 2 pp.

[K] acknowledgements list: to follow contents list if a complete verso or $\frac{3}{4}$ page is available; otherwise to follow preface

Arabic pagination starts at fo. 1

The main text of a book usually starts on a right-hand page, but there are exceptions: for example, in a book of musical pieces, each of which occupies two pages, it is essential that each piece starts on a left-hand page. In that case it is probably better to number the preliminary pages in arabic, especially if the preliminary matter ends on a right-hand page. If you are left with a blank right-hand page before the first page of text, try to put something on it; if there is nothing else, you can repeat the book title as a kind of half-title.

Verso of half-title

This page may be used for a list of other books in the series or by the same author, for a list of the series editors (or editorial board) if this will occupy too much space for the half-title, for a frontispiece printed on text paper, or, if necessary, for a dedication (see below). If the list of books includes some published by another firm, give the publishers' names, so that your sales department does not receive orders for them.

Frontispiece

A frontispiece should never be turned on the page, but it may be possible to print a landscape-shaped photograph upright on the page if the sides are masked. It may be possible to switch the frontispiece and one of the other half-tones.

Title page

Prepare a sheet with the complete wording. See that here, and on the half-title, the title, style for volume number (usually arabic), form of author's name and his description are the same as on any brief for the jacket designer. If you are at all doubtful about any of these points, check them now, as changes at a later stage are a nuisance to the sales and publicity departments as well as being expensive.

There is no need for a colon between the main title and sub-title, as the layout will make the division clear. It is usual to omit punctuation at the end of displayed lines on the title page, unless this would be misleading.

The number of the edition (if not the first) should be given (see chapter 15). The form of the author's name should be in accordance with his own preference; the inclusion of his qualifications and position will depend on the proposed market for the book. If the author dies before his book is published, some publishers put 'the late' on the title page; in any case any degrees or personal honours will be omitted; his academic position, if any, may be retained as still being relevant, though it should be preceded by 'formerly' or 'sometime'. A 'publisher's note' may be necessary in the preliminary pages to explain that someone else prepared the typescript for publication or saw the book through the press.

The name of the translator, artist or person who wrote the foreword may also need to be given on the title page.

The publisher's name or device should appear. Some publishers give the place and date of publication as well.

Verso of title page

It is useful to have duplicated sheets giving the standard wording, with spaces for the information that is different for each book.

The following should be included (for reprints and new editions see chapter 15):

publisher's full name and address

publication date if this has not been given on the title page

copyright notice, and possibly a notice about information retrieval. In
a book of plays or music there may be a note about performing rights
International Standard Book Number
Cataloguing in Publication data
printer's name and address
some publishers also give information about the typeface etc.

Publisher's name and address. Watch for circumstances that will entail
some variation from the usual wording. For example, the address of an
American branch will be omitted if your firm does not have the American
rights for a book, or decides, on the grounds of cost, not to obtain
American rights for items in an anthology.

Copyright notice. The familiar © copyright notice was introduced by
the Universal Copyright Convention (the UCC). Signatories to the
UCC (and they include the UK (1957), the USA (1955) and the USSR
(1973)) give each other copyright protection within their individual
countries provided that 'from the time of first publication' all copies
'bear the symbol © accompanied by the name of the copyright proprietor and the year of first publication'. The UK (in common with a
lot of other countries – but not the USA or the USSR) belongs to a much
older copyright union which is usually referred to simply as 'Berne'
(where it was first formed, in 1886). Berne does not require a particular
copyright notice of its members; nor, with the major exception of the
USA (where need for the © copyright notice is a part of internal legislation), does the law of most countries absolutely require it. It is simply
needed to acquire UCC protection, and since most countries are members of UCC it follows that it is sensible (wherever possible) to include a
proper © notice in all publications.

Nowadays there are only two circumstances where it is impossible to
include a © notice.

The first is a reprint of a work which was originally published before
the country in question became a signatory to the UCC. Thus, in the
UK, no work in its original form first published by a UK publisher before 27 September 1957 is entitled to a © notice. If the work has a new
introduction, then we may have only

Introduction © [copyright proprietor] 198–

A © notice for the text will only be possible if it appears, post-1957, in
a significantly different form: a new edition of a Shakespeare play, for

123

example, is entitled to a © notice if it is significantly different – in punctuation, spelling, or whatever – from any version which is known to have been published before.

The second case where a © notice should not be added is where the work when first published did not contain a notice because of the conditions of the manufacturing provisions of the old US Copyright Act. Briefly, before the new US Copyright Act of 1976 it was necessary, except under certain special circumstances, to omit a © notice altogether in the case of a US-authored work manufactured outside the USA but intended for import into the USA. Since 1 January 1978, this prohibition no longer exists, and a © notice can be included in all works entering the USA but must not be applied retrospectively to works that have already entered the USA without a © notice in deference to the old Act.

Under the Universal Copyright Convention the copyright notice should appear 'in such location as to give reasonable notice of claim of copyright' (by US law on the 'title page or page immediately following'). The correct form is:

© copyright proprietor, year of first publication

Sign, name of proprietor and date should follow each other closely, ideally in a single line; the contract should tell you who the copyright holder is. Watch out for circumstances that may entail a different copyright line. For example:

(*a*) If your firm is publishing the British edition of a book first published in the USA, the copyright date will be the date appearing in the US edition. As well as the date of first publication, there may be an earlier date if the author registered an earlier version of the work, such as a performing version of a play, at the Library of Congress. There may also be a later date, the date of renewal of copyright.

(*b*) *Translations*. There may be two copyright notices, one for the original work (if it is still in copyright) and one for the translation. The one for the translation would probably be:

English translation © [copyright proprietor] 198–

(*c*) *An edition of a text* would have a copyright notice for the text (if it was still in copyright) and another for the editorial material, which might read:

Introduction and notes © [copyright proprietor] 198–

(*d*) *An anthology* would need acknowledgements for the individual items (see section 3.6); and the acknowledgements for some US items would include copyright dates. The copyright notice for the book should be qualified, and might read:

Introduction, selection and notes © [copyright proprietor] 198–

(*e*) *Reprints and new editions.* See section 15.3.

Notice about information retrieval. Some publishers include the following, or a similar, notice:

All rights reserved. No part of this publication may be reproduced or transmitted in any form or by any means, electronic or mechanical, including photocopy, recording, or any information storage and retrieval system, without permission in writing from the publisher.

Publication date. The date of first publication should be given, plus the date of first publication by your firm (if this is different) and the date of all your reprints and new editions (see chapter 15). Some publishers do not give the original publication data if they are not the original publisher, but say, for example,

First published in Great Britain 1981

Other publishers give not only the original publication date but also the original publisher.

If the title, content, etc., have changed, this should be made clear:

First published as *Four Metaphysical Poets* 1934
Second edition, with a new chapter on Marvell, published as *Five Metaphysical Poets* 1964

If the book is a translation of a published work, the title in the original language should be given, together with the original publication date and the name and address of the original publisher. (See also section 11.6.)

The International Standard Book Number (*ISBN*) is always ten digits, and is divided into four parts separated by spaces or hyphens:

group identifier (of one to three digits), identifying the language or geographical area in which the book was published. The group identifier o (zero) includes the United Kingdom, USA, Australia, Canada, Eire and South Africa.

publisher prefix, identifying the publisher. This prefix may be of two to seven digits, depending on the size of the publisher.

title number, identifying the particular edition and binding of a particular book. The title number may consist of one to six digits, depending on the length of the group identifier and publisher prefix.

These three parts – group identifier, publisher prefix and title number – always total nine digits.

check digit, to pick up errors in transcribing the other nine digits. The check digit is always one digit: 1 to 9 or x (ten). When an ISBN is fed into a computer the first digit is multiplied by 10, the second by 9 and so on. For example, a book published by the Cambridge University Press might have the following number:

group identifier	publisher prefix	title number	check digit
0	521	05875	9

The computer would carry out the following calculation:

$$\begin{array}{cccccccccc} 0 & 5 & 2 & 1 & 0 & 5 & 8 & 7 & 5 & 9 \\ 10 & 9 & 8 & 7 & 6 & 5 & 4 & 3 & 2 & 1 \end{array}$$

$$0+45+16+7+0+25+32+21+10+9 = 165$$

If the total can be divided by 11, the number is a valid one.

There is a different ISBN not only for each book but for each edition and binding (e.g. hard-cover, paperback, limp), so that a bookseller can simply use one number to order the paperback of Hazel, *Cotton trade* (3rd edn). Where two or more books are sold as a set, there is a number for each volume and also one for the set, and all these numbers should appear and be identified in each volume. They may be set out as follows:

ISBN 0 521 05875 9   hard covers
ISBN 0 521 05876 7   paperback

ISBN 0 521 05875 9   vol. 1
ISBN 0 521 05876 7   vol. 2
ISBN 0 521 05874 0   set of two vols.

If your firm is co-publishing with another firm, and providing the preliminary pages that will appear in the copies they sell, see that their

ISBN is included. If they have their own title page and verso, the latter will contain their ISBN and not yours. If the same preliminary pages are to be used by both publishers, both ISBNs must be included and identified:

Oxford University Press   ISBN 0 19 826160 8
Cambridge University Press ISBN 0 521 07705 2

The relevant ISBN should also appear at the base of the back cover if there is no jacket, or at the base of the back of the jacket if there is one.

For full information about ISBNs, see *International Standard Book Numbering* published by the Standard Book Numbering Agency Ltd, 12 Dyott Street, London WC1A 1DF.

Cataloguing in Publication (CIP) data are provided by national libraries such as the British Library and the Library of Congress, from preliminary pages sent to them by the publisher; the data are printed on the verso of the title page (as in this book) so that other librarians need not spend time and money cataloguing the book themselves but can quickly make it available to library users. The data, augmented by details such as estimated price and publication date, also appear in the *British National Bibliography* and allied services, from which the librarian can select titles in advance of publication. Publishers thereby achieve earlier, and in some cases higher, sales.

The data should not be altered in any way without asking the Library first.

Printer's address. Books must carry the name of the country in which they were printed. Books printed in the United Kingdom must also include the printer's name and address. If the type is set in one country and printed in another, only the second country (and printer if necessary) need be identified, but publishers often give more than the minimum information.

Epigraph
It is usually sufficient to give the author of the quotation and the title of the work from which it is taken, without page or line number.

Contents page
All non-fiction works should have one comprehensive contents list, not one per part or a separate one at the beginning of an appendix of tables: it is easier for the reader to have only one place to look. There will

be rare exceptions to this rule; but be sure that an exception is justified.

The heading should be 'Contents' not 'Contents list', 'List of contents', 'Table of contents'.

The list should contain all the preliminary material except the following: half-title, any lists on p. ii, title page and verso, dedication or epigraph. Lists of illustrations etc. are called 'List of...' in the contents list, though their own headings are just 'Illustrations', etc. If the foreword has been written by someone other than the author, his name should appear in the contents list (and in some cases on the title page too) as well as at the beginning or end of the foreword. The contents list should also contain all endmatter such as endnotes (called 'Notes' or 'Notes to the text'), bibliography, glossary and index; if there is more than one index, the title of each one should be given.

It is difficult for a reader to find what he wants if the contents list is too detailed. Look critically at any list containing more than one grade of subheading. Second-grade subheadings may be run on as a paragraph instead of occupying separate lines; but this makes each item and its page number more difficult to find.

See that all parts and chapters (and subheadings where appropriate) appear in the list, and that they tally in wording, numbering (preferably arabic), spelling, hyphenation and capitalization of special words, both between text and list, and also with each other. The word 'Part' is usually retained in the part title; but the word 'Chapter' occupies more space and can anyway be taken for granted, so it is usually deleted. 'Appendix' may be deleted before each appendix number if there are many of them, provided you add 'Appendixes' above the first one. Chapters should be numbered in one sequence even if the book is divided into parts. There is no need for a point between the number and the title. The authors of individual chapters should be given; their academic positions may be included here if this will not clutter the list too much, or otherwise in a separate list of contributors or at the beginning of the relevant chapter. In a book of reprinted essays the details of original publication may be given in the contents list if they are not complicated, or otherwise in a list of acknowledgements.

If the title of the book appears at the top of the page, cross it out. Add 'o' after the first item, so that the printer does not forget to leave room for the page numbers. Ring any folio numbers that may be given for the various items, so that the printer does not set them; if he did set them, it is conceivable that no one would check them and they would appear in the finished book.

If, after your checking and the consequent alterations and additions, the list is rather untidy, have it retyped. Contents lists are best typed in upper- and lower-case, with initial capitals only for the first word of each item and any proper names: typographical treatment should be left to the designer. If the layout is complicated, consult the designer before having the list retyped.

Other lists

As I have already mentioned, lists of illustrations, abbreviations, contributors and so on, are called 'List of...' in the contents list and in their headlines; but the words 'List of' are omitted from the heading above the list. There should be no full point after the item number or at the end of any item; *'facing p.* oo' is used only for illustrations which are not in the text pagination, for example plates printed on art paper or pullouts. Check that all lists tally in spelling, capitalization and hyphenation with the captions etc. to which they refer, though the items may be given in a shorter form.

There may be no list of illustrations if the reader is unlikely to want to refer to them separately from the relevant text. If the frontispiece is the only plate, it may appear as the first item in the contents list: title on the left, '*frontispiece*' above the page numbers. The source can be given in a separate note, say at the end of the contents list.

If there is no list of plates and the plates are bound in separately, each leaf that is tipped in, and the first and last plate of any group or wrap-round, should have '*facing p.* ooo' printed at the foot of the page, so that the binder knows where to place them.

List of illustrations

If half-tones and line illustrations are numbered in one sequence, the list will probably be called 'Illustrations' rather than 'Figures'. If they are numbered separately the individual lists will be headed 'Plates', 'Figures', 'Maps', so that each item can begin with just a number.

For text illustrations add 'oo' at the end of the first item. If the plates are to be grouped, add '*Between pp.* oo *and* oo' below the heading 'Plates' or above each group. If they are not to be grouped, add '*facing p.* oo' after the first item.

It is not necessary to include the whole of the caption in the list; one needs only enough to identify the illustration. If each has a different source it may be most helpful to put the source at the end of each item; but if all the plates come from two or three sources, it is less repetitive to acknowledge them in a separate note at the end of the list or in a separate list of acknowledgements. In some cases the copyright holder will ask for the acknowledgement to be given immediately below the illustration.

List of tables

A list is necessary only if the tables are likely to be consulted independently of the text; but if the author has provided one, consult him before omitting it.

Preface, foreword, introduction

An introduction that is an essential part of the main book should be in the arabic pagination but need not be called chapter 1: mathematicians may call it chapter 0; others may leave it unnumbered.

A purely personal note by the author about how he came to write the book should be called 'Preface' and included in the preliminary pages. It is often signed and dated; if the book is on a subject which dates quickly the author may wish to give the date when he finished the type-script (to make it clear that the book takes no account of new discoveries after that time); in other cases an author will acknowledge help with proofs or index, and any date should take account of that fact. Try to persuade the author to use the latest possible date, or his book may look out-of-date.

If the preface is by someone other than the author, it should probably be called 'Foreword' or 'Editorial preface'. If the same preface or 'note to the reader' is used in each book in a series, make sure it applies fully to the present one.

Acknowledgements

General acknowledgements of help are best included in the preface, but acknowledgements of sources of copyright material are best listed separately, unless each acknowledgement immediately follows the relevant quotation or illustration (see section 3.6).

List of abbreviations

This is usually placed as near as possible to the beginning of the text, preferably on a left-hand page, so that the reader can refer back to it easily. See that all the necessary abbreviations are included and that they agree with the author's usage in the text and footnotes. Check the alphabetical order.

Other items

These may include a list of contributors, a note on sources or editorial conventions, or a list of notation. If there is such a note, see that its title indicates its content correctly, and that the content tallies, so far as you can tell, with what the author has actually done in the text. If you think an explanatory note is needed, send the author your suggested wording.

8

Indexes

For general background to this chapter I suggest you read M. D. Anderson's *Book indexing* (Cambridge Authors' and Publishers' Guides). There is also a British Standard, BS 3700: *Preparation of indexes*.

I should explain some of the terms I shall use. A simple entry comprises a *heading* and one or more *page references*:

> earthquakes, 24, 96

A complex entry consists of a heading (which may or may not be followed by page references) plus *sub-entries*, each consisting of a *subheading* followed by page references:

> limestone, 2, 55
> crinoidal, 128
> fossils in, 110, 114
> magnesian, 130

Sub-entries may start on a fresh line (as in the last example) or they may run on between semi-colons:

> limestone, 2, 55; crinoidal,
> 128; fossils in, 110, 114;
> magnesian, 130

If there are *sub-sub-entries*, the sub-entries are likely to be broken off and the sub-sub-entries run on between semi-colons:

> Cambridge University, 114–18
> architecture, 160
> colleges: Corpus Christi,
> 227; Jesus, 150
> rivalry with Oxford, 114

If an entry or sub-entry is too long to fit on to one line, the continuation lines or *turnover lines* (such as the second line of the sub-entry 'colleges' in the last example) have to be indented more than the start of a sub-entry, so that the two cannot be confused.

8 Indexes

8.1 *What needs to be done*

The publisher must be satisfied that the coverage, length and general organization of the index are satisfactory. Although a professional indexer will do a competent job, the author may well know more about the subject or the needs of the likely readers and should see a copy of the index before it is sent for setting.

You should ensure that the material is legible and arranged in the way most helpful to the reader. Check the organization and order of entries and sub-entries, and also the wording, capitalization, punctuation, use of italic and elision of numbers. Mark space to be inserted before each new letter group if the index will be longer than one page. See that there is a note at the beginning of the index to explain any unusual system.

Before passing the typescript on, write the author's name and the abbreviated book title at the top of the first folio, and give the number of the printed page on which the index is to start: 'To start on p. ....' The first index may start on a right-hand page if length is not a problem. The second (if there is one) usually starts on a fresh page but may run on from the end of the first. A general index usually comes last. If you did not include the index(es) in your list of headlines, or if their titles have changed since then, put a note on the first folio: 'headline to be...' The headline should give the name of the individual index, not just 'Indexes'.

Make sure that the printer knows how much to indent turnover lines and broken-off sub-entries, and where to insert 'continued' lines (see p. 146).

Authors and indexers should provide the index in the form of double-spaced typescript. Printers will accept cards that are numbered, but they will charge more because of the extra time taken to handle individual cards; and if the cards are handwritten, the cost will be still higher. If you are sending cards, see that they are correctly numbered and securely fastened in bundles or in a box.

8.2 *General organization*

Choice of heading
The choice of the first word of the heading is very important, because this will decide the position of the entry in the index. Are items indexed

under the right word? Are page references split between two synonyms that should be combined? Are there some entries that no reader of this kind of book would look up?

The British Standard on indexes says: 'Main headings should normally be nouns (qualified or unqualified) rather than adjectives or verbs on their own.' Some authors do use adjectives, and this can work satisfactorily in a few cases; but the heading should never be used as both noun and adjective in the same entry (see below).

The index should, of course, use the same spellings and accents as the text, but if old-fashioned or idiosyncratic terminology or spellings appear in quotations, the correct modern form should be used in the index, with a cross-reference from the other form where necessary.

An index of first lines is the only one in which 'a', 'an' and 'the' start an entry (but see 'Proper names' below). In other indexes the article is usually omitted; if it forms part of a book title or is necessary to make the sense clear, it may be placed at the end of the entry heading.

When to combine entries

If a word is used in both singular and plural forms in the text, only one form should be used in the index:

not bishop, duties of	*but* bishops	*or* bishop(s)
bishops, incomes of	duties	duties
	incomes	incomes

This rule does not apply, of course, if the two forms have different meanings, e.g. damage, damages.

When a word has more than one meaning, there should be a separate entry for each meaning, with an explanatory phrase to show which meaning is intended:

> Bath (Avon)
> bath, zinc

For the order in which to place words with identical spelling, see under 'Alphabetical order' below.

Proper names which merely share the same first word should not be grouped in one entry; for their order see p. 138.

London, 81–4, 91	*not*	London, 81–4, 91
London, a poem, 81		*a poem*, 81
London, Jack, 184		Jack, 184
London School of Economics, 83		School of Economics, 83

Watch out for the author who uses the heading as noun and adjective in the same entry:

> child
>> adolescent
>> labour
>> mortality
>> pre-school

Proper names

References to a peer should be collected under the title or the family name, whichever is the more familiar to the reader; if both forms are used in the book, or the peerage is a recent one, provide a cross-reference from the other form. The same principle should be followed when indexing married women. Names such as Russia and USSR, Ceylon and Sri Lanka, may be indexed separately if the distinction is necessary; but if so there should be a cross-reference. If the author uses in the text a name which is likely to be unfamiliar to some readers – perhaps a real name instead of a well-known pseudonym such as Mark Twain – add a cross-reference from the familiar name.

Saints, kings and popes are indexed under their forenames; places, institutions, Acts of Parliament, book titles, etc., are placed under the first word after the definite article (if any):

William IV, king of England	*but*	King William Street
		King Lear
Thérèse of Lisieux, St	*but*	St Louis, Missouri
Lewis, John	*but*	John Lewis Partnership Ltd

Also indexed under the forename are early names in which the second part is a place name rather than a surname, e.g. Philippe de Mézières under Philippe, John of Salisbury under John, Giraldus Cambrensis under Giraldus.

Compound personal names, whether hyphenated or not, should be indexed under the first element of the surname:

> Maugham, W. Somerset
> Vaughan Williams, Ralph

Compound place names such as Upper Slaughter, Lower Slaughter, Great Yarmouth, North Shields, South Shields, should be indexed under the first element; but do not change the author's system without consulting him.

Table 8.1. *Prefixes that should start the index entry*

Language	Preposition only	Article only	Preposition and article
Dutch	No	No	No (exception: ver)
English	Yes	Yes	Yes
French	No	Yes	Yes, if one word: Du Bellay, Joachim, but La Fontaine, Jean de
German	No	—	Yes, if one word or elided
Italian	Yes, except di or d' preceding a title of nobility	Yes	Yes
	In names of people living before the nineteenth century the prefixes de, de', degli, dei, de li, indicating descent from a noble family, usually follow the name, e.g. Medici, Lorenzo de'		
Portuguese	No	—	No
Spanish	No	Yes	No

Data from *Names of persons: national usages for entry in catalogues* (see p. 137).

Names of natural features such as rivers, lakes, seas and mountains should be indexed under the second element:

> Everest, Mt
> Seine, R.

There are two exceptions to this rule. (1) If the word for mountain etc. is in another language, e.g. Ben Nevis, Glen Affric, Eilean Donan, then the name is indexed under the first element. 'Loch' is sometimes treated as 'Lake', sometimes placed first. This different treatment of foreign names applies also to the definite article: foreign definite articles stay at the beginning of such names:

> La Paz
> Las Vegas
> Los Angeles

(2) If the name of a geographical feature is used as the name of an area or town, it is not inverted, e.g. Cape Town.

For Dutch, French, German, Italian, Portuguese and Spanish names starting with a preposition and/or an article, see table 8.1. Names naturalized in Britain or the United States are usually indexed under the prefix:

> Goethe, J. W. von   *but*   De Quincey, Thomas

Some indexers put the preposition at the beginning of the entry but do not count it in the alphabetical order; this is an acceptable system.

For other points about foreign names, see Anderson, *Book indexing*, pp. 20–1. Do not forget that the family name is the first element in unwesternized Chinese and Japanese names, so that they should not be inverted; and watch out for honorific terms as in U Thant. Spanish names often include two surnames. If you want fuller information about proper names, consult *Names of persons: national usages for entry in catalogues*, definitive edition edited by A. H. Chaplin and Dorothy Anderson (International Federation of Library Associations, 1967).

Alphabetical order

Alphabetical order can be either word by word (as the index to this book) or letter by letter (as the glossary), in each case counting only as far as the first comma or other mark of punctuation, and then starting again. See that the same system is used throughout the index.

In the word-by-word method, short words precede longer words beginning with the same letters, and hyphenated words are sometimes counted as two words unless part is a prefix or suffix which cannot stand alone. Words with apostrophes are treated as single words.

Word-by-word	*Letter-by-letter*
PLA, *see* Port of London Authority	partitioned schoolrooms
part-time employees	part-time employees
partitioned schoolrooms	PLA, *see* Port of London Authority
Port, William	Port, William
Port Sunlight (Ches.)	Portinscale (Cumb.)
Portinscale (Cumb.)	Port Sunlight (Ches.)

In word-by-word indexes, sub-entries may be in order of the first significant word (see below).

Abbreviations. M', Mc are treated as though they were spelt Mac; St as though it were spelt Saint. Other abbreviations consisting of one or more letters of a word (e.g. Dr, Mrs) are arranged as they are spelt. Groups of letters such as BBC may be treated either as a single word or as a series of single letters; see PLA in the example above.

If chemical formulae are to be arranged in alphabetical order, each element is treated as a separate word, and subscript numerals are ignored except in otherwise identical formulae:

$$CO$$
$$CO_2$$
$$CS_2$$
$$CaCO_3$$

Headings consisting of the same words should be in the order:

people
places
subjects
titles of books, etc.

Forenames (and other names with titles or appellations only) should precede surnames with inverted forenames or initials and other appellations:

John, king of England
John XXI, pope
John, Anthony

Kings of each dynasty or country should be in numerical order, the dynasties or countries being in alphabetical order.

In personal names with transposed forenames, an entry with a title preceding the forename is usually placed after a similar entry without a title, and such titles are in alphabetical order; but the order of titles is subordinate to the order of forenames:

Dixon, Sir Andrew	Dixon, Thomas
Dixon, Dr Bruce	Dixon, Dr Thomas
Dixon, Charles	Dixon, Sir Thomas

Foreign words. The British Standard on alphabetical arrangement (BS 1749) says that alphabetical arrangement of entries in a foreign language should follow English alphabetical usage, unless all the entries are in a foreign language. Where an accent is the only difference between two items, the item without the accent comes first. In all other cases, the presence of diacritical marks does not affect the order: for example German ö and Danish ø should be treated as o and not as oe, and Polish ł as l. Tell the author if you propose to alter his order, as some authors are anxious to show that they know the difference between, say, ø and o; if the index does not follow English alphabetical order, an explanatory note should be added at the beginning.

Foreign-language indexes. In languages with Roman alphabets, the letters treated differently are usually those with accents; but note that in Spanish ll and ch are treated as separate letters following the l and c entries respectively. In languages transliterated into the Roman alphabet, the order may bear no resemblance to English alphabetical order.

Numbers and Greek letters are alphabetized as though they were spelt out, except in chemical prefixes (see below).

Chemical prefixes. Most such prefixes, for example m, r and t in front of RNA, are ignored in alphabetization. *Cis-, trans-* and *cyclo-* may or may not be taken into account; roman prefixes such as iso- are taken into account.

Sub-entries and sub-sub-entries

If an entry contains more than six page references, or a reference spans more than nine consecutive pages, it should usually be broken down into sub-entries. On the other hand there should not be a sub-entry for every page number. Passing mentions should not normally be indexed.

Broken off or run on? There is little point in breaking off sub-entries which are in chronological or numerical order. Otherwise the decision depends on the space available, the complexity of the index and the type of reader it is intended for: for example one might break off sub-entries in a school book, for extra clarity, if it would not add much to the length.

If sub-entries are to be broken off, break off the first one too, even if there are no general page references following the heading; in that case no punctuation is needed after the heading. If, however, there are no general page references and only one sub-entry, the sub-entry should be run on:

coal   *but*   coal, industrial uses, 72, 76
    domestic use, 15, 45
    industrial uses, 72, 76

Sub-sub-entries are usually run on between semi-colons if the sub-entries are broken off, between commas if the sub-entries are run on between semi-colons. It is extravagant to break off sub-sub-entries: not only do they occupy more lines, but the extra indention for turnover lines leaves a very narrow measure. If sub-sub-entries must be broken off, but they only occur in two or three entries, it may be better to indent turnover lines differently in those entries.

Order. Check the order, which can be:

alphabetical, for categories. The alphabetical order may be 'order of
  first significant word', that is, it may disregard such words as 'and',
  'at', 'in', 'of', so that the sub-entry headings need not be inverted to
  bring the significant word to the beginning
chronological, for events
numerical, that is, order of first page reference

I myself find numerical order unhelpful.

Alphabetical and chronological order can be used in the same index: for example a history of Newfoundland might include some biographical entries and also one on fisheries which would be divided into kinds of fish. The two kinds of order can be used in the same entry: a group of biographical sub-entries in chronological order may be followed by an alphabetical group of the subject's writings or the topics on which he expressed views: 'on slavery, 156; on women, 134'.

If the sub-entries are broken off and the order requires so much correction that it cannot be marked clearly with arrows, you may indicate the final order by ringed numbers; but if the entry is split between two folios, and there is not a complete sequence of numbers on one folio, transfer all the sub-entries to a separate folio so that the keyboard operator can see all the numbers at the same time.

If the sub-entries are run on and the order is wrong, the whole **entry** should be retyped.

Cross-references

Check that the cross-references refer to existing entries, are correctly worded and make it clear what the entry heading is: for example '*see* social alienation' is no good if the heading is in the form 'alienation, social'; '*see* Brontë' is not enough if there are entries for more than one Brontë.

If the reference is to one entry which contains only a few references, it is better to have all the page references in both places than to make the reader go from one entry to the other. What one must not have is half the page references in one place and half in the other.

It may be helpful to have a cross-reference from a common abbreviation to its full form (or vice versa), or from a synonym or an alternative form of a proper name to the form used in the book.

Wording. If the entry is purely a cross-reference, the heading is followed by a comma and '*see*' in italic. If the cross-reference is only part of the entry, '*see also*' is more appropriate than '*see*'. In cross-references to italic headings 'see' and 'see also' can be roman.

The items within a cross-reference should usually be in alphabetical order. The items may be separated by commas if none of them contains a comma. However, if it is necessary to cite the whole of an inverted heading such as 'alienation, social', or if the author cites both heading and subheading ('coal, as a domestic fuel'), a semi-colon will be needed between all cross-references in the book. It is not necessary to refer to the subheading if it will be clear which one is intended; it will be enough to say '*see also under*' followed by the heading(s). Where a cross-reference includes a general description, rather than the actual names, of the entries, this description should be in italic: for example an entry on trade might end '*see also individual commodities*'.

Position. If the cross-reference helps to show the limitations of the entry in which it appears, some authors prefer to place it immediately after the heading and before the general page references. For example:

alphabetization (*see also* proper names), 18, 19

shows that the page references for alphabetization do not cover the order of proper names (which is a matter of which part of the name should come first rather than of alphabetical order).

If the cross-reference is a final sub-entry, it should be treated like the others; if there is a cross-reference from a sub-entry, it should be treated like a sub-sub-entry:

religion, 10–11, 107–11, 274	religion, 10–11, 107–11, 274
and myths, 11, 19, 29–31	and myths, 11, 19,
and ritual, 8–11, 29, 129	29–31; *see also* gods
see also gods, priests	and ritual, 8–11, 29,
	129; *see also* priests

8.3 *Style within the entry*

Capitalization

It is now usual to use lower-case for headings that do not have capitals in the text. However, if the author or indexer has capitalized all the headings, it may not be worth changing his system if nearly all the headings are proper names or if a large number of words are capitalized in the text and you would have to spend a good deal of time checking headings against the text.

Sub-entry headings should always be lower-case (except, of course, for proper names).

Wording

Keep wording and punctuation to a minimum, provided the sense is clear: in the following sub-entry neither the 'of' nor the comma is necessary:

> Napoleonic wars
> effect of, on Norwegian agriculture

In an exceptionally involved index it may save wordiness if an abbreviated form of the main heading (usually the initial letter and a full point) is included in some sub-entries:

> bird
> angel in form of b.
> b. mother makes human mother ashamed
> choice between b.s as best messenger

Although one should avoid wordiness, the entry must be full enough to be self-explanatory. The author of an introductory textbook provided an index with entries such as:

> post-neonatal
> projection
> quasi-stable
> quota system
> rhythm method
> separation
> supply

Punctuation

It is usual to put a comma after the heading if it is followed by page references, though one may decide to have a fixed space instead. If there are no general references and the sub-entries run on, put a colon between the heading and first subheading, so that there is no confusion as to what the second subheading is a subheading of:

> Canterbury: archbishop of, 1, 71; disturbance in, 250

If the sub-entries are broken off, there is no punctuation at the end of the main entry, whether or not there are any general page references.

Page references are usually separated by commas, but it is acceptable to omit all commas before page numbers, though retaining semi-colons and commas between run-on sub-entries and sub-sub-entries. In that case the space between page references is standardized and the columns are unjustified. There is usually no point after 'n' (note).

> limestone 2 55; crinoidal
> 128; fossils in 110n 114;
> magnesian 130

There should be no punctuation at the end of an entry, or at the end of a broken-off sub-entry or sub-sub-entry.

Page numbers

If two entries or sub-entries cover similar ground, see that no page references are obviously missing from either. One is quite likely to find:

	fossils in limestone, 54, 110n, 126
and	limestone
	...
	fossils in, 110n, 114

Pairs of numbers, except teens, are usually elided (see section 6.9). General page references should be placed before sub-entries, not interspersed among them, even if the sub-entries are in chronological order.

Exact references such as '101–6' are preferable to '101ff'; but you may not have time to check the vague references against the text in order to change them. '*Passim*' references should also be avoided as far as possible. If the author has a reference 'chap. 6 *passim*', it is more helpful to the reader if the page numbers of chapter 6 are given instead of (or as well as) the chapter number.

The author should distinguish between 65–6 (a continuous discussion of the topic) and 65, 66 (two separate mentions). The reader usually identifies the author's fullest treatment of the topic by the number of pages of continuous discussion (that is by a reference such as 65–9). If the author wants to distinguish the most important references in some other way, bold or italic could be used. Some authors like to put the important references first; such a system should perhaps be explained in a note at the beginning of the index, though the use of italic or bold for this purpose is common enough not to need explanation.

Bold or italic may be used for other things, for example to distinguish pages on which illustrations appear; such a use should be explained in a note.

If the index covers two or more volumes paginated separately, the volume number should be given before the first page reference to each volume (or anyway the second volume) in each entry and sub-entry.

In a combined reference list and author index, the page references to the publication being indexed usually run on from the bibliographical reference and are set within square brackets and/or in italic to distinguish them from the page numbers which are part of the bibliographical reference:

Goldschmidt, V. M. 1954. *Geochemistry*. Oxford, Clarendon Press. [*148*]

Gray, H. B. 1964. Molecular orbital theory. *Journ. Chem. Educ.* **41**, 1–12. [*196*]

If there is a list of references at the end of each paper, the author index will usually distinguish the pages on which those lists appear from references to the authors in the text of each paper (perhaps by the use of italic figures), so that the reader can see at a glance where he can find the details of the papers cited.

In an index of passages cited, sub-entries are usually broken off and the page references ranged right; or the reference to the original work may be in parentheses:

Homer, *Iliad* (2.4), 44–8, 60–1

For classical books see also section 14.1.

References to numbers other than page numbers

If a book is divided into numbered items, the index will probably refer to the item numbers rather than page numbers. Such an index can be set at the same time as the text. Except in bibliographies, where the system is common, there should be a note at the beginning of the index saying that references are to item numbers.

References to notes

Notes should be indexed only if they give additional information about a topic or person.

In any case a footnote need not be indexed if there is already a reference to that page: '16 and n' is unnecessarily full, because anyone looking at the relevant text on page 16 will find the reference to the footnote; however, some authors insist on retaining this kind of reference. References to footnotes also cause difficulty when a subject is discussed over two or more pages: '27n–28n' (meaning pages 27–8 and notes on both pages) looks odd, and so does '27–9n'. And what about any notes on the intervening pages?

Endnotes should be indexed under the page on which they appear, not the page on which they are referred to in the text. The note number should be given.

References to notes should be in the form '169n' (or '169n.') or, if there are several notes on the page (and the author gives the note number in the index typescript), '169 n. 3' (or '169 n3', '169n3').

References to illustrations

Illustrations should be indexed if they are likely to be consulted independently of the relevant text; page references for text illustrations may be distinguished by being underlined for italic or being followed by '(fig.)'. In the former case there should be an explanatory note at the beginning of the index.

Indention

If sub-entries are run on, all turnover lines are usually indented 1 em. If sub-entries are broken off and any sub-sub-entries are run on, sub-entries are indented 1 em and all turnover lines 2 ems. If both sub-entries and sub-sub-entries are broken off, sub-entries are indented 1 em, sub-sub-entries 2 ems, and all turnover lines – in that entry, at least – are indented 3 ems.

If only the sub-entries are broken off, and the typescript shows the system of indention correctly, you need only mark the indention of the first sub-entry and the first turnover line, and add a general note: 'sub-entries indented 1 em, turnovers 2 ems'.

Layout

You should decide whether the sub-entries and sub-sub-entries need to be broken off or should run on. You may also mark indention and the spacing of such things as '16n'. Otherwise layout is usually the designer's responsibility. If the author asks for unusual typographical conventions or layout, discuss them with the designer.

Number of columns per page. Most indexes have two columns, but an index of passages cited may have three columns, and an index of first lines or combined list of references and author index is likely to have one column. An index with a great many long entries may be set in one column.

Unjustified setting is becoming more popular because one can avoid the great variations in word spacing that occur when an index contains long words that are difficult to break, such as proper names.

When an entry runs from one page to the next, the printer should repeat the entry heading, and if necessary the sub-entry heading, at the top of the left-hand column. Although this repetition is really only necessary on a verso, having it at the beginning of every page means that it will be possible to move the index back or forward a page at proof stage if this turns out to be desirable.

146

9
Other parts of a book

9.1 *Page numbers*

There is no need for you to give instructions about page numbers, apart from saying where the arabic pagination is to begin (see p. 120). However, you may find it useful to have some general background information.

Printers use the word 'folio' to mean a printed page number as well as a sheet of typescript (and also a format very little used for books). It is used of printed page numbers in general, as in the phrase 'folios are at the foot of the page', rather than the number of a particular page: one does not say 'fo. 236' to mean p. 236 of a printed book; 'fo. 236' always refers to sheet 236 of the typescript.

Page numbers may be placed at the foot of the page or in the same line as the headline. They are usually in the headline if the book contains mathematics, because a page number at the foot might be confused with displayed mathematics; but if each chapter starts a fresh page, and therefore that page has no headline, the page number will be moved to the foot of the page, and enclosed in square brackets if necessary to avoid confusion with mathematics.

Page numbers are omitted from all blank pages and from the half-title and its verso, the title page and its verso, the dedication or epigraph page and any half-titles to parts; also from the last page of the book if page numbers are usually at the foot.

The number is also omitted where there is a turned table or figure, or where a table or figure occupies more than the usual depth, provided that this will not mean too many pages without numbers.

Although no number is printed on these pages, they are, of course, included in the page numbering. However, any half-tones printed on different paper from the text are not usually included in the page numbering, though a very large plate section may be.

9.2 *Headlines*

Headlines are unnecessary unless they help the reader to find a particular part of the book. If the chapters have no titles, only the book title can be used for headlines, and their only function would be to help to fill the page. Most non-fiction books do have headlines, but it is worth asking yourself in each case whether they are necessary. Headlines are usually omitted if illustrations are to be extended into the top margin, or if as much text as possible must be fitted on to each page of a fairly simple book.

If the exact form of each headline cannot be decided until the book is paged, and so the headlines cannot be keyboarded with the rest of the book, they are more expensive. Such headlines should be avoided where possible, but they are needed in dictionaries and catalogues to show what is included on each page or pair of facing pages.

What should be used for headlines
Headlines should help the reader to find a particular part of the book; choose whatever you think will be most useful. The title of the larger section appears on the left, that of the smaller on the right:

	left-hand	*right-hand*
	part title	chapter title
	chapter title	main section title
or	contributor's name	title of paper

To use the section title may cost more if the sections are short, as the printer may not set and insert the headlines until he has paged the text and knows how many he needs of each one.

In dictionaries, headlines usually contain the first and last items on the page; in catalogues there may be a section title and the names or numbers of the first and last items on the page – or the first item on the left-hand page and the last item on the right-hand.

If chapter and/or section numbers are used for many cross-references, they should be included in the headline, unless sections are numbered by chapter (e.g. 2.1, 2.2) and are less than two pages long, in which case the section headings in the text will be sufficient guide. If there are end-notes, *either* the chapter number must appear in the text headlines, in which case the headline to the notes will be 'Notes to chapter 6', *or* the relevant page numbers of the text must appear in the headline to the notes 'Notes to pp. 86–9'; the second alternative is probably more helpful to the reader, though it does mean that the headlines cannot be completed until the book has been paged. The headlines should give the numbers of the relevant pages only, not the page numbers for the whole of the relevant chapter.

Where the headlines are chapter title (left) and section title (right), and the first section title does not come at the beginning of the chapter, give the chapter title as the right-hand headline in that chapter until the section titles begin. Where a new section starts at the top of a page, the chapter title or an abbreviated form of the section title should be used for the headline, in order to avoid having identical headings one above the other (for example, see p. 133). Where a new section starts below the top of the page, the title of the new section should be used as the headline.

Preliminary pages. The headlines are usually the same on both sides, for example 'Preface'. Headlines for lists of plates and so on are in the form 'List of plates' rather than 'Plates'.

Appendixes. The headlines are usually 'Appendix 1' on the left and the appendix title on the right.

Bibliography and indexes. The headlines are usually the same both sides. Give each index its own headline, for example 'Index of passages cited'.

Pages that should have no headline. Headlines are omitted above headings that intentionally start new pages (e.g. chapter or part headings); above all turned illustrations and tables; above text illustrations and tables that extend beyond the type area (except at the foot) and are not turned. Headlines are included above headings that accidentally occur at the heads of pages (including chapter headings in a book with run-on chapters); above text illustrations and tables that fall within the type area and are not turned.

Length

Long chapter titles are not usually split between the left-hand and right-hand page, because one may be left with a nonsense headline if the chapter ends on a left-hand page or there is no headline on a page containing an illustration or table. If you cannot easily shorten the titles to fit on to one page, ask the author to provide shortened forms, telling him the maximum number of letters and spaces available, worked out from headlines in the pattern volume or specimen. If you provide short forms yourself, send the author a list: a change in the headlines at proof stage can be very expensive.

If page numbers are set beside the headline, there should be space between the two. Allow for this when calculating the length.

Style

Headlines are often set in spaced small capitals or upper- and lower-case italic. There are no italic small capitals, and some designers prefer not to have roman words in an italic headline, so the titles of literary works, or foreign words that are italic in the text, may be distinguished by being enclosed in inverted commas. As inverted commas tend to give words a self-conscious look, it is probably better not to distinguish foreign words if the roman/italic distinction cannot be retained. If such a distinction is important, tell the designer in case he is able to retain it. If necessary, warn the author that quotes will be used for titles, etc.

In upper- and lower-case headlines, initial capitals are normally used only for the first word and proper names; tell the printer this if you are not sending him a list. Say whether accents should be used on capitals.

Copy for the printer

Provide the printer with a list if shortened titles are to be used, unless the headlines will differ from page to page and the printer knows the exact form they should take. The list should be headed with the author's name and short book title, and should cover the preliminary pages and indexes as well as the text, bibliography and endnotes; and it should give the exact wording and capitalization (and accents and inverted commas where appropriate). Check the list after it is typed: a mistake in a chapter title can be very expensive if the chapter is long; and a mistake in the book title would be even worse. If a chapter or section title – or the book title – is changed at typescript stage, make sure that the new form is included in the list of headlines as well as in the contents list.

9.3 *Headings*

Headings to preliminary and end matter do not need to be identified in any way; nor do chapter headings if they are numbered and are marked to start on a fresh page. If they are unnumbered or are not to start on a fresh page, they should be labelled 'chapter heading'. For headings to parts see section 3.4.

Chapter headings

The word 'chapter' is often omitted from the chapter heading. If the chapter titles are abnormally long, you may want to persuade the author to shorten them. Long headings can be off-putting and they are difficult to design effectively.

Subheadings

Try to confine subheadings to a maximum of three grades in typematter of each size, except in reference books. In running text a reader finds a great variety of headings confusing rather than helpful; and it is difficult for the designer to specify more than three kinds of heading that will be sufficiently distinct from one another and from table headings, headlines, etc.

In letterpress books marginal notes and headings are expensive and should be avoided. In all books they will entail wider margins, and unless the margins are very wide there will be space for only a word or two, so that a long heading may straggle a long way and be difficult to read.

It is unnecessary to number the headings unless the numbers are used in cross-references. If the author has treated similar sections inconsistently, giving some a number and a title, and others a number only, ask him to make them consistent one way or the other. The introductory section to each chapter need not have a heading. If the sections are introduced by a centred number, some authors omit 1 if it occurs immediately below the chapter title, to give the page a neater appearance; so the first section number to appear is 2. I suggest you do not introduce such a system yourself. For numbering systems, see p. 28.

Coding the subheadings

The designer, working from your coding of the typescript, will specify the typographical style for the headings, and say whether those on a separate line are to be centred, full out or indented. It is for you to see that the hierarchy is logical and clearly marked in the typescript, and to decide whether the lowest grade heading can be run on at the beginning of a paragraph instead of occupying a separate line: in general these run-on headings should not be used to introduce sections of more than a page or two.

The subheadings should be coded in pencil in the margin, by a letter or number in a square, according to their place in the hierarchy. Sub-headings in sections to be set in smaller type (e.g. appendixes, bibli-ography, theorems) should be coded differently from those in text type, because the designer specifies the type size as well as the style for each code letter. If you code the headings before the designer has decided whether the displayed material in the text will be set in the same size as the bibliography and any appendixes, a complicated book might need several codes:

> chapter heading: uncoded
> text type: A, B, C
> displayed material in text: X, Y, Z
> appendixes: 1, 2, 3
> bibliography: i, ii, iii

Make sure that the coding in the designer's specification and any specimen pages corresponds with the coding in the typescript.

Style

Warn the designer about any factors that may affect the style of the sub-headings, for example if they are very long or very short, or contain Greek, arabic figures, lower-case symbols, etc., or if any chapter does not contain the first or an intermediate grade. As subheadings are often set in small capitals or italic, one has the same problem as in headlines, of distinguishing titles of literary works or foreign words that are italic in the text (see section 9.2). If the roman/italic distinction is important, tell the designer.

Point out to him also any places where a heading introduces only one or two paragraphs out of the many that follow, so that he can suggest a way of indicating the end of the passage covered by the heading. In textbooks there may be examples, or theorems followed by proofs, that are too long to set in italic, and the author may be very anxious that they should not be set in small type for fear that they should be regarded as less important than the main text. To put space before and after them may break the book up too much; conversely in a book already broken up by much displayed mathematics, such a break may not show up. It may be best to begin them with a run-on heading and to indent them or indicate the end by a symbol; the designer will be able to suggest a suitable device. Make sure that the end is clearly indicated in the typescript.

You should do any editorial marking necessary. For instance, headings occupying a separate line should not be followed by a full point, whereas those which are to run on usually have one. In upper- and lower-case headings it is normal to have an initial capital for only the first word and proper names; see that the capitalization will be clear to the printer, for example if the heading has been typed in capitals. Add any inverted commas or symbols necessary to make the distinctions mentioned in the two preceding paragraphs. Make clear whether the first line after a heading that occupies a separate line should be indented or not.

9.4 *Footnotes and endnotes*

Endnotes or footnotes?
Whether the notes are to be endnotes or footnotes will depend on the kind of note, the economic factors and the author's view. Endnotes are not as convenient for the reader, but they are usually cheaper than footnotes: they do not have to be fitted on the text page; and, unlike footnotes numbered by page, they do not have to be renumbered by the printer. However, they are usually set in a larger size than footnotes, and so paper and printing might cost a little more.

A book may have both footnotes and endnotes: if it will appeal to general readers as well as scholars, one may relegate to endnotes the sources which few readers will want to follow up, but retain as footnotes the additional pieces of information which the general reader may enjoy but which cannot easily be fitted into the text. In an edition of a text, the editorial notes may be printed as endnotes, to distinguish them from the original footnotes; or the original notes may be printed as endnotes if they are thought to be less useful to the reader; or there may be two sets of footnotes (see below). Where there are both endnotes and footnotes, the endnotes are keyed by number and the footnotes by symbol.

Footnotes
Very long footnotes should, if the author agrees, be taken into the text or made into appendixes. Very short notes, such as cross-references or short sources of quotations, may be taken into the text too. Try to move

into the text any mathematics containing superscripts and subscripts: the printer may not have characters small enough for use with footnote size type.

Footnotes may sometimes be shortened by omitting information already given in the text: for example, if the author and title are mentioned in the text, the footnote need give only publisher, place and date. In fact there is a movement towards omitting publication details from footnotes unless they are of particular significance, provided there is a full bibliography; and this is another way of cutting down the number of footnotes.

Style. All footnotes should end in a full point. Some publishers start footnotes with a lower-case letter if they begin with one of the following abbreviations: *c*., e.g., i.e., l., ll., p., pp. and possibly cf., *ibid.*, *op. cit.*, *loc. cit*. If you decide to retain the lower-case forms, and the printer is not familiar with this style in your books, explain the system on your style sheet.

Some printers prefer to have the footnote copy in one group, because it is usually set in a smaller size than any other part of the text. If the footnote copy is at the end of each chapter, give the folio number for the relevant notes on the first folio of each chapter.

Text indicators. In order to avoid having an indicator in a heading or subheading, a general note to a chapter may appear without an indicator at the foot of the first page. It should be clearly identified for the printer.

Check that all other notes have text indicators and that no notes are missing. It is very important that this should be got right at the typescript stage: if the compositor finds that a note or its indicator is missing when he is dividing the book into pages, he will have to stop work and wait until you can tell him the correct position for the indicator or obtain the missing footnote from the author.

In science and mathematics books footnotes are relatively rare. Symbols are used as text indicators, to avoid any confusion with superscript figures in the text; the series starts with a dagger if an asterisk is used in the mathematics. The sequence is * † ‡ § ‖ ¶, repeated in duplicate if necessary.

In other books footnotes are usually keyed by superscript figures. Symbols may be used if there is no likelihood of cross-references to notes on pages that contain more than one note.

In books set in Monotype, the footnotes may be numbered from 1 on each page, the correct number being inserted by the compositor as he pages the book. In slugset or filmset books it is much cheaper to number the footnotes in one sequence throughout each chapter, because renumbering the footnotes and the text indicators when the book was paged would usually mean resetting the line of text containing each indicator and the first line of the footnote; make sure that the numbering in the typescript is correct and contains no gaps or added numbers such as 15a.

Some publishers number footnotes within each chapter in sequences of 1–9, that is, the first nine notes in the chapter are numbered 1–9, the tenth 1 again, the eleventh 2 and so on. This avoids the clumsy appearance of two- and three-digit indicators, but of course it causes duplication of numbers if there are more than nine footnotes on any page. One publisher who uses this system allows the sequence to end before 9 or go beyond it if a note has to be omitted or added; and this gives more flexibility than a system of numbering in one sequence through the chapter, when an addition may entail a note 63a or renumbering to the end of the chapter.

Indicators in the text are less distracting to the reader if they are moved to the end of the sentence or to a break in the sense; but if the author is discussing specific words, it would mislead the reader if the reference was moved. Consult the author if you are in doubt. For aesthetic reasons, text indicators are placed after punctuation (except dashes), unless the reference is to a single word at the end of a sentence or of a parenthetical phrase. Most printers will follow a general instruction to move the indicators without your marking them; but stet any indicators that should not be moved after punctuation.

If there are two successive text indicators to the same footnote, they may fall on different pages when the book is set in type. If the footnotes are numbered throughout the chapter, it does not matter that there is a second reference 68 on the page following note 68; but if the notes are numbered afresh on each page, the footnote should be repeated if it is short, or if it is long the second note could be 'See preceding note', or 'See p. ooo, n. o' if other footnotes intervene. Write the additional footnote into the copy, but ask the printer to omit it if both indicators do fall on the same page.

Books containing more than one set of footnotes
There may be two or more sets of footnotes in an edition of a text. If some are original and some editorial, the editorial ones should be

distinguished: they could be keyed differently (perhaps the editor's by number, the author's by symbol), or enclosed in square brackets or followed by '[Ed.]'. It is sufficient to use one of these devices; but if one of the first two is used, it should be explained in the preliminary pages.

There will often be more than one kind of editorial note, for example one textual, one about content; sometimes there are three kinds. Textual notes often start with a line number and so do not need to be keyed into the text; but line numbering is expensive, and the line numbers for prose passages are not known until the text has been typeset, because the printer does not follow the original line for line as he does with verse.

If the text has a prose translation facing it, the two will probably differ in length, and the notes may be so arranged as to compensate for this, because one kind of note is likely to occupy more space than another. If the notes apply to both text and translation (i.e. are about subject matter rather than textual points) they cannot be keyed by line number, because the two versions cannot easily be set line for line.

Endnotes

Endnotes are usually numbered in one sequence throughout each chapter. See that all the notes have text indicators and vice versa, and that the numbering contains no gaps or added numbers such as 15a. For the placing of text indicators at a break in sense in relation to punctuation, see under footnotes above.

Endnotes are difficult to find if they are placed at the end of a chapter, but they may have to be placed there if there are to be offprints; otherwise they should be placed just before the bibliography. They should be headed 'Notes' or 'Notes to the text', and the chapter number and title should appear as a subheading above the notes for each chapter. If the chapter number is included in the text headlines, the headlines to the notes could be 'Notes to chapter o'; but it is probably more helpful to the reader if the relevant page numbers are given in the headline (see section 9.2).

If footnotes become endnotes. If the author typed the copy for the notes at the foot of each folio, it may take a little longer before the printer sends the first batch of proofs, as he will have to keep the typescript until he has checked the proof of the endnotes against the copy. It is, of course, more convenient for the printer if the endnote copy is separate from the text; but he would not be happy to receive text pages of various lengths from which the notes had been cut; and it is probably not worth the expense of photocopying or retyping all the notes. The copy for the chapter headings within the endnotes would have to be provided separately.

You will have to renumber the notes and indicators, unless they are already numbered by chapter rather than by page.

More information may have to be given in the notes now that they will not appear on the same page as the relevant text. A book title and page number – or just a publication place and date – may be sufficient in a footnote if the other details are mentioned in the text; but it is irritating to have to keep checking back to the text from the endnotes if one is looking back through the notes for a book mentioned earlier.

Notes to letters and documents

Notes are sometimes placed at the end of the relevant letter or document, sometimes at the foot of the page, sometimes at the end of the book. If the document is long, notes at the end of it may be difficult to find: if the book contains many long documents it may be sensible to combine two systems and to place the notes either at the foot of the page or at the end of the document, whichever comes first; for example, if a document runs from p. 63 to the middle of p. 69, the notes for pp. 63–8 would be at the foot of the relevant page, and those for p. 69 immediately after the end of the document. By using this system one can number the notes throughout each document without any ambiguity if two short documents, and therefore two notes numbered 1, appear on the same page.

Notes to tables

Notes should be placed immediately below the table and should use a different system of indicators from the footnotes or endnotes. See section 9.5.

Marginal notes

If an author wants to retain marginal notes, consult the production department; it can be expensive to use the margin in letterpress books (see section 9.3), and marginal notes are not usually necessary.

Superscript numbers referring to a bibliography

See section 10.3.

9.5 *Tables*

First of all, consider whether a table is the best way of presenting the data, or whether a graph might be better. The data in a table can more easily be compared with data elsewhere, but a graph shows trends and interrelationships more clearly. See whether some material presented in ordinary sentences might be clearer if it were tabulated.

Provide copy that the printer can follow easily. If some numbers that are run on in the typescript are to be tabulated, have them retyped in tabulated form. If a big table runs across two folios, see that the line spacing on the folios is the same: a difference of half a line in the spacing of all the items would mean that the lines would get out of step and the printer would not be able to tell which line ran on to which. For other points about large tables see below.

Watch for illogical or wasteful presentation of tables. A table with several columns, but few items in each column, may be fitted on to a page more easily by altering the axis (see fig. 9.1). Make sure that by doing this you are not making it difficult for the reader to compare this table with others; if there seems to be no snag, tell the author what you propose, and have the table retyped in its new form.

See that the structure of the table is clear: for example whether two or three columns should be grouped under one heading; this grouping may be shown by a horizontal line or a brace (bracket) below the shared heading. If the table is complex and is not very well laid out, have it retyped. Leave the exact spacing to the designer or printer, but indicate where extra space is needed; if a table contains a large number of rows, the designer may ask the printer to leave extra space after every four, or five, to help the reader's eye to follow the correct line along.

It is not necessary to separate the tables from the rest of the text. If the author provides some tables on separate sheets, include them in the folio numbering and mark the best position in the margin of the text: 'Table 11 near here from fo. 115'.

Tables may be set in small type or footnote size, or the size may vary from one table to another according to their size and complexity, so it is best not to ask for a particular size. However, if the tables are not on separate sheets it may be necessary to mark their exact extent: it is sometimes difficult for a printer to distinguish between a general note that is part of the table, and a comment that happens to follow in the

	Heading A	Heading B	Heading C	Heading D	Heading E	etc.
Item 1	xxxxxxxxx	xxxxxxxxx	xxxxxxxxx	xxxxxxxxx	xxxxxxxxx	
Item 2	xxxxxxxxx	xxxxxxxxx	xxxxxxxxx	xxxxxxxxx	xxxxxxxxx	

would fit better as

	Item 1	*Item 2*
Heading A	xxxxxxxxxx	xxxxxxxxxxx
Heading B	xxxxxxxxxx	xxxxxxxxxxx
Heading C	xxxxxxxxxx	xxxxxxxxxxx
Heading D	xxxxxxxxxx	xxxxxxxxxxx
Heading E	xxxxxxxxxx	xxxxxxxxxxx
etc.		

Fig. 9.1 A table with many columns and few items in each column may fit on to a page more easily if column headings become side headings and vice versa.

text (see fig. 9.2). If the printer could be certain of placing the table exactly where it is in the typescript, the distinction would not matter, but there may not be space for the table at the foot of the relevant page, in which case the table and its notes would have to be moved to the next page and the intervening space filled with text. A pencil line in the margin may be used to show the extent of the table and its notes; some publishers draw a double vertical red line beside the table itself, including the column headings and any notes, but not beside the table heading, which may be set in text type rather than the smaller size used for the table itself.

As some authors expect tables to be placed exactly where they occur in the typescript, they may use such phrases as 'the trade figures are as follows', or 'the trade figures in the table' even if there are several tables in the chapter. Even authors who number their tables may expect them to be in exactly the relevant place. Warn the author that the printer could find it difficult or impossible to place tables of more than four or five lines exactly where they appear in the typescript, unless they may be split between two pages; and perhaps your firm asks its printers to place tables at the head or foot of the page. The author may prefer his tables to be split (if necessary) rather than moved; or he may feel that if they cannot be placed in the exactly relevant position they would be better grouped at the end of the chapter or in an appendix. If the author insists that the tables must be placed as in the typescript (and

Lendon boys' school may be taken as an example of a school which was run efficiently and secured good, if not enthusiastic, reports. With Trinity it was among the earliest to introduce pupil-teachers.

<u>Hyson Green boys' school, 1854</u>

Present 55

Reading	Letters and monosyllables	25 boys
	Easy narrative	14 "
	General information	0 "
Writing	On slates from copy	7 "
	On paper	27 "
	(15 were not writing)	
Arithmetic	Four rules and below	12 "
	No advanced work	
Extra subjects	History	15 "

This was a poor school which earned a series of bad reports at this time. It will be seen that the curriculum was in effect confined to reading and writing.

In 1873 the local Inspector, Mr Capel Sewell wrote a letter to the chairman of the School Board, which gives some information about the condition of the elementary schools at the time when the School Board took over.

Fig. 9.2 Why one should mark the extent of a table. If the table cannot be placed exactly where it is in the typescript, the sentence following it may have to be turned into a general note to the table.

says that they may be split), say so in the margin beside each one. If they may be split only in certain places, give the necessary instructions.

Because they are likely to be moved, tables of more than four or five lines should be numbered, and references to them changed from 'as follows' to 'in table 6'. If a table is in the middle of a paragraph in the typescript, and is followed by a new sentence, write 'run on' beside it, or the keyboard operator may start a new paragraph.

If two tables share a number, persuade the author to let you renumber them as two separate tables; otherwise their structure may become very complicated. If two tables should appear in the same opening, so that they can be compared, note this in the margin.

If some numbered tables have titles and others do not, you might suggest to the author that the tables will look more consistent and be more useful to the reader if all of them do have titles.

Large tables

You may not know whether a table (or how much of it) can be fitted on to a page or a double-page spread, either upright or turned on the page; this can be left to the designer's and printer's expertise, but you should give them the following information.

Say how a table occupying more than one folio runs on from one folio to the next (fig. 9.3). Give this information on the first folio of each table, either in diagrammatic form as in fig. 9.3(*b*) or in a note such as: 'Table 2.2 is divided into "a" and "b". Both parts, i.e. fos. 41–2 and 43–4, run on horizontally and may be divided at any vertical line in the typescript.'

Say where each table may be split: see sample note in the preceding paragraph. If you are not sure, ask the author. If he says that the whole of certain tables must be visible at the same time, this may mean a pullout, which would be expensive. If you are not sure exactly how much the printer will be able to fit into each page, ask him to repeat column and side headings at the beginning of every page or opening. It may be a helpful reminder if you ring, on the second and subsequent folios, the headings which are to be repeated only at the start of each fresh page (or left-hand page). In the example given above, the headings to be ringed would be all the items in the left-hand column, because the table runs on horizontally. If the table ran on from the foot of each column, the column headings should be ringed.

The table number is usually repeated at the top of each page:

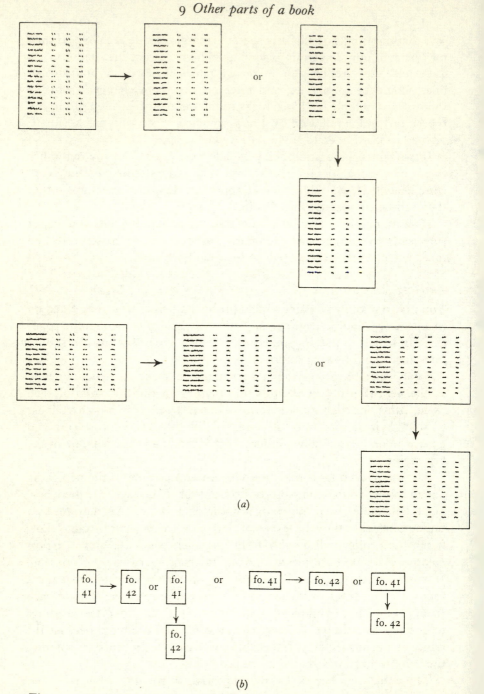

(a)

(b)

Fig. 9.3 If a table occupies more than one folio, it may not be clear to the printer how the folios relate (a), unless you tell him. The instruction may be in diagrammatic form (b).

'Table 6 *cont.*' Consider whether a shortened form of the title should also be given. If the table is turned on the page and runs across an opening, the table number, and probably the column headings, would only be given once. Give the printer the necessary instructions. Say whether the notes should appear on the first page only, on the last page only, or on every opening.

Say which tables must face the same way, in order that one may be compared with the others.

The parts of a table

Mark capitalization and punctuation; headings and items should have no full point. Ditto marks should be eliminated by using subheadings or by repeating the relevant word.

Rules. Vertical rules are expensive in letterpress books, and are almost always unnecessary, so publishers avoid them. If the tables are complex, warn the author about this and ask him whether any rules are essential; any essential ones must be identified in the typescript. Some tables have a diagonal rule in the top left-hand corner; if the rule is essential, point these tables out to the designer.

Table heading. See that headings are consistent in content and style, and keep capital letters to a minimum. The title, usually preceded by 'Table 1', should be as short as possible, though without the use of unnecessary abbreviations. The reader wants to be able to see at a glance what the subject of the table is, and any general information may be given in a note below the table or below the title. If the same unit applies throughout the table, for example '00,000', it is usually given in parentheses below the title and above the column headings.

Column headings are usually in roman rather than italic nowadays. See that they are consistent in content and style, and contain the minimum necessary information. All units and percentages must be identified, and multiples of units must be expressed unambiguously: '10^3 kg' is better than 'kg ($\times 10^3$)'. It is better to put the unit or % in the column heading than beside each number. Long headings to columns should be avoided, if necessary by using numbers or letters with a key below the table. The headings should have an initial capital for the first word and proper names only.

Side headings. Where possible, the author should use the same terms in similar tables, but only, of course, where the same terms apply: for example census figures may cover slightly different areas in different years, because of a change in boundaries. If the author uses spans such as 1–10, 10–20, 20–30, ask him whether they should be 11–20, 21–30 and so on, so that the spans do not overlap. Mark up any subheadings, and indent turnover lines; you or the designer should tell the printer how much to indent them, and also whether the setting may be unjustified.

Totals. The word 'Total' is usually indented or set in small capitals, and there is a rule or extra space above the total.

Numbers, etc. If the decimals in any column have different numbers of digits after the decimal point, it should be to indicate the accuracy of the result; but some authors are lax about this, and you may want to query it. See that the decimal point is preceded by a digit (a zero if necessary); say whether a low or medial decimal point should be used, and alter decimal commas to points. Mark decimal points to align vertically; if the columns contain words rather than numbers, say how the items and any turnover lines should be aligned.

If you are using spaces rather than commas to indicate thousands, four-figure numbers should be spaced to align with larger ones. Check totals, but do not worry if percentages come to 99 or 101; the individual figures may have been rounded up or down.

Em rules do not mean the same thing as zero, so do not try to make them 'consistent'; but if the author uses em rules, spaces, unexplained letter symbols such as x, leaders (two or three points), 'NDA' and 'NA' (see below), ask him what the distinction is. If some tables contain minus quantities, em rules should not be used to indicate a lack of data.

Notes are placed immediately below the table, though some publishers place any general note immediately below the table title. There are three kinds – sources, general notes and notes to specific parts of the table – and the same order should be used throughout the book. See that the notes are consistent in style and that any sources are adequate; and obtain any permission necessary for the use of any tables taken from other publications. Notes to specific parts of a table should be keyed differently from footnotes: symbols or superscript roman lower-case letters may be used, or superscript figures if these are not used for footnotes or in the table. If the author uses *, ** etc. to indicate degrees of probability, do not change the double asterisk to a dagger. The sequence of note indicators should read across the columns: an indicator in the first line of the second column precedes an indicator in the second line of the first column. If a table occupies more than one page or opening, it may be necessary to repeat the relevant notes in each opening.

Unfamiliar abbreviations should be explained, but the following may need no explanation:

DK – don't know	N – number
GDP – gross domestic product	NA – not applicable/available
GNP – gross national product	ND, NDA – no data available (i.e. data sought without success)

Tables that include artwork

Watch out for genealogical or similar tables for which artwork will be needed. If there is also a heading or footnote that is not to be included in the artwork, send the printer a photocopy of the folio, with the artwork area ringed; it is easy to forget to do this, and to realize only at proof stage that the heading or note is missing; and of course it may then be difficult to find the copy for the relevant heading or note, and equally difficult to find space to fit it in.

9.6 *Appendixes*

Appendixes are usually set in small type, as they are less important than the text; but they may be set in text type if they contain complicated mathematics or special sorts or footnotes; or because it is necessary to distinguish long quotations or other displayed material to be set in small type; or if they are short and small type is not used elsewhere in the book.

Appendixes usually precede any endnotes and bibliography. Tell the printer whether each appendix, or only the first, is to start a fresh page: this depends partly on length and partly on whether the appendixes are closely related in subject matter; tell the author if you are planning to run them on. If the book is divided into parts, each preceded by a half-title, there should be a half-title before the appendixes too.

The headlines are usually 'Appendix 1' on the left and the appendix title on the right.

Appendixes to individual chapters usually run on. In a book that has a list of references at the end of each paper, the appendix precedes the references. If the appendix is long enough to need headlines, these should probably be 'Appendix to chapter 5' on the left and the appendix title on the right.

9.7 *Glossaries*

In a book about, say, India or Spain, the author may need to use a number of foreign words. These should be explained at their first occurrence in the text; but if they are used more than once they should also be listed in a glossary, which is usually placed immediately before the bibliography and index (if any) so that it can be found easily.

Check the coverage of any glossary the author has provided; see whether he has omitted some difficult words and included some that are unnecessary. Check also the alphabetical order, the use of italic and the punctuation. Glossaries can be difficult to lay out clearly, because they may contain various kinds of information in a very short form: for example, an entry might consist of a French headword, part of speech, meaning of headword, and discussion which might include other French words or phrases. One could perhaps italicize all the French and put all meanings within inverted commas; the decision would vary according to the material involved, and it would be sensible to consult the designer if the material was complicated. However, most glossaries are simpler than this, and you should avoid the use of inverted commas if you can. If the glossary is set in a single column, turnover lines are indented, so that the headwords stand out; if headwords and definitions are in separate columns, the turnover lines of the definitions may not be indented.

IO

Bibliographical references

It is not necessary to back every piece of information by a reference, for example to a dictionary or general encyclopedia. However, the sources of quotations, the grounds for controversial statements, and acknow-ledgements of other people's work should be given.

There are three relevant British Standards: BS 1629: *Bibliographical references*; BS 4148: *Specification for the abbreviation of titles of period-icals*, Part 1: *Principles*, Part 2: *Word-abbreviation list* (see p. 312); and BS 5605: *Citing publications by bibliographical references*.

The four usual methods of referring to manuscript sources and publications may be called the short-title system (see section 10.1), the author–date system (see 10.2), reference by number only (see 10.3) and the author–number system (see 10.4). The first system is used in most general books, the second mainly in science and sociology books, the third and fourth less frequently. For lists of further reading see section 10.5.

This chapter does not cover what could be called the *op. cit.* system. *Op. cit.* tells you no more than the author's name on its own would, and so is unnecessary; and if there is no bibliography, or if there is more than one work by the same author, the reader might have to search back through a hundred pages to find the full reference to the book. *Op. cit.* may, however, be retained if it refers back only a page or two; so it is used more often in endnotes than in footnotes.

The exact punctuation and order within the references does not matter, provided all the necessary information is given clearly and consistently. For example, a few authors omit punctuation when there is no chance of ambiguity, and so include no commas in references to journal articles because the parts of the reference are distinguished by the transition between roman / roman in quotes / italic / non-italic figure / parentheses.

If you cannot use the author's system, tell him what you propose to do. If more than one system is used in a multi-author book, consider whether it is worth introducing a consistent system; if a great deal of work would be involved, it may not be, but it will depend on the level of the book.

Whatever the system, you should see that every reference in the text and notes tallies (form and spelling of author's name; date; wording, spelling and capitalization of title; publication place; and page numbers where relevant) with the bibliography or list of references. If there are discrepancies, send the author a list. *Punctuation* of references in footnotes and endnotes, however, does differ from the punctuation in a bibliography.

The spelling should not be made to conform to the style used in the rest of the book: titles of publications are treated like quotations. For capitalization see pp. 171–2 and 173. It is sometimes difficult to work out from the typescript what should be italic; if you are at all doubtful, ask the author.

A list called 'References' or 'Works cited' should include all the works cited in the text or notes, and no others. A 'Bibliography' may contain either more or less than the author has cited: if it contains only a few fewer, it is worth querying the omissions with him; if it contains many fewer it should be called 'Select bibliography'.

10.1 *Short-title system*

FORM OF REFERENCES IN NOTES

The most common form of the short-title system is to provide a full reference only at the first mention, though it may be better to give a full reference at the first mention in each chapter if there are a great many footnotes and (*a*) the book in question is not included in the select bibliography, (*b*) there is no bibliography, or (*c*) the bibliography is a list of further reading not arranged as an alphabetical list. Hart's *Rules* allow for short titles being used throughout, which is all right if all the works are listed in the bibliography.

First reference to a book
This should consist of:
(1) author's initials or forename (style same as bibliography), followed by
(2) author's surname

(3) book title, underlined for italic except for unpublished theses (roman in quotes) and manuscript sources. See pp. 171–7

(4) editor, compiler or translator, if any. If there is no author, the editor or compiler will appear in (1) and (2)

(5) the series, if any, plus volume or number in the series. The series name should not usually be underlined (see p. 179)

(6) the edition (if not the first). See p. 179

(7) number of volumes, publication place, publisher and date (all in parentheses). See pp. 179–81

(8) volume (if more than one) and page number: vol. and p. can be omitted if there is no ambiguity (see p. 181). If not all the volumes were published in that year, the volume number should precede the place

The reference is often punctuated as in the following examples:

J. A. Hazel, *The growth of the cotton trade in Lancashire*, 2nd edn (4 vols., London, Textile Press, 1956–7), vol. 3, p. 2

P. Carter, *Frognal to Englands Lane*, London Street Names Series, vol. 4 (London, Textile Press, 1938), p. 45

A colon should be used to separate title and subtitle; the title of another work included in an italicized title should be (italic) in inverted commas.

The Chicago *Manual of style* and the *Style book* issued by the Modern Humanities Research Association recommend that items (4)–(7) should be omitted, provided the book is included in the bibliography, though dates of publication may be given if relevant to the argument. If the author's name and the book title are given in the text, his initials and the publication date (if either of these is needed) could be given in the text as well, thus saving a note.

Subsequent references to a book

Such references should contain:

(1) author's surname

(2) short title – see p. 177. (The author's name may be sufficient if there is only one entry under that surname in the bibliography.)

(3) volume and page number

> e.g. Hazel, *Cotton trade*, vol. 4, p. 102

For the use of *ibid.* and *loc. cit.* see pp. 178–9.

First reference to an article in a book

In place of item (3) at the top of p. 169 one has:

(*a*) title of the article, not underlined but usually in inverted commas and with a capital only for the first word and any proper names. (Italic words within the title remain italic; words in quotes take double quotes.)

(*b*) 'in'

(*c*) editor's name followed by '(ed.)' (editor), or '(eds.)' if there is more than one editor

(*d*) title of book underlined for italic

or (*c*) may follow (*d*), in which case the editor's name will be preceded by 'ed.' (edited by) and 'in' may be omitted, e.g.

Noam Chomsky, 'Explanatory models in linguistics' in J. A. Fodor and J. J. Katz (eds.), *The structure of language* (Englewood Cliffs, NJ, Prentice-Hall, 1964), pp. 50–118

or

Noam Chomsky, 'Explanatory models in linguistics', *The structure of language*, ed. J. A. Fodor and J. J. Katz (Englewood Cliffs, NJ, Prentice-Hall, 1964), pp. 50–118

Subsequent reference to an article in a book

If the book is listed under its editor in the bibliography, the subsequent reference will be:

Chomsky, 'Explanatory models' in Fodor and Katz, *Structure of language*, p. 72

or the short title of the article and/or the book may be omitted if there will be no confusion with another publication:

Chomsky in Fodor and Katz, p. 72

If the book is listed in the bibliography under the author of the article, subsequent references will probably be:

Chomsky, 'Explanatory models', p. 72

First reference to a journal article

This should contain:

(1) author's initials or forename, followed by

(2) author's surname

(3) title of article, not underlined but usually in inverted commas, and with a capital only for the first word and any proper names (see p. 173). Italic words in the title remain italic; if the title is in inverted commas, any within the title must be double

(4) name of journal, underlined; this can be abbreviated provided the abbreviation is well known, self-explanatory, or listed in the preliminary pages. See p. 173

(5) place, if there is more than one journal with the same name (see p. 180)

(6) volume number in roman or arabic figures (vol. not needed), plus issue number if the volume is not paginated continuously. See pp. 181–2

(7) year, in parentheses

(8) page numbers(s) (p., pp. not needed). Some authors give the first and last pages of the article, followed by the relevant page; see p. 182

punctuated as follows:

J. L. Carr, 'Uncertainty and monetary theory', *Economics*, 2 (1956), 82–9

After a journal abbreviation ending in a full point, the comma may be omitted to avoid double punctuation.

Later references to a journal article
These should consist of the author's surname and either the journal title, volume number, etc., or else a shortened form of the article title:

Carr, 'Uncertainty and monetary theory', p. 82
or Carr, *Economics*, 2 (1956), 82

References to newspapers
These usually give only the title (see pp. 173–4) and the date of issue.

PARTS OF THE REFERENCE

Author's name
Authors' names should not be inverted in footnotes or endnotes.

Capitalization in titles
In English titles it is still usual to capitalize the first and other chief

171

words, though there is a move towards capitalization of first word and proper names only, especially in the titles of journal articles. Follow the author's system provided it is consistent. (Watch out for the definite or indefinite article beginning a sub-title.) If an author says that inconsistent capitalization follows the title pages of the books concerned, and even words such as 'of' and 'the' are sometimes capitalized, press him to standardize. Readers are likely to think that the author (or copyeditor) has been careless rather than scrupulous.

In running text, capitals help to distinguish titles that are set in roman in quotes (such as those of journal articles or poems) from quotations: similarly, fully capitalized book titles are more easily distinguished from other italic phrases. If only the first word has an initial capital, article titles must be in quotes in text and footnotes, though this is not necessary in the bibliography.

Many publishers use the same capitalization in the notes and bibliography. However, one or two recommend capitalization of all major words in the notes, but minimum capitalization in the bibliography.

Minimum capitalization can make long lists of titles easier to read. However, to implement a system of minimum capitalization might involve you in numerous decisions as to whether particular words (for example government, Puritan, non-conformist, labour) should be counted as proper names.

Some authors do not count *The* and *A* as the first word if they are capitalizing first word and proper names only; but this system looks inconsistent and should be discouraged. See p. 176 for the capitalization of foreign titles.

Poems

Poems may be italic or roman in quotes. Italic should be used for long poems which are virtually books in themselves; Hart's *Rules* add 'any other poems divided into books or cantos'. The MHRA *Style book* recommends italic for longer poems, roman in quotes for poems which form part of a larger volume or other whole. Such systems may look inconsistent even if they have been consistently applied, and you may find it difficult to check them if you do not know all the poems. If the author has no consistent system, it may be best to treat all poem titles in the same way, provided that one does not need to make a distinction between the titles of individual poems and the title of the collection of which they are a part (e.g. *Lyrical ballads* or *Songs of innocence*).

Avoid the abbreviation ll. for 'lines' if lining figures are used. If you decide to retain the abbreviation, see that the typescript makes it clear that ll. and not 11 is wanted. References to poems divided into stanzas and lines, or books, cantos and lines, are usually in the form iv. 8 or ii. ix. 16. All such groups of numbers divided by points may be spaced or closed up, but of course they must be consistent.

Plays

Titles should be italic. References to act and scene are usually in the form Act 3 Scene 4; or, if line numbers are given, iii. iv. 235 (or iii. 235 if there are not both acts and scenes). Commas (followed by word spaces) may separate the parts of the reference if the numbers are readily distinguishable as in these examples. If all the numbers are arabic, points must be used. Full capitals are used for act numbers followed by lining arabic figures.

Essay and article titles

Such titles are usually roman in quotes, though the quotes are not essential in a bibliography. Italic may be used for essay titles in a book discussing the essays, if the journals or collections in which they appeared are not mentioned and so the distinction between roman in quotes and italic is not needed.

It is usual to capitalize only the first word and proper names if the titles are roman in quotes.

Journal and newspaper titles

These should be italic. They may be abbreviated if the abbreviations are explained or self-explanatory. Note that *ELH* and *PMLA* (without points) are actual titles.

It is usual to capitalize the first and chief words, whatever style is used for other titles; there is then less discrepancy between journal abbreviations such as *JPE* and other unabbreviated titles. BS 4148 specifies that in journal abbreviations either all initial letters, or only that for the first element, should be capitalized.

The is usually omitted from all journal and newspaper titles in bibliographical references; but in a sentence the preceding 'the' is usually italicized in the following titles:

The Cornhill Magazine	*The Financial Times*
The Daily Telegraph	*The Lancet*
The Economist	*The Listener*

The Observer	*The Tablet*
The Scotsman	*The Times* (but the *Times of India*)
The Sunday Times	

(For a fuller list see Herbert Rees, *Rules of printed English* (1970), para. 235.) Of course, where the definite article does not refer to the newspaper, as in 'the *Times* correspondent', it will be lower-case roman.

For the inclusion of the place of publication see p. 180. In references to English-language daily newspapers published in the United States, the name of the city of publication is usually italicized as part of the title; see the Chicago *Manual of style* (12th edn), p. 354, para. 15.67.

Editions of texts

It is probably best to cite editions under the author's name, e.g.

John Locke, *An Essay concerning Human Understanding*, ed. J. W. Yolton

However, if the emphasis of the book is on the editor's work, it may be better to use the form:

J. W. Yolton (ed.), John Locke: *An Essay concerning Human Understanding*

If an edition is very frequently cited a concise short title should be used.

MSS and unpublished documents

The titles of unpublished theses and other unpublished books and articles are usually roman in quotes; unpublished theses should be labelled as such, and the name of the University given: Unpublished Ph.D. thesis, Birmingham University, 1967.

The titles of manuscript collections should be roman without quotes, and such citations should contain the name of the depository and a full reference following the usage of the depository concerned, e.g. British Library, Additional MS 2787, though parts of the reference may be abbreviated, provided that the abbreviation is explained or self-explanatory, e.g. ULC Add. 3963.28. Do not try to make references to one collection consistent with those to another. The titles of individual manuscripts should be enclosed in quotes:

E. Topsell, 'The Fowles of Heauen', *c.* 1614. Huntington Library, Ellesmere MS 1142

In reference to folios it is better to use fo. and fos. or fol. and fols. rather than f. and ff. Avoid the use of superscripts for v (verso) and r (recto). If manuscript references contain roman numbers followed by v or r, mark a small space before the letter; if it is followed by ff, mark a small space after it: fols. xii v ff.

Government and other official papers
Follow the author's system as far as you can, and beware of the following pitfalls. In references to Command Papers follow the author's use of C, Cd, Cmd and Cmnd as these refer to different series:

1–4222	1833–69
C 1–9550	1870–99
Cd 1–9239	1900–1918
Cmd 1–9899	1919–56
Cmnd 1–	1956–

Some documents, such as Hansard, are numbered by column rather than by page, so do not add p. before all arabic numbers.

In scholarly books it is not necessary to spell out or explain standard abbreviations such as Cal. S.P. Dom. Follow the author's use of roman or italic, provided it seems to be consistent.

The Chicago *Manual of style* has a section on the citation of United States documents.

Statutes
See section 14.2.

Law reports
See section 14.2.

Classical references
See section 14.1.

Biblical references
Books of the Bible should be roman, not italic. If chapter numbers are arabic, a point or colon must be used between chapter and verse number: Genesis 8.7 or 8:7. Roman lower-case chapter numbers may be followed by a point, comma or space (viii. 7, viii, 7, viii 7); but the abbreviations v. and vv. (verse, verses) should be spelt out to avoid confusion with chapter numbers.

A series of verses within one chapter is separated by commas (Genesis 8.7, 11, 13). A series of references in different chapters is best separated by semi-colons, to avoid confusion in mixed references such as 6:4, 5; 8:9.

A long passage within one chapter has an unspaced en rule between the verse numbers (6.4–11). A passage continuing into another chapter may have a spaced en rule if the parts of each reference are spaced (6. 8 – 7. 2), provided that there can be no confusion with parenthetical dashes: but 'to' may be better (6. 8 to 7. 2). If the en rule *is* to be spaced, make this clear in the typescript. References to a passage continuing into another chapter should consist of chapter numbers both sides of the en rule (chapters 6–8) or chapter and verse numbers both sides of the rule (6.2–8.35), but not chapter and verse one side and chapter only the other, e.g. 6.6–8 must not be used to mean chapter 6 verse 6 to the end of chapter 8.

Roman Catholic translations of the Bible deal differently with the books which the Authorized Version gathers under the title of 'Apocrypha'. Also those Roman Catholic translations that have been made from the Latin Vulgate often differ from the Authorized Version in their names for certain books of the Bible and in their numbering of the Psalms. The Ten Commandments are not itemized as such in the Bible, and the official Roman Catholic numbering differs from that found in Anglican prayer books.

Foreign works

In all modern European languages except English and French, and in Latin and transliterated Slavonic languages, capitalization in the titles of books, essays, poems, etc., follows the rules of capitalization in normal prose. That is: the first word and all proper nouns (in German all nouns) take an initial capital, and all other words take a lower-case initial.

Translations of the titles (where necessary) are usually roman in square brackets following the original titles. If Greek or Cyrillic type is used only in notes and bibliography, the author should perhaps be asked to substitute transliterated titles.

In general, publication details should be in English. When citing German, Spanish and French works, for example, B(and), t(omo) and t(ome) should be replaced by vol(ume).

Similarly it may be better to give the place of publication in English throughout; the author ought in any case to follow some consistent system. If the places are not to be anglicized, consider whether the less familiar names should be followed by the anglicized forms in square brackets.

French references. See Hart's *Rules* (38th edn, p. 92) for the capitalization of book titles. Only the initial letters of the first word and of proper names are capitalized, unless the first word is the definite article, in which case the first noun and any preceding adjectives take an initial capital, e.g. *Les Femmes savantes, La Folle Journée, A la recherche du temps perdu*. Authors may capitalize only the first word and proper nouns, and this is acceptable. Some French bibliographical abbreviations are given in appendix 7.

German references. All nouns in titles should be capitalized. If ß is used only in the notes and bibliography, ask the author whether 'ss' may be substituted. If he thinks the distinction important, tell the printer to follow copy. Some German bibliographical abbreviations are given in appendix 7.

Russian references. Use a capital for the first word and proper nouns only, in titles of literary works, newspapers and journals. Unless sloping Cyrillic type is to be used, titles of books and journals may be set in roman type: within a passage of Russian they would be enclosed in *guillemets*; in a list of references or in passages of English the *guillemets* would be omitted.

Short title

The short title should lead one unerringly to the right entry in the bibliography. An author's surname is not enough if he has written more than one book or if there are two authors with the same surname; and easily distinguishable short titles should be used for books with similar names. Abbreviations should be self-explanatory, though a frequently cited source may be abbreviated further, provided the abbreviation is given in a list preceding the text (if there are footnotes) or at the beginning of the endnotes or the bibliography; to give such an abbreviation only after the first full reference in a note is not as helpful to the reader, because he may not remember where the first full reference occurred. Abbreviations should be italic if the full form would be italic. Consult the author before abbreviating titles of books not listed in a select bibliography.

The short title should not usually include an ellipsis; however, authors of books containing a number of titles in unfamiliar languages such as Polish or Russian may use short titles consisting of the first few words of the title plus an ellipsis. Do not initiate such a system yourself without consulting the author.

I think the easiest way to ensure a consistent system of short titles is to mark up a copy of the bibliography. If one ticks each item there when it is first cited in a note, and indicates the short title used in the second citation by ringing it or deleting the other words of the title in the bibliography, one knows at a glance whether a book has already been cited and what its short title should be. I myself note the folio number in the margin, in case I need to refer back.

Ibid.

Ibid. can refer only to the immediately preceding reference, or part of it, e.g. '*Letters*, p. 515' may be followed by '*Ibid.*' (= exactly the same reference) or '*Ibid.* p. 518'. Do not, however, use *ibid.* if there are two references in the preceding note; and if an author uses *ibid.* only for an identical reference, do not extend its use to those which are not identical. If *ibid.* contains an implicit volume number and you are putting p. before page numbers only where there is no volume number (see p. 181), it is better to be inconsistent and include p. after *ibid.*

Ibid. – like *idem*, *op. cit.* and *loc. cit.* – may be roman or italic, provided all are treated in the same way throughout the book. Some publishers omit the comma after them, to avoid double punctuation.

The printer's compositor can no longer be asked to change *ibid.* to author and short title in the first reference on a left-hand page when he pages the book: this involved a good deal of new setting, which was expensive. Beware of the author who amplifies *ibid.* in the first reference on each folio of typescript, because the pages of the printed book will fall differently and two references to the same book might appear as:

[1] *Ibid.*
[2] Hazel, *Cotton trade.*

Idem, loc. cit., op. cit.

These Latin terms should be avoided, but if an author insists on using them, their use should be restricted as follows. *Idem* or *id.* may be used instead of repeating the author's name in successive references, though there seems no advantage in using this slightly shorter form. *Op. cit.* may be used with the author's name to denote the same book as cited in a recent reference; similarly *art. cit.* may be used to refer to an article. *Loc. cit.* may be used with the author's name to indicate the same page and work as in a recent reference.

Series

The series name should not be underlined if there is a volume title; but some record society volumes may contain two or three works and have no volume title, in which case the individual works are roman in quotes and the series name is italicized. If there is only one work in such a volume, the name of the work will be italic and the series name roman.

Some series of volumes are not true 'series' (open-ended groups of individual volumes) but multi-volume works, in which case the title of the whole work is used in place of, or precedes, the volume title and is italic, e.g. *New Cambridge modern history*, vol. VIII. If the volume title is given it should be in italic also.

There is no need to expand NS (= new series), but it should be underlined for small capitals except when lining figures are used or small capitals are not available.

Edition number

The author should cite the edition he has used, even if it is not the latest one. Hard-cover editions should usually be cited, though it may be useful, in a book for schools, undergraduates or the general reader, to mention a paperback edition.

Some authors indicate the edition by a superscript number after the title, e.g. *Usage and abusage*^{2}, or a subscript number before the publication date, e.g. $_2$1969. This is acceptable except in the author–date system; but as it may be an unfamiliar convention to some readers, the more conventional style of '2nd edn' before the parentheses could be substituted. Be consistent in your use of 'second edition' or '2nd edn'. The edition number is sometimes included in the parentheses with place, date and number of volumes.

Publication place and publisher of books

It is best to give both place and publisher, and authors should be encouraged to do this. However, if the author gives only the place or only the publisher, you may decide to follow his system. If he gives only the place in some references and only the publisher in others, it is easier to opt for place, as finding the publisher may call for considerable research. A list of the addresses of British publishers may be found in *British books in print* (London, Whitaker); American addresses are in *Books in print* (New York, Bowker). An author who usually gives only the place may add the publisher of books and pamphlets published by societies or individuals; this information may be helpful and should be retained.

Place. Some authors give all publication places except London (or Moscow, or whatever is the most usual place); others give places only for books published outside the United Kingdom. There should be a note at the beginning of the bibliography to explain such a system.

Give enough details to prevent confusion between two places with the same name, e.g. add Mass. after the Massachusetts Cambridge, if the Harvard University Press is not mentioned. Include the name of the state if the town is not well known in Britain, e.g. say Englewood Cliffs, New Jersey (or NJ). Note that Dover is usually Dover Publications, New York, not Dover, Kent.

If both place and publisher are given, it is all right to omit the place if it is implicit in the publisher's name, for example Cambridge University Press.

If the place of publication is not known, n.p. (no place) is used instead. If the place is ascertainable but does not appear in the book, it is enclosed in square brackets. It is best to reserve square brackets for uncertain data in references, and not to use them to avoid having two sets of round brackets, one inside the other.

Publisher. Publishers' names may be shortened if this is done consistently and short forms are unambiguous, e.g. EUP could be Edinburgh University Press or English Universities Press, ULP could be University of London Press or University of Liverpool Press, Arnold could be Edward Arnold or E. J. Arnold. Be consistent about the use of 'and' or '&' in publishers' names.

Hyphens, rather than en rules, are normally used in group names such as Appleton-Century-Crofts in bibliographical references.

Publication place of journals

It is necessary to give the publication place to distinguish journals with the same name:

Bookman (London)	*Ann. Phys.* (*Paris*)
Bookman (New York)	*Ann. Phys.* (*NY*)
Nature, London	

Publication date

The date should be of the edition consulted. If the work referred to has no date in it, and its date of publication is not known, n.d. (no date) takes its place; if the date is ascertainable but does not appear in the book, it should be enclosed in square brackets.

Multi-volume works. See p. 182 for the position of the date in relation to the volume number. If publication is not yet complete, it is usual to put a space after the en rule, e.g. 1930– .

Journal references. The date is usually in parentheses between volume and page number.

Volume and page number

Vol. and p. in references to books, poetry and documents. Follow the author's system if it is consistent and sensible. One system is to include vol. and p. only where there is any possibility of ambiguity, that is, where both volume and page numbers are arabic, or where there is an arabic or roman number on its own and it may not be clear whether the number refers to a volume or a page: a small capital roman 'one' can look like a non-lining arabic 'one', and a small capital roman v or x could be mistaken for a lower-case roman number. There should be no ambiguity if all unidentified numbers are page numbers, that is if volume numbers are preceded by vol. when they appear on their own and if arabic volume numbers (and roman ones if they also occur in the book) are separated from the page number by a colon when they appear together. If there are also references to lines of poetry, it may be as well to include p. for the page references.

If p. is used for some page references it should be used consistently, but do not add p. indiscriminately before arabic numbers: some documents are referred to by column, paragraph or folio.

Remember to use pp., not p., if more than one page is cited. This includes references such as pp. 21f, pp. 36ff. Remember that f and ff should be consistently spaced or closed up to the preceding number. Page numbers are usually elided (see section 6.9).

Do not use v. as an abbreviation for 'volume'.

Vol. and p. in journal references. There are devices that will usually distinguish volume and page numbers without the use of vol. and p.

In science books the volume number is normally bold; but if for some reason it would be expensive to use bold (for example if this is the only bold needed in a slugset book), the volume number must be distinguished in another way: italic could be used in place of bold, or 2, 3 could become 2:3 or vol. 2, p. 3.

In other books the style is '2 (1963), 3', with the volume number before the date and the page number after it; but if the reference also contains an issue number and the volume number is arabic, it may be clearer to say '2:1 (1963), 3' or 'vol. 2, no. 1 (1963), p. 3', rather than '2, 1 (1963), 3'. With a roman volume number there is no problem: 'II, 1 (1963), 3' is self-explanatory. (See p. 257 for order of journal references in legal books.)

Some authors give the first and last page numbers of a journal article, immediately followed by the page relevant at this point, e.g.

Camb. J. Pub. 5 (1971), 121–32, 128

or　　　　　　*Camb. J. Pub.* 5 (1971), 121–32 (p. 128)

The second form is recommended in the *MHRA style book*.

Arabic or roman for volume numbers. Follow the author's system if it is consistent and sensible. See that it will be clear to the printer whether an arabic or roman figure one is wanted: some typists type II for 11 (eleven), others type lll for III (roman three).

Roman volume numbers should be marked for small capitals (if available) unless lining figures are being used. However, there are no italic small capitals, so any roman numbers within a book title (e.g. *Sessional Papers II, 1916–17*) will have to be full capitals.

Order of volume number, date and page numbers. The volume number should come *before* the publication date for a book if not all the volumes were published in that year. If the author is apparently inconsistent, ask him if he is following this system.

BIBLIOGRAPHY

All books with bibliographical references in the text or notes should have a bibliography or list of works cited. Consult the author if there is no bibliography in the typescript, and warn him that you will not be able to check the references for consistency of content. If the bibliography omits a few of the works cited, ask him about the omissions; if it omits many, call it 'Select bibliography'.

School books may contain lists of 'Further reading' (see section 10.5).

These may omit some or all the works cited in text and notes, and will probably contain some not cited.

See that the list is correctly named. Check the order of the entries, and see that they are consistent in the amount of information they contain, the order in which it is given, and the punctuation.

Position

A few authors prefer to have the bibliography in the preliminary pages but it is usually placed before the index. This is a better place than before the endnotes, because it is easier to find.

Even if there is a separate bibliography for each chapter, they are best grouped at the end of the book for ease of reference, unless there are to be offprints. Lists of further reading in school books, however, *are* usually at the end of each chapter, because each forms part of the individual teaching unit.

List of abbreviations

Some authors include a list of abbreviations at the beginning or in the body of the bibliography; but if the abbreviations are also used in the footnotes the list is better placed in the preliminary pages. Italic abbreviations should normally be used for italic titles.

Subdivisions

The author should be dissuaded from subdividing the bibliography too much; if he does, it may be difficult for the reader to find a specific reference. Documents and manuscripts are best listed separately because they do not fit into a list arranged alphabetically under author; documents are probably best grouped by country and department, manuscripts by depository and collection. Works by a man who is the subject of a book are best separated from books *about* him, and may be listed chronologically or alphabetically.

Order of entries

In an alphabetical list, the order is of authors' surnames; government documents or anonymous works are listed under the first word, not counting the definite or indefinite article. (For points about alphabetical order see section 8.2.)

More than one work by the same author. His own writings usually precede books he has edited. Each group should be arranged alphabetically or in date order; or articles may follow books; but the same system should be used throughout the bibliography. Works by a single author precede works by that author in collaboration with others.

Editions should be entered as they are cited in footnote references (under author or editor). If they are cited under the editor, there should be a cross-reference from the author's name.

Form of entry

If the references are embedded in discussion they should be in the same form as in the notes (see above); but in an alphabetical list the author's surname should precede his initials or forenames, and in all lists the punctuation is usually simplified.

Carr, J. L. 'Uncertainty and monetary theory', *Economics*, 2 (1956), 82–9
Chomsky, Noam. 'Explanatory models in linguistics' in J. A. Fodor and J. J. Katz (eds.), *The structure of language*, Englewood Cliffs, NJ, Prentice-Hall, 1964, pp. 50–118
Hazel, J. A. *The growth of the cotton trade in Lancashire*, 2nd edn, 4 vols., London, Textile Press, 1956–7

In works listed under their titles a definite or indefinite article at the beginning of the title is usually omitted.

Authors' names are normally set in upper- and lower-case nowadays; if they are typed in capitals, mark any letters that might confuse the printer, for example the L in MacLehose.

The author's name is not usually repeated for the second or succeeding references, but is indicated by indention: say 1 em, with 2 ems for turnovers. However, his name *should* be repeated when he appears as a member of a new group of authors:

Bloggs, A. J. First publication. Turnovers
   indented 2 ems
  Second publication, indented 1 em
Bloggs, A. J., and Jones, X. Y. First publication

Otherwise one may get commas hanging in space:

Bloggs, A. J. First publication. Turnovers indented
  2 ems
 , Smith, R. S., and Jones, X. Y. First publication

If the author particularly wants rules to represent a repeated author's name, one does not need to repeat the name when the co-authors change:

Bloggs, A. J. First publication
— and Jones, X. Y. First publication

Two rules may be used to indicate that the first two authors remain the same, and so on. If you think rules should be retained, tell the designer.

Although the name of the first author should be inverted, the names of second and subsequent authors need not; it does not matter, provided a consistent system is used. It is quite common to omit the comma between the author's initials and 'and', to avoid double punctuation in, for example:

Brown, H. W., Forbes, A. S. and Smith, S. D.

If the author's name does not appear in the work cited, it should be enclosed in square brackets.

Articles. Encourage the author to give the first and last (or at least the first) page number(s) of an article. If he cannot trace them all, it is better to include those that are available than to omit them all for the sake of consistency.

Comments. If each item is followed by a comment, consult the designer about a suitable way of distinguishing the comment from the reference.

10.2 *Author–date system*

This system, known in one of its typographical variants as the Harvard system, gives author and year of publication in the text and the full reference in a 'list of references' (see p. 187).

Check that all published works referred to in the text are included in the list, and vice versa: a wrong date can be altered fairly easily at proof stage, but the addition of a reference or the name of a second author in the text would be expensive. Personal communications and other unpublished works, such as theses, may be excluded from the list, in which case a full reference should be given in the text.

Form of text reference

The author's name, date of publication and page reference (if one is needed) are given in parentheses: 'the synthesis of amino acids (D'Arcy,

1920, pp. 131–8) amazed...'. The reference may be simplified still further, by omitting the first comma and substituting a colon for the second and pp.: '(D'Arcy 1920: 131–8)'. If the author's name forms part of the sentence, it is not repeated in the reference: 'the synthesis of amino acids by D'Arcy (1920, pp. 131–8) amazed...'.

If the author published two or more works in one year, these are labelled 1920a etc. (with the letter closed up to the preceding date and perhaps italic). If more than one is included in one text reference one says 1920a, b.

It can sometimes avoid ambiguity if '&' is used instead of 'and' between the names of joint authors: e.g. 'in the work of both Smith & Brown and Jones & Robinson'; but if the author has used 'and' throughout it is not worth changing. The same system should be used throughout, though '&' can be used in the parentheses and 'and' in running text.

Et al. should be used consistently; for example references to works by three and four authors may give all the authors at the first mention and be shortened to 'Smith *et al.*' thereafter, provided there are not two different groups of authors headed by Smith with the same date; and if there is no cause for confusion, five names or more are shortened to 'Smith *et al.*' even at the first mention. Or three and four authors may be abbreviated at the first mention. Now that *et al.* references are becoming more and more common, ambiguity is sometimes avoided, not by giving all the names, but by labelling those with the same year 1920a etc., even though the second and later authors are not the same: e.g. Jones, Norman, Hazel & Robinson 1962 would become 'Jones *et al.* 1962a' and Jones, Smith and Robinson 1962 'Jones *et al.* 1962b'. If a and b are used in this way, it is probably sensible to order the list of references according to system (3) on p. 187.

The person's initials should be included in two kinds of text reference: where there are papers by two authors with the same surname, and where the reference is to a personal communication not included in the list of references, e.g. '(N. C. Brock, personal communication)'.

Where several references are cited together in the text they may be placed in alphabetical or chronological order, or in order of importance, but one system should be used consistently throughout.

See that the following are consistent: the inclusion or omission of a comma between the author's name and the date, the use of '&' or 'and' for joint authors, and the use of *et al.*

A few authors make the reference into a separate 'sentence', with a full point inside the parentheses, if it applies to more than just the preceding sentence.

The references should be in one alphabetical list, or one list for each chapter.

Position

The list of references may be placed at the end of the individual paper of a multi-author work if there are to be offprints; otherwise it should probably be at the end of the book, which is easier to find than the end of a chapter.

Order of entries

For alphabetical order of authors' names see section 8.2. Each author's publications are listed chronologically within the following groups.

Works by a single author are listed before those which he wrote in collaboration with others.

The *joint works* may be grouped in any of the following ways:

(1) alphabetically by second author (irrespective of the number of authors), so that the order would be Jones 1965, 1969; Jones & Abrams 1968; Jones, Abrams & Smith 1966; Jones, Norman, Hazel & Robinson 1962; Jones & Smith 1965.

(2) author with one other, in alphabetical order of second author; author with two others; and so on. The order would be Jones 1965, 1969; Jones & Abrams 1968; Jones & Smith 1965; Jones, Abrams & Smith 1966; Jones, Norman, Hazel & Robinson 1962.

(3) if there are a very large number of *et al.* entries, it may make them easier to find if works by two authors are grouped as in (2) and those by three or more are listed chronologically, whatever the name of the second author. The order would be Jones 1965, 1969; Jones & Abrams 1968; Jones & Smith 1965; Jones, Norman, Hazel & Robinson 1962; Jones, Abrams & Smith 1966. If the author is differentiating those published in the same year by labelling them a and b, the a, b etc. will of course have to appear in the list: Jones, Norman, Hazel & Robinson 1962a; Jones, Smith & Robinson 1962b.

187

If you plan to use system (3), make sure the author understands and approves of it; and add an explanatory note at the beginning of the list of references.

Form of entry

See that the entries are consistent in the amount of information that they contain, the order in which it is given, and the punctuation. If the author divides his list of references by chapter, see that adequate information is given at the second or subsequent mention: 'Bloggs (1969), see above' could involve the reader in looking through the lists for all previous chapters until he found the full citation. It is best to give a full citation at each occurrence in the lists.

Authors' names are usually set in upper- and lower-case nowadays, and if so should be marked accordingly.

The name of the author may be repeated for the second or subsequent reference, or it may be indicated by indention. If indention is used, the author's name should be repeated when he appears as a member of a new group of authors:

Bloggs, A. J. 1960. First publication. Turnovers
   indented 2 ems
  1961. Second publication, indented 1 em
Bloggs, A. J., & Jones, X. Y. 1959. First publication

Otherwise one may get commas hanging in space:

Bloggs, A. J. 1960. First publication. Turnovers indented
  2 ems
, Smith, R. S., & Jones, X. Y. 1955. First publication

If the author particularly wants rules to represent a repeated author's name, one does not need to repeat the name when the co-authors change. Two rules may be used to indicate that the first two authors remain the same, and so on. If you think rules should be retained, tell the designer.

The name of the first author should be inverted. The names of second and subsequent authors need not be inverted; it does not matter, provided a consistent system is used. It is quite common to omit the comma between the author's initials and '&', to avoid double punctuation in, for example:

Brown, H. W., Forbes, A. S. & Smith, S. D.

See that the use of '&' or 'and' is consistent.

The date (followed by 'a' etc. if necessary) immediately follows the name of the author(s), so that the reader can easily find 'D'Arcy 1920a'. In science books it is often within parentheses.

Article titles, if given, should have a capital only for the first word (plus proper names and German nouns) and should not be in inverted commas.

Journal and book titles should be underlined. In unabbreviated journal titles and in book titles it is still common practice to capitalize all the principal words, though there is a move towards minimum capitalization.

Journal titles may be given in full; or standard abbreviations may be used either for all journals or for the most familiar ones. Follow the author's system, and consult the editor if you are in doubt as to which system to use in a multi-author book. BS 4148 specifies that in journal abbreviations either all initial letters, or only that for the first element, should be capitalized. Lists of abbreviations may be found in BS 4148, Part 2. *Word-abbreviation list*, the *International list of periodical title word abbreviations* prepared for the UNISIST/ICSU-AB Working Group on Bibliographic Descriptions, *The International list of standard title word abbreviations* (ISDS), and in specialized publications such as the following:

The Journal of Physiology: suggestions to authors
Institute of Biology list of abbreviations of biological journal titles taken from the World List
Handbook for Chemical Society authors

Edition number. See p. 179.

Place and publisher of books and journals. See pp. 179–80 above.

The complete reference would read something like the following:

Eckstein, P. & Zuckerman, S. 1960. Morphology of the reproductive tract. In *Marshall's Physiology of Reproduction*, ed. A. S. Parkes, vol. 1, part 1, pp. 43–154. London, Longman
Heller, H. & Lederis, K. 1958. Paper chromatography of small amounts of vasopressin and oxytocin. *Nature, London,* **182**, 1231–2
Wood, R. H. 1961. *Plastic and Elastic Design of Slabs and Plates*. London, Thames & Hudson

No comma is needed after the journal title, though one is normally included except after an abbreviated title ending in a full point. The volume number should be marked for bold, unless the book is to be slugset, in which case it may be cheaper to avoid bold; in that case use italic or put a colon between the volume and page number, or add vol. and p(p)., e.g. '113: 847–59' or 'vol. 113, pp. 847–59'. If there is no volume number, put p. or pp. before the page number(s).

COMBINED LIST OF REFERENCES AND AUTHOR INDEX

If the reference list is to double as an author index, return the list to the author when you have edited it, so that he can fill in the page numbers from his proofs when he gets them. He should return the list when he sends the subject index. The page numbers should be entered at the end of each reference in square brackets or underlined for italic, to distinguish them from the page numbers in the reference (see p. 144).

There are usually cross-references from second and subsequent joint authors to the main author.

10.3 *Reference by number only*

In this system each publication or group of publications is numbered in the order in which it is referred to in the text; the text reference is just the relevant number. There is usually a separate numbering sequence, and list of references, for each chapter.

The advantage of this system is that two or more references may be indicated by a single number; its disadvantages are that it is very diffi-cult to find a particular author's publications in the list of references, and that if the text references are to be in numerical order they will have to be renumbered every time a reference is added or omitted. Sometimes authors try to remove the first disadvantage, by numbering the publi-cations in alphabetical order; but this means that the entries *must* be renumbered if the order is wrong or there is an addition or deletion.

In a science book the figures (which may be superscripts) will probably have to be placed within square brackets or possibly paren-theses, to distinguish them from other numbers or superscripts. This can make the numbers very bulky, and some authors object to their following the punctuation as note indicators do:

Smith,[146] Jones,[147]

In a variation of this system there is a consolidated reference list for the whole book, with a separate numerical sequence for each letter:

that is, one for all (first) authors beginning with A, and so on, so that Allen 1965 might be A1 and Abelard 1962 might be A2. The text references are in the form: 'noted by Gurney (G11)'.

LIST OF REFERENCES

Position

As I have already said, there is usually a list of references for each chapter or paper – placed at the end of the individual paper if there are offprints, otherwise usually at the end of the book because they are easier to find there.

Form of entry

In this kind of list of references there is no need to invert the author's name or to place the date immediately after it. Some authors run-on all the references that share one number; but it is probably clearer for the reader if each publication is set out on a separate line.

Some authors, repeating a reference cited in an earlier chapter, may give just a cross-reference:

18. See chapter 6, no. 10

It is more useful to the reader if the full reference is given at each occurrence.

Otherwise the general style should follow that of either the short-title system (see section 10.1) or the author–date system (see section 10.2).

10.4 *Author–number system*

This system is similar to the author–date system except that each author's publications are numbered and the reference in text or notes is 'Jackson (14)'.

LIST OF REFERENCES

Position

There is usually one list at the end of the book.

Form of entry

Authors' names are inverted and immediately followed by (1); authors' names need not be repeated before items with exactly the same authorship, but they should be repeated (and a new sequence of numbering started) when the authorship changes in any way:

Bloggs, A. J. (1) First publication. Turnovers
    indented 2 ems
  (2) Second publication, indented 1 em
Bloggs, A. J., and Jones, X. Y. (1) First publication
  (2) Second publication

10.5 *Lists of further reading*

Lists of further reading may be divided by chapter or by subject, and often contain comments. They may omit some or all of the books cited in the text and any notes, and will probably contain some not cited.

Position

If each chapter is a completely separate unit, the lists may be best placed at the end of the relevant chapter; otherwise a list subdivided by subject may be placed at the end of the book.

Form of entry

Each section of the list may be in alphabetical order, in which case the authors' names should be inverted; but the date need not follow the author's name. Alternatively, the books may be listed in order of importance, subject matter, date, etc., or may be embedded in paragraphs of discussion. See that the author has used a consistent and helpful order.

The general style should follow that of either the short-title system (see section 10.1) or the author–date system (see section 10.2).

II

Literary material

11.1 *Quotations*

Identify any quotations that are to be set off from the main text, if they are not clearly distinguished in the typescript. Make sure that it will be immediately clear to the keyboard operator where such a passage is to begin and end, if the quotation starts and finishes in the middle of a line in the typescript. See that sources are sensibly placed.

Tell the author about any changes you propose to make in his treatment of quotations, because this is something about which he is likely to feel strongly.

Layout

Prose. Has the author a sensible system for deciding which quotations should be displayed, that is, spaced off from the main text and set in smaller type, or with less leading, or in italic and/or indented? It is usual to display prose quotations of more than 60 words, unless there are fewer than ten of this length. One may, of course, decide to display quotations for other reasons:

(*a*) One may run-on those that form an integral part of the sequence of the author's argument, and display examples on which he is commenting.

(*b*) One may display small quotations when they are of exactly the same kind as those over 60 words, or where long and short ones are grouped.

(*c*) One may display all the quotations that the author has displayed in the typescript.

In order to give the beginning of the passage a neater appearance, some publishers do not indent the first line of a displayed prose quotation, even if it was originally the beginning of a paragraph. However, if a quotation is dialogue and the first speech is only one line, it looks better to indent the first line.

193

Be cautious about using small type for lists if it is also being used for prose quotations, in case the lists might appear to be quoted.

Verse. It is usual to display verse if there is at least one complete line. If the author runs some verse on in the text, consider whether it should be displayed or, if not, whether line breaks should be indicated by capital letters (if the original had them) and/or oblique or upright strokes; strokes are the only completely clear way. If a displayed verse quotation starts with a broken line, the first word should be indented to approximately its true position in the complete line.

If it may not be clear to the printer whether a quotation is verse or prose – for example a Latin verse quotation with no capitals at the beginnings of the lines, or German prose which happens to have a capitalized noun at the beginning of each line – say 'break lines as copy' where appropriate. If you are not sure yourself, ask the author.

If one or two verse quotations include the poem title, tell the designer, so that he can specify the type to be used for them; if they are rare, he may miss them when he looks through the typescript.

Plays. If there are quotations from different plays, it is probably sensible to standardize the layout and typographical style used for speech prefixes (speakers' names) and stage directions, unless the differences have some significance.

Quotations in footnotes cannot be set in a smaller size of type, and prose quotations may be better run into the text than indented. Verse quotations are usually displayed, though they may be run on with oblique or upright strokes to indicate line breaks.

Inverted commas ('quotes')

When to use them. Displayed quotations have no inverted commas at beginning and end, unless there is any possible ambiguity. If quotations are distinguished only by the use of inverted commas, and more than one paragraph is quoted, an opening inverted comma should appear at the beginning of each paragraph. If you run-on a quotation displayed in the typescript, remember to add inverted commas.

Dialogue, of course, retains its own inverted commas even when displayed in small type; but displayed quotations from plays never need inverted commas, provided at least one speech prefix is included in the quotation.

Single or double quotes. Single inverted commas are normally used except for quotations within quotations; since quotations displayed in small type have no inverted commas at beginning and end, quotations within them will have single inverted commas.

In books containing transliterated Arabic, it is sensible to use double quotes to avoid any confusion with the ʿain and *hamza*, which are indicated in the standard system of transliteration by a single opening and closing quote respectively.

Some authors have their own system of inverted commas, which they are anxious to retain: for example double quotes for speech and single for thoughts, or double quotes for quotations and single quotes for words or phrases used in a special sense. If you retain an unusual system, tell the printer, so that he does not try to 'correct' it.

In more complex books, inverted commas may be used to convey at least four things:

(1) mentioning the word:

> 'John' is a four-letter word

(2) mentioning the meaning of a word:

> 'John' means 'God is gracious'

(3) quoting what someone else has said:

> 'John', he said

(4) 'sneer' quotes:

> 'John' Smith, alias Ebenezer Crumpet Smith

Philosophers, logicians or linguists may want to distinguish (1) from (2); (3) and (4) hardly ever cause problems, because it is usually clear when quotes are being used in these ways. One can use single quotes for (1), (3) and (4), and double for (2); or double for (1), (3) and (4), and single for (2); or single for (1) and double for all the others. Ask the author what his system is; and if you cannot follow the subtle distinctions in usage tell him you will follow copy. If long quotations are to be displayed, ask the author whether they should be enclosed within the appropriate inverted commas. If a phrase is quoted within a quotation, check whether the phrase should be within single or double inverted commas: the usual rule of single first, then double within single, will, of course, not apply.

Punctuation and closing quotes. The usual rule in Britain is that the closing inverted comma precedes all punctuation except an exclamation mark, question mark, dash or parenthesis belonging only to the quotation. The position of the full point depends in theory on whether the sentence quoted is a complete one; as it is impossible to be certain about that without checking the original source, publishers usually follow a rule of thumb. BS 5261 recommends that where a complete sentence is quoted at the end of the main sentence (so that, logically, both would have a full point in this position) the full point should follow the inverted comma:

> I have often heard you say 'It cannot be done'.

Hart's *Rules* recommend that in such a case the point should precede the inverted comma. An author who is a textual scholar may place the full point according to whether it is part of the quotation; so do not make his system consistent without consulting him. American authors place the inverted commas *after* commas and full points, so explain the British rule to them if you propose to use it.

When a quotation is broken by words of the main sentence, and then resumed, the punctuation before the break should follow the inverted comma unless it forms part of the quotation.

Style within quotations

Follow copy for capitalization, italic and punctuation, and normally for spelling (unless the quotation is the author's own translation). However, it is usual to normalize typographical conventions such as the use of single quotes, en or em rules for parenthetical dashes, italic/roman punctuation and the position of punctuation with closing quotes. Tell the author what you plan to do, and try to dissuade him from retaining unnecessary distinctions. If he insists, warn the printer that he must follow copy for those particular points.

Some authors think they should retain the original punctuation at the end of displayed quotations even if it looks odd within the sentence: for example a quotation at the end of a sentence may end with a comma, or a quotation in the middle of a sentence may end with a full point. In my experience, authors who have insisted on retaining this system at typescript stage, have changed their mind at proof stage; so try to persuade them to change the system before the book is sent for setting.

If some words are omitted from a quotation, indicate the omission by an ellipsis of three points. This may be preceded or followed by a full point or other mark of punctuation; but, as full points are differently spaced from the points of an ellipsis, the printer must be able to see at a glance whether the first or last of a group of four points is to be a full point. Some publishers nowadays use a standard ellipsis of three points, not preceded or followed by a full point, because many authors type anything from two to five full points and it is impossible to tell, without checking the source, whether the sentence preceding the ellipsis has been quoted in its entirety. If the author wants to retain full points, make sure that it is clear where he wants them, and warn the printer to follow copy. If the author wants to distinguish the omission of one or more paragraphs (or several lines of verse) from the omission of a few words, a row of points on a separate line may be used.

It is usual to omit ellipses at the beginning and end of quotations, unless they are necessary for the sense. It is, after all, clear that the quotation is only an extract from the original work and is not complete in itself.

In transcriptions of inscriptions, etc., a point, hyphen or en rule may be used to indicate each missing letter, and the number of points or rules must be followed exactly.

Other conventions may not be worth preserving, for example full points for 'Mr' and 'Mrs' in characters' names which appear frequently both in quotations and in surrounding commentary. Discuss the conventions with the author, and inform the printer accordingly.

For the retention of old or idiosyncratic spellings, and the use of '[*sic*]', see section 11.5.

Make sure that square brackets are used for anything added within quotations by someone other than the original author. As few typewriters carry square brackets, the author may use parentheses or he may close and reopen the inverted commas. Ask the author if you do not know which should be parentheses and which should be square brackets. It is not usual to place ellipses in square brackets; but if the author quoted used ellipses himself, it will be necessary to distinguish the two kinds. For the use of parentheses in translations see p. 210.

If the author underlines certain words for emphasis, he should say '[my italic]' at the end of the quotation.

Accuracy

Spot-check easily accessible quotations, to see how accurate the author is; try to use the same edition as he has, because different editions of a poet's work may differ in punctuation etc. If the author is not reliable, you may need to return the typescript to him to check thoroughly. Check against each other all quotations that appear twice, for example words and phrases quoted in discussion of a longer quoted passage.

Translations

In a book on poetry in another language, where there are likely to be many translations of different lengths, translations of longer, displayed passages may be displayed below them or given in footnotes; but translations of short passages should be in parentheses in the text.

Copyright

As you go through the typescript, look for quotations that will need copyright clearance (see section 3.6). Check that permission has been obtained where necessary.

Sources

Sources should be spot-checked for accuracy, and it is worth checking that, for example, four lines of verse are not called lines 44–8. It is probably enough to give the number of the first line unless some lines have been omitted. See that sources are short, clear and consistent.

Sources for displayed quotations may be set in parentheses, full out right on the following line (or the last line if there is room); but if the sources are short they may be placed just before the colon introducing the quotation. It is more expensive and less helpful to the reader to put short sources in footnotes; but if there is a special reason for placing sources there, the note indicator is best placed at the end of the quotation rather than in the phrase introducing the quotation.

Even with quotations that are not displayed, it may be better to give the source in the text rather than in a footnote. See whether this would break up the author's argument too much, and whether it would mean having parts of the text retyped after you had inserted the sources. It probably depends on how frequent and how long the sources are: a large number of page references to a single book would probably be better in the text.

Before and after displayed quotations

Look at the punctuation introducing the quotation. If the author's system is not satisfactory, a colon (*not* a colon and a dash) may be better.

If the author interpolates a phrase such as 'said X' after the first phrase of a long quotation:

> 'I came into this kingdom,' said Queen Mary, 'under promise of assistance...'

there are three ways of dealing with it.

(1) The whole quotation can be displayed, with 'said X' in square brackets:

I came into this kingdom [said Queen Mary] under promise of assistance...

(2) The first part of the quotation can be in text type, in inverted commas, only the part after 'said X' being displayed:

> 'I came into this kingdom,' said Queen Mary:

> under promise of assistance...

(3) The interpolated phrase can be reworded (if necessary) and moved to precede the quotation, all of which can be displayed:

> Queen Mary said:

> I came into this kingdom under promise of assistance...

The third alternative is the clearest for the reader, but ask the author before making the change.

If the author displays two or three quotations together, he may not space them out in his typescript, because his use of inverted commas makes it clear that they are separate. Mark space to be inserted between them if you are not retaining the inverted commas.

Make sure it is clear to the printer whether the line following the quotation is a new paragraph or should start full out.

11.2 *Poetry*

As I have already mentioned, poetry should be identified as such on the typescript if it is not obvious at a glance whether a displayed quotation is prose or verse.

Layout

Poetry may be set in text type if this will not mean a large number of turnover lines, and if small type is not needed for prose quotations. It may be visually centred; but it is cheaper to align it all (apart from indented lines and turnovers, of course) either full out or indented. Displayed verse never needs inverted commas unless these were part of the original or unless the verse looks like prose and is therefore indistinguishable from the main text.

See that the author's system of indention is sensible and will be clear to the printer; mark the indention of individual lines if necessary. You should in any case distinguish turnover lines in the original by using a run-on mark, and see that the printer is told where any turnover lines in your own edition should start. In 'concrete' poetry, warn the printer that he must follow the layout of the lines exactly.

Where a line of verse is split to indicate a caesura, make clear to the printer that the space must be retained.

At the foot of each folio where this is not absolutely clear, indicate whether a space should be inserted after the last line on that folio, or whether the verse should run straight on to the next folio.

If long stanzas must not be split between recto and verso or verso and recto, tell the printer and warn the author that pages will have to be left short. If stanzas may be split, ask the printer not to separate rhyming lines if he can avoid it.

Warn the designer if some poems in the book do not have titles, unless the first line may be used as a title if the poem has no name. His design may rely on the title to give prominence to the beginning of each poem.

Accents to indicate scansion

Use -èd rather than a mixture of -èd and -éd, unless the author wants to retain the distinction; but do not add an accent without the author's approval. Elided syllables may or may not be indicated, e.g. 'riven', 'riv'n' or 'rivn'.

Indexes

Books of poems usually have an index of first lines, plus an index of authors if there are many and they are not arranged alphabetically in the book. Indexes of titles are more unusual.

11.3 *Plays*

List of characters

The list should be on a left-hand page facing the beginning of the play, so it will often be preceded by a half-title, to avoid a blank right-hand page. See that all the characters are included in the list and are spelt the same way as in the play itself.

Stage directions

Stage directions are usually set in italic, often with the names of speaking characters distinguished by being set in roman, either small capitals or upper- and lower-case; single sentences often do not end in a full point.

There are various conventions: two hypothetical ones are listed below, to show you what to look out for when you brief the designer. Authors and editors of plays usually have strong views on layout and the style for stage directions.

Convention A, for, say, a Shakespearian play with very few stage directions. In this convention all entrances are centred, all exits full out right.

Convention B, for a modern play with discursive stage directions. In this convention all broken-off stage directions may be indented, say 2 ems.

(1) *Description of scene*

centred

full measure

(2) *Entrance or other action between description of scene and first speech*

centred

either full measure, as continuation of (1), or broken off in square brackets

(3) *Phrase between speech prefix and first word of speech*

in square brackets, with no initial capital and no full point at end; precedes colon or point

in square brackets, with no initial capital and no full point at end; precedes colon or point

(4) *Similar phrase in middle of speech*

in square brackets, with initial capital but no full point at end

in square brackets, with initial capital but no full point at end

(5) *Full sentence in middle of speech*

    centred on a separate line, with capital at beginning and full point at end, but no square brackets

    if applies to speaker, run on in speech; if applies to someone else, probably broken off. In both cases in square brackets, with capital at beginning and full point at end

(6) *Full sentence between speeches*

    as (5)

    broken off within square brackets

(7) *Exits*

    full out right, often preceded by opening square bracket. If refers to speaker, 'Exit' is placed at end of last line of his speech, if there is room. If 'Exeunt' on a line by itself

    if brief, perhaps full out right, preceded by opening square bracket. If long, probably broken off in square brackets

Speech prefixes

Characters' names are usually abbreviated and set in small capitals, though italic upper- and lower-case may be used if long names are given in full; the disadvantage of italic is that it may not be clearly distinguishable from stage directions or any italic in the first line of the speech. See that abbreviated forms are consistent and unambiguous. In old-spelling texts, the speech prefixes are often made consistent, even though the original inconsistent spellings are retained in the dialogue.

The speech prefix is usually set at the beginning of the first line of a speech, followed by a colon, full point or space, the remaining lines of the speech being indented. Editors of French plays may want to follow the French convention of centring the character's name above the speech, but this is extravagant of space, so ask whether it is really necessary to retain the convention.

Broken lines in verse plays

If a line of verse is split between two or three speakers, the beginning of the second (and third) speech aligns with the end of the preceding one.

Act and scene numbers

Act and scene numbers that did not appear in the original edition (for example in a Shakespeare play) are usually set full out right in letterpress books, rather than in the outer margin, to save expense. Points are usual between act, scene and line number, though commas may be used if different kinds of figures are used for acts, scenes and lines. The usual convention is, of course, capital roman numerals for act numbers, lower-case roman for scene numbers, and arabic figures for line numbers.

Headlines

The act and scene number should appear in the headline. It may be set in a short form (for example v. iii) at the inner edge of each page; or in a fuller form it could be used as the right-hand headline or 'Act one' left and 'Scene five' right.

Performing rights

If the play is in copyright there may need to be a notice in the preliminary pages about performances.

11.4 *Anthologies and collections of essays*

With an anthology of modern poems the greatest problem for the copy-editor is likely to be the wording and placing of acknowledgements to suit both British and American copyright-holders (see section 3.6). A full source and acknowledgement may be given at the end of each piece; or only the author's name and the title of the piece may be given in the text, all the acknowledgements being listed in the preliminary pages. In a volume of reprinted papers, the source may be given immediately below the heading of each paper, in a footnote on the first page of each paper, or in the contents list.

In an anthology of poems and prose pieces, should the author's name or the title of the piece be given the greater prominence? A child's interest is more likely to be caught by an intriguing title, but the author's name may be more important for older readers. One needs to consider also the best position for any notes on individual authors, pieces or textual points: should one make the anthology look more inviting by printing some or all of the notes at the end of the book, or should one keep them with the text, where they are more easily referred to? If the latter, should a note on the individual author precede the piece(s) by him, and should notes on specific textual points be at the foot of the relevant page; or should all the notes follow the pieces by that author? The answer will depend on the kind of reader for whom the book is intended, and on the degree of economy that must be achieved. For information about editorial apparatus, see section 11.5.

The headlines may need some thought: if there may be two or more items in an opening, it will not be satisfactory to have the author on the left and the title of the piece on the right.

Some problems of consistency arise: for example should all the items be given titles if some have them; should spelling, or the indention schemes in verse, be made consistent? Again it depends on the level of audience and kind of material; but one should not depart from the original style without good reason.

If essays are being reprinted photographically, one cannot attempt to impose any consistency other than of 'chapter' headings and headlines. If the essays are being reset, capitalization and spelling in the text should be made consistent, and a consistent system of bibliographical references should be imposed if this will not cause a disproportionate amount of work. The author may edit his essays for republication; see that he makes clear to the reader how much he has altered the essays, perhaps to make them less out-of-date. If the essays have already been published in a book, there may be cross-references that will have to be expanded or omitted; also the bibliographical references may be incomplete because a full form was provided in a list at the end of the original publication.

11.5 *Scholarly editions*

In what follows, 'volume editor' is used to mean the editor of the particular book or text, as against the publisher's editor.

How closely to follow the style of the original
Very occasionally a document may be reproduced facsimile; more often it will be edited and reset. The volume editor and publisher must decide how closely the edition should follow the original; and the decision will depend on whether they want to make available what the author said, or the way in which he said it. Old-style spelling or lavish capitalization may act as a barrier between the modern reader and the argument; marginal notes and superscripts may make the book more expensive. Some volume editors are so scrupulous about following the text exactly

that they lose all sense of proportion and retain things that have no significance, for example the non-indention of certain paragraphs in handwritten letters. Some useful guidance will be found in *Art and error: modern textual editing*, edited by Ronald Gottesman and Scott Bennett (Indiana University Press and Methuen, 1970).

Obtain the volume editor's agreement to any changes you propose to make from the style in his typescript, and see that the preface or textual note makes clear how closely the text has been followed.

Converting handwritten material into type. Once one converts manuscript (via typescript) into type, one is not producing a facsimile edition, and there is no point in retaining features which belong to manuscript: for example, single underlining becomes italic, double underlining small capitals. Ampersands are usually spelt out, because they look very obtrusive when set in type.

Typographical conventions. It is usual to normalize typographical conventions such as the use of single quotes, en or em rules for parenthetical dashes, italic/roman punctuation and the position of punctuation with closing quotes. Some volume editors want the original printer's house style retained, including such practices as renewing the inverted commas at the beginning of every line. Try to dissuade the volume editor from retaining unnecessary distinctions; but if he insists, warn the printer to follow copy for the things you list. It is not enough to say just 'follow copy', because the printer will not know how far you mean him to do so, for example whether the material must be set line for line, whether he must follow the original for italic/roman punctuation, etc.

Layout and headings. It is usual to standardize the layout, unless this would mislead the reader, as it might in transcribed inscriptions. If inscriptions must be transcribed line for line, say so; for prose it is more usual to show line breaks in the original by a single vertical or oblique line. Page divisions in the original may be indicated, if necessary, by double vertical or oblique strokes, with the original page or folio number between the strokes or in square brackets after them.

Marginal headings may be taken into the text as subheadings, used as headlines, printed as footnotes or omitted. In litho books they may be retained; but consult the designer. If they are retained, they usually appear in the outer (wider) margin, rather than in the left-hand margin as they may have done in the original manuscript. Warn the volume editor about this.

In editions of correspondence, the address of the sender and/or addressee may be omitted unless it has any particular significance; but there should be a sensible system. If the date is part of the heading to each letter, it may be omitted from the letter itself. If the address and date are included, it is usual to follow the original as to whether they are placed at the beginning or end of the letter, but not for the exact position; the line divisions in the parts of the valediction may be followed, but not the exact position of each part or of the signature. Signatures may be set in small capitals.

Spelling, superscripts, capitals, italic and punctuation. In textual studies and definitive editions of pre-nineteenth-century works, modern diaries, notebooks and letters, old or idiosyncratic spelling is often retained, with the exception of i/j, u/v and long s. Some founts today have no long s, but if long s is to be retained, f is not an adequate substitute: a roman f has a complete crossbar, where a long s (ſ) has only a tiny stroke at the left-hand side; similarly an italic long s (ʃ) is like an italic f but without any crossbar.

Superscript letters and tildes (nunnation marks) in contractions are normalized to modern usage unless there are good reasons to the contrary.

Spelling errors are rarely worth preserving; where they are, '[*sic*]' should be inserted only where the mistake changes the sense, for example 'he' for 'she'.

In making seventeenth- and eighteenth-century works available for their subject matter rather than for textual study, the volume editor may capitalize and italicize according to the more moderate modern practice, and may also repunctuate in the modern style. In editions of correspondence it is usual to provide a missing capital letter at the beginning of a sentence, and a missing full point at the end of one.

Editorial changes to the text

Author's alterations, additions and deletions. A published edition usually provides the final or 'best' version of the text if more than one version exists. The 'best' version may include words from various versions, plus the volume editor's own conjectural readings; and he should make clear in the preface, or in notes at the relevant points, exactly what he has done. He will normally annotate only the variants that change the sense, or additions or alterations in the manuscript that indicate a significant change of mind on the author's part; but if he is discussing the author's alterations to a draft of a poem, the only clear way may be to publish the text with crossed-out words and alterations immediately above them.

If some material deleted by the author is of particular interest, it may be printed in a footnote, or it may be printed in the text and suitably annotated.

Editorial omissions and additions. Unless they are covered by a general note in the preliminary pages, all omissions and additions should be clearly identified. Omissions within a paragraph are usually indicated by an ellipsis of three points; if the volume editor wants full points to be retained, he must include them in the copy and make clear whether they precede or follow the ellipsis. Omissions of one or more lines of verse or one or more paragraphs of prose are usually distinguished from smaller omissions.

Editorial additions should be within square brackets. If you think some of the parentheses in the typescript should be square brackets, ask the volume editor.

Copy for the printer

If the edition is to be reset from a nineteenth- or twentieth-century edition, and the volume editor has made very few changes, the edition itself or clear black photocopies of it are probably the best copy. See p. 26 for how to mark photocopies. Photocopies of earlier printed versions are often much more difficult to read, and should be replaced by double-spaced typescript. If the volume editor refuses to have the text typed, because of the risk of introducing errors, he should mark up the photocopies as clearly and simply as possible, with a minimum of marginal marks; ask him to show you one or two sample pages so that you can ensure that they will be sufficiently clear for the printer.

Preliminary pages

The copyright notice will probably have to be qualified, because the text itself may not be in copyright; or there may need to be two notices, one for the text and one for the editorial material. If the text has already been published, the date of first publication should usually be given on the verso of the title page, in addition to the date of your own edition.

If the author wrote a preface or introduction to the text, the volume editor's introduction will have to be called 'Editorial introduction' or something similar.

Although one may feel that the arabic pagination should start with the text itself, remember that the editorial introduction will be indexed and that large numbers can be clumsy in roman numerals.

Notes

If the volume contains a number of separate texts, such as letters or inscriptions, each text may have an introductory headnote. The other notes may be placed at the end of the relevant text, or at the foot of the page, or at the end of the book (see section 9.4).

A volume of correspondence may have biographical notes. If there are a large number of people who appear only spasmodically, it is probably best to have all the biographical notes in a separate section preceding the index, so that the reader can find the relevant note easily. If the biographical material is included in the notes to the document, it may be as well to proof the book in galley first: minor characters may be identified at a late stage, or the editors may realize that someone identified in a note on p. 52 also appears on p. 26; if the biographical note cannot be found by looking at the first page number given for that person in the index, the relevant references should be distinguished typographically.

Glosses

If all the glosses for verse are short, and there is no chance of confusion as to which word is being glossed, each gloss may be placed beside the relevant line and the glossed word need not be identified. However, it is more economical to place the glosses at the foot of the page or the end of the poem or extract, each gloss being preceded by the line number (if any) and the word which it explains; the catchword may be in italic, with the gloss in roman, or vice versa if the text editor wants the catchword to appear exactly as in the text.

If the glossed or annotated words must be identified in the text, superscript figures may be used as with ordinary notes; or each annotated word may have an asterisk.

Check that any catchwords and line numbers are correct.

Line numbers

Consider whether line numbers are really necessary. The line numbers for prose passages or for passages that contain both prose and verse (for example some scenes in Shakespeare's plays) cannot be known until the text has been typeset, because the prose will not be set line for line; so the line numbers cannot be inserted in the notes until the text is set.

Lines are usually numbered in fives or tens, and the numbers are placed at the right, within the text measure. They are on the same side of the page on both left-hand and right-hand pages, so that they can be keyboarded with the text before the page division is known. The right-hand side is more suitable for verse, because there is more space there.

In notes and sources avoid the abbreviation 'll.' for 'lines' if lining figures are to be used. If you retain the abbreviation, make sure that the typescript makes it clear that 'll.' and not '11' is wanted.

Check that line numbers in notes and glosses are correct.

Plays. A line of verse split between two or three speakers counts as one line, and stage directions are ignored in the numbering; if they are referred to in a textual note the line number may be given in the form '139.1' (line 139 plus 1).

Parallel texts. If the text has a facing prose translation, only the lines of the original text will be numbered, because no prose translation can be exactly line for line.

Illegible or missing letters in the original

Where a known number of letters in an inscription are totally illegible, it is usual to indicate each illegible letter by a point, hyphen or en rule, and so one must keep the same number as in the typescript. Where the letters are almost illegible but may be guessed at, the conjectural letters may be placed within angle brackets. It does not really matter what conventions the volume editor employs, provided that they are easy for the printer to set, consistently used, and easy for the reader to follow. They should be explained in the preliminary pages.

The following is a typical set of conventions for a book on inscriptions:

[ ] enclose letters supposed to have been originally in the text but now totally illegible or lost
( ) enclose letters added to complete a word abbreviated in the text
⟨ ⟩ enclose letters either omitted or wrong in the text
{ } enclose letters which are superfluous in the text
⟦ ⟧ enclose letters thought to have been present but later erased. Underlining is sometimes used instead of double square brackets
vacat indicates a vacant space in the text
| marks the beginning of a line
‖ marks the beginning of every fifth line

209

.... represent lost or illegible letters equal in number to the number of dots
—— represents an uncertain number of lost or illegible letters

You will find other sets of conventions explained in published editions of correspondence, etc.

Parallel texts

A foreign text may have a translation on the facing page; or two versions of the same text may be printed on facing pages for comparison. Discuss with the volume editor which version should be on the left-hand page and which on the right-hand. A translation should probably follow the original and so be on the right-hand page.

Consider whether the printer will be able to understand a foreign text sufficiently to be able to keep the two versions in step (to the nearest line) when he pages the book. If not, you will have to arrange the paging yourself when galley proofs are available.

11.6 *Translations*

There is now a British Standard on the presentation of translations: BS 4755.

The translation, not being the original text, may usually be made consistent with your house style. Find out whether the author, translator or volume editor is to answer any queries you may have. Abbreviations and acronyms, such as those of names of organizations, should be translated into their English equivalent (if any), or spelt out – and if necessary translated – at their first occurrence.

If the volume editor has also translated the text, he may be so familiar with the text that he does not look at his own translation when he quotes passages in the introduction, but translates them afresh in slightly different words. Check this if you can do so fairly easily.

If the volume editor wants occasionally to cite the original foreign word or phrase in the translation, parentheses may be used for this word or phrase and square brackets for editorial interpolations.

Where the foreign author translated quotations from an English source into his own language, see that these quotations are not translated back into English but are taken direct from the original source.

Preliminary pages. The translator's name should be given, either on the title page or in the preface. If the text has been published in the original language, the original title and the date of publication should be given on the verso of the title page; if the translation was made from a second or later edition, the number and date of the relevant edition should be given. A copyright notice for the translation is essential, and there may need to be one for the original edition as well. The British Standard says that the following should also be given:

the place or country of the original publication

the name and address of the original publisher

the name of the language from which the translation was made (which may not be the original language).

Translator's notes. Observations by the translator (whether in brackets in the text or in a footnote) should of course be distinguished from the translated material; the British Standard recommends that they should be preceded by the words 'Translator's note'.

Bibliography. If the bibliography is reprinted from the original, it may be necessary to transliterate titles given in other alphabets, to add information about English editions of works cited and to anglicize bibliographical terms such as 'vol.' and the place of publication.

12

Multi-author and multi-volume works

12.1 *Books with more than one author*

This section is primarily concerned with contributory works such as symposia, where each paper or chapter is written by a different person, but of course the same kinds of problem are found in books written jointly by two or three authors: the typescript is likely to be more inconsistent, and one needs to know which author to consult about queries and whether the other(s) should receive carbon copies of all letters.

In what follows, 'volume editor' is used to mean the editor of the particular book, as against the publisher's editor.

What the volume editor can be expected to do

All the contributions should pass through the volume editor's hands before they reach the publisher; but the extent and quality of the work he does depends very much on his experience and efficiency, and also on the time at his disposal. He may receive contributions over a period of weeks, months or even years, and he may forget what he did to the first contributions by the time he receives the later ones. He will almost certainly have to hurry over the last contributions, which may reach him late or incomplete.

It is helpful if the volume editor and copy-editor can meet as early as possible to draw up instructions for the contributors. Such a meeting gives the copy-editor the chance to explain to the volume editor why certain faults in typescripts can delay a book, and to emphasize that, if the volume editor and his contributors are careful about these points, the publisher and printer will be able to deal with the typescript more quickly once it reaches them.

Impress on him that he must be responsible for the quality of the book, and for obtaining the contributors' agreement to any changes he makes in their chapters. Discuss whether all queries should be sent to him; if there is time, it is best to send questions about content (missing or unintelligible material) to the contributor, with a carbon copy to the volume editor.

After the meeting the publisher can send the contributors a list of the agreed instructions. In this way, the volume editor may be able to see that all or some of the following are done:

(1) If the book is to be published quickly, he should send batches of papers as soon as he finishes his work on them, especially if there are some illustrations to be redrawn or special sorts to be ordered.

Preliminary pages

(2) If the contents list has not already been agreed he should send one as early as possible, showing the order in which the contributions are to be printed; also a list of contributors, with their appointments, if the volume is to contain one, so that the copy-editor can check names and appointments against the information given at the beginning of individual papers.

Text

He should see that:

(3) the text is well written

(4) there are no incongruities in conference papers, arising from the fact that the words were first spoken: for example, discussions may have been typed from a tape recording full of unfinished sentences; or a paper may start 'I had intended to talk to you today about...' He should see that discussion and paper hang together: some contributors revise their papers in the light of questions asked during the discussion, and the typescript of the discussion may include questions already answered in the preceding text

(5) consistent conventions are used for such things as abbreviations, capitalization, nomenclature or short titles for works referred to by more than one contributor, or that a list of the preferred forms is provided for the copy-editor; and that abbreviations are explained where necessary

(6) handwritten additions are legible

(7) subheadings are of not more than three grades (or whatever number has been agreed) and they are coded A, B or C in the margin

(8) references to papers and books are in the agreed style and tally with the list of references or bibliography

(9) a list of headlines is provided if the titles of the papers are long

(10) bold, italic, Greek and other symbols are clearly identified

213

Illustrations

He should see that:

(11) adequate originals are provided for half-tones and line drawings and these are numbered in separate sequences (where appropriate) and clearly identified by the contributor's name

(12) separate typewritten lists of captions are provided for each

(13) the position of all text illustrations is marked in the margin of the typescript

(14) all conventions, such as abbreviations, are consistent in all figures and with the text, and all lettering is in English

(15) the top of a photograph is marked on the back if necessary, and those parts of photographs which must or may be omitted are indicated

(16) any grids to be retained in graphs are indicated

The publisher may also ask him to see that contributors obtain permission to use all copyright material.

The arrival of an urgent typescript

If time is short, the typescript will arrive in batches. Even if the first batch of papers arrives well before the due date, it is worth looking at them as soon as possible to see whether the volume editor is doing the right things, so that one can, if necessary, brief him more fully before he works through the other papers.

Check the contents list and ask the volume editor whether it shows the correct printing order: provisional lists are often revised, as some papers may never arrive.

The typescript should not normally be sent for setting until it is complete, but you may not receive all the contributions by the due date. The production department will be able to tell you whether the printer can deal most conveniently and quickly with two or three large batches or with a number of smaller ones. The printer may be asked to provide page-on-galley proofs; but if some of the papers to appear at the beginning of the book are not available, he will not be able to assign page numbers to page proofs of the others. The index cannot, of course, be made until the page numbers are known. It may be better to have galleys: the publisher's design department can mark the page division on these, and, once the first chapters are in proof, page numbers can be assigned so that the indexer can start work.

How much to do to the typescript

If the volume editor has not dealt with points (3) to (10) above, you will, of course, have to do as much as you can within the time available. Your style sheet for the printer should make clear whether or not (or how far) the chapters or papers are consistent with one another; each one must, of course, be consistent within itself. If the contributions are not consistent when they reach you, your decision as to how far to make them consistent will depend on the kind of book it is.

(*a*) If it is not a collection of papers but a book with a beginning, a middle and an end, designed to be read right through – the sort of book that does not give the contributor's (or co-author's) name below the title of his chapter – then the book should be treated as a single unit and a consistent system of capitalization, spelling and italic should be imposed throughout.

(*b*) Conference papers have to be published quickly. The contributors may be inexperienced, but you will have time to rewrite only those pieces which are really ambiguous, misleading or obscure. These volumes usually have a consistent style for subheadings, bibliographical references, abbreviations, spelling, spelling-out of numbers, etc.

(*c*) For Festschriften and other volumes with eminent contributors, the publisher and volume editor may decide that there is no need for complete consistency between contributions, and that contributors may retain, for example, American spelling and their own system of nomenclature and bibliographical references.

(*d*) If collections of already-published papers are to be reprinted photographically, it is not possible to impose any consistency other than of 'chapter' headings and headlines. If the papers are to be reset, capitalization and spelling in the text should be made consistent, and a consistent system of bibliographical references may be imposed. See that the papers are complete in themselves: that any cross-references are clear and that bibliographical references are complete.

Paging

If there are to be offprints, each paper will probably start on a right-hand page; the list of references or bibliography will usually run on from the end of the paper, as will any discussion of that paper; but discussion covering more than one paper will start on a right-hand page.

Notes

If there are to be offprints, endnotes will be placed at the end of each paper, preceding the list of references. Otherwise they will probably be at the end of the book, just before the bibliography.

References and bibliographies

If there are to be offprints, the list of references or bibliography will usually run on from the end of the paper; a list of references may do so even if there are not to be offprints.

In science books the author–date system (see section 10.2) is normally used; if some contributors have failed to include the titles of journal articles, and there is not time to obtain them, it is probably better to keep article titles in some lists of references, and so leave the volume inconsistent but more useful to the reader, than to omit those that have been provided. The list provided by the contributor may not contain all the references in the text; if you cannot obtain the missing references from the contributor in time, add the authors' names to the list and ask the printer to leave space so that the rest of the reference can be added at proof stage. If some contributors have numbered their references, it may not be worth changing these to the author–date system.

If the reference lists or bibliographies are to be at the end of the book, consult the volume editor as to whether they would be more useful if amalgamated. If they are amalgamated they must be made consistent. Publishers do not always attempt to achieve complete consistency between separate lists if time is short, though obviously one must make sure that a book is shown with the same author, title and date in each list in which it appears.

Abstracts or summaries

If the volume editor sends abstracts or summaries, discuss with him whether there is any real need to include them. If they replace a missing paper they should be treated as if they were a paper; if not, they should probably be omitted or could form the first section of the paper.

Headlines
In categories (*b*) to (*d*) on p. 215, the headlines are likely to be the contributor's name on the left and the paper title on the right. If the contributors were not asked to provide shortened titles, a list of proposed headlines should probably be sent to the volume editor for approval.

Copyright
The copyright situation for some of these volumes is complicated: for example some institutions for whom scientists work retain the copyright in papers written by them.

Contributors' names and appointments
In collections of papers the contributor's name usually appears below the paper title; his appointment may appear there or in the contents list or in a separate list of contributors in the preliminary pages.

If the author of a scientific paper has moved from the institution at which he carried out the research, that institution is usually given under his name at the beginning of the paper, with his present address in a footnote (if it is known in time) or at the end of the paper, in the form: 'Present address...'.

For books in category (*a*) on p. 215, the contributors' names are likely to appear in the contents list. If there are only two or three authors, and no volume editor, the authors' names will appear on the title page, and the special responsibility of each for certain parts of the book will probably be explained in the preface rather than in the contents list.

Illustrations
In a collection of independent papers, figure, table and plate numbering will start afresh in each paper and the plates will probably be grouped at a convenient place near the end of the paper. It helps the printer if you give the number of figures, tables and plates on the first folio of each paper. If illustrations in different papers should be related in size, scale or conventions, tell the designer.

In books in category (*a*), figures, tables and plates are each numbered in one sequence through the book, and the plates may be in one group.

See also points (11)–(16) on p. 214.

If the book has to be produced quickly, only really bad drawings can be redrawn; the rest will merely be relettered; and the volume editor will check all the illustrations. If there is a little more time and several figures have been redrawn, it will be better to send the artwork (photocopies whenever possible) to the individual contributors, because their originals may have contained errors or ambiguities. Discuss this with the production department.

Offprints

If some papers have more than one author, tell the production department whether there are to be, say, twenty-five offprints per paper or twenty-five per contributor. If there are introductions, discussions or plates, say whether there are to be offprints of those also, and who should receive them. In general, plates or pages of text which belong to different offprints are not backed up; but consult the production department about the cost. Each offprint must carry the following information on the first page or a cover: book title, editor's name, copyright owner and date, publisher's name and 'Printed in [country]'.

Proofs

Give the production department a list of the contributors' addresses, making it quite clear which part of the text and which plates, if any, are to go to whom. If the contributor's name appears at the beginning of the paper, there will be no problem, but if it appears only in the preliminary pages, write the chapter number beside each contributor's name on the list.

Make clear who is to receive the marked proof and the typescript. The revised proof will go to the volume editor only, but the practice with first proofs varies. As contributors do not always deal with proofs quickly, the marked proof may be sent to the volume editor, with the typescript if he has no duplicate; the contributor in any case receives a copy of the proof and should be asked by the publisher to send his corrections to the volume editor within a certain time. The volume editor is asked to collate his own and the contributor's corrections – or to correct the proof on behalf of the contributor if the latter does not send corrections by the due date – and to send the marked proof to the publisher. Things become more complicated, of course, if there are two volume editors, or if the marked proof is to go to the contributor and some papers have two authors.

218

12.2 *Works in more than one volume*

There are four main kinds of work in more than one volume.

(1) Books which are an integral whole and published at one time, but which cannot be fitted into one volume.

(2) Books which can be divided chronologically (e.g. histories, journals, correspondence, biographies) or by subject (e.g. essays, bibliographies), etc. These may be published at one time or volume by volume.

(3) Books which consist of two parts published simultaneously, of which one is likely to have a larger sale than the other: some people buying the complete book, others only the more general volume.

(4) Series. As series are published over a long period and are likely to be consulted singly, they will be similar in general appearance (style of subheadings etc.), but may differ in such conventions as spelling. This section is not concerned with books in this fourth category.

The editor and the sales offices decide whether books in categories (1) to (3) should be sold separately or only as a set. In general, those in category (1) will be available only as a set, and those in (2) and (3) will be available separately, though if those in (2) are published simultaneously they may be sold only as a set. Those sold separately should, of course, be complete in themselves. For those sold as a set, the copy-editor should do what seems most helpful for the reader.

Books sold only as a set may be paginated consecutively, but this is not necessarily more useful to the reader, because he will not remember exactly where the volumes divide, so cross-references may need a volume number. If the volumes are paginated consecutively, the arabic pagination in volume 2 will start with the next odd number after the last page number of volume 1; the prelims will be paginated separately, starting with i in each volume.

The book will almost certainly have only one index, but here again the reader will need some reminder as to where the volumes divide, either in a note at the beginning of the index or by the inclusion of the volume number before the first page reference for each volume, e.g. 1.8, 159, 354; 2.396. Parts, chapters, illustrations and tables will usually be numbered in one sequence even if the volumes are paginated separately.

Although it is more useful to the book-buyer to have only one bibliography and one index to consult, the library-user will probably find it helpful to have the complete contents, showing the division into volumes, in each volume, or at any rate in volume 1. He may also need a list of abbreviations and a glossary in each volume.

Volumes sold separately. The contents lists will cover only the relevant volume, and each volume will have its own list of abbreviations. The note on editorial conventions may or may not be repeated in each volume; if it is, see that it contains all the conventions relevant to that volume, and that, if it contains a large number that are not, it is clear to the reader that the list contains the conventions for the complete work and not just that volume.

Each volume may have a complete index, perhaps consolidated into a final index volume; or a partial index with a complete index in the final volume; or no index until the final volume.

Numbering of volumes

The volumes should normally be numbered in arabic; if there is a special reason for roman numbering, tell the designer.

Preliminary pages

Half-title and title page. See that the volume number and volume title are included.

Imprints page. If the volumes are to be sold as a set each volume should give the ISBNs for all the individual volumes and also one for the set (see chapter 7).

Contents list. If the volumes are to be printed simultaneously and sold only as a set, should each volume contain the complete contents list showing the division into volumes? If the volumes are not to be printed simultaneously it will, of course, be impossible to include page numbers for later volumes.

Preface. Should this be repeated in each volume?

Lists of illustrations and tables. There is no need to include the complete list in each volume, unless the illustrations are relevant to the whole work. If the contents list covers all the volumes, and the list of illustrations only one volume, the latter should probably be headed 'Illustrations in volume 1' to make the distinction clear.

Lists of abbreviations should probably be printed in each volume: it is not worth the trouble of pruning such lists in order to include only the relevant entries in volumes 2, etc., of books that will be sold as a set. In any case there should probably be a complete list in volume 1.

Acknowledgements. Consider whether the relevant acknowledgements should be included (or repeated) in the relevant volume if the book is to be sold as a set, or whether it is enough to have a consolidated list in volume 1.

Cross-references

The volume number must be included in references that will fall in one or the other volumes, if the volumes are to be paginated separately; it may be helpful even if they are to be paginated in one sequence.

Consistency

The volumes should be consistent in spelling, capitalization, etc. If the volumes will be published over a number of years, keep a full note of the conventions for use with the next volume. However, one may decide not to follow earlier volumes for minor conventions that are no longer house style. Consult the author or volume editor if you wish to change the style.

If the same editorial note is included in each volume, see whether in fact it should be modified for the current volume.

Illustrations

If a map is relevant to more than one volume, it should probably be repeated, in which case it may be less confusing to number the maps in a separate sequence in each volume, even if the book is to be sold only as a set. The map would then be included in the relevant place in the numbering for each volume.

If the volumes are not all to be published at once, or if there are a very large number, it is better to number the illustrations separately in each volume. Otherwise the numbering may become very cumbersome; and without a volume number it may be difficult to tell which volume contains the illustration.

Sending the book for setting

The printer will probably treat each volume as a separate unit, because each represents a book to be printed and bound. So send the first volume for setting before the rest, if it is completely ready, and return it for press before the rest if you have been able to complete the contents list etc.

13

Science and mathematics books

The complicated notations used by scientists and mathematicians pose special problems and so require more than usually detailed marking up by the copy-editor, even for those printers who specialize in this kind of setting. This chapter attempts to give some working principles for the choice of nomenclature and its clarification for the printer. The books listed in section 13.7 are all valuable for reference. For the physical sciences at least, the summary of standard notation in reference (1) on p. 243 is indispensable, and a list of mathematical sorts, such as (7), is useful; a list of the usual contents of a mathematical matrix case is given in appendix 8 below. Most journals issue instructions or recommendations to authors, which can be a source of information for specialized books.

Nomenclature

For all nomenclature follow where possible the conventions of the Royal Society set out in (1): the Royal Society's recommendations for units of measurement follow the Système International (SI). If the author uses conventions which differ from those of the Royal Society, consult him before changing them.

English

Scientists and mathematicians often use terms which have not yet become absorbed into general scientific language and may be quirkily hyphenated and capitalized. The use of the minimum possible hyphenation and capitalization will make decisions easier: it will usually be obvious whether to make compound terms into two distinct words or one: and if a lower-case t is used in Cauchy's theorem it will not be necessary to worry about the e in Maclaurin's expansion or the c in Liebig condenser. Watch out for systems that are not immediately obvious: there is, for example, one which says that where a prefix to a word starting with a vowel ends in one itself there should be a hyphen only if the vowels are the same: tetra-acetate and tri-iodide, but tetraiodide and triacetate. Note that a hyphen is commonly used to join a single-letter prefix to the word it qualifies, and so: X-ray but cosmic ray, β-ray but beta ray. See also p. 109.

When two or more hyphenated terms are condensed in the same phrase the hyphens should be left hanging (α-, β- and γ-rays) and identified as hyphens if the printer could confuse them with, say, minus signs.

Abbreviations

Unusual abbreviations should be spelt out or explained when they first occur; what is unusual will, of course, depend on the level of the book. Examples are drugs and reagents such as ACTH, and techniques such as n.m.r. Except in the very few cases where small capitals are by convention always used (see pp. 236–7), capitalized abbreviations should be set in full capitals *without* points, lower-case abbreviations (except those of units) *with* points. (See also sections 13.3 on units and 13.5 on biology.)

Useful lists of abbreviations and contractions are contained in (1) p. 43, (6) pp. 21–45, (10) pp. 21–7.

13.1 *Structure of science books*

Headings and headlines

If mathematics containing superiors, fractions or bold, for example, occurs in headings and headlines it may restrict their typography. Point this out to the designer before the book is designed or estimated.

Footnotes

The more complicated the content of the book, the more reason there is to persuade the author to eliminate footnotes. If footnotes are added to a page already fragmented by small type, displayed equations and formulae, the effect can be very messy. It should also be remembered that mathematical setting of any complexity becomes more difficult to read as well as to set in a footnote size of type; unavoidable mathematics in footnotes should be pointed out to the designer before the book is estimated.

Choose indicators carefully to avoid confusion with scientific or mathematical nomenclature: symbols are usually best, but it may be necessary to dispense with the asterisk and start with a dagger. In tables having a large number of notes, superior roman or italic lower-case letters can usually be used without ambiguity. Use different indicators for footnotes to text and notes to tables.

See also pp. 153–5.

References

Science books most commonly use the author–date system: see section 10.2.

Equations

In books which contain both mathematical and chemical equations number these in separate sequences; the numbers will need to be differentiated typographically by using, for example, bold for the chemical equations.

Check that the numbering sequence is consecutive (whether the author numbers every equation or only those to which he refers). The numbers should be on the right, and no leader dots are needed. If more than one equation is allocated to an equation number, the number should be centred vertically and the equations may be linked on the right-hand side by a large brace.

It is preferable to punctuate equations in the same way as any other written statement. The alternative system of using no punctuation at all after displayed material is acceptable if consistent; as it is not always possible to predict just what the printer will display, give him a general instruction.

An equation will be displayed if it has been displayed in the type-script, or if it has been run on but cannot be squeezed into the remainder of the line without being broken. The latter is a potential source of inconsistency, and while printers can generally be relied upon to use intelligent discretion over displaying single equations or formulae which have been typed as part of running text, one should keep an eye open for potentially inconsistent sequences or cases of inconsistent displaying/running-on by the author. It is generally preferable to mark for display any run-on equations that may produce inconsistency. Equations should not be run on if some fractions will be more than one line deep (see p. 231).

Guidance should be given on where to break long equations, if it is possible that they will be too long for the line. They should not be broken in the middle of a term; e.g.

$$2(x-y-z) = (x-y-z)+(x-y-z)$$

could be broken before $=$ or $+$, but not inside any of the brackets. A product $(\ldots)(\ldots)$ may be broken between brackets, with the implied operator $(\times)$ carried over to the next line.

Corrections in proof to the spacing in equations are relatively easy with Monotype setting, but with film or typewriter setting it will probably be necessary to reset the whole line.

Illustrations

See chapter 4. The following points are of special importance in science books.

Transfer as much peripheral matter as possible to the caption (see pp. 45–6), but tell the author when you send him the artwork, so that he is not worried by the omission.

However, scales on photomicrographs etc. are better than magnifications, though possibly more expensive. Not only are they more graphic, but they avoid the need to recalculate magnifications when photographs are reduced. If magnifications are given in the captions, remember to check the proofs against the artwork and make any adjustments, if the author has not done so.

Graphs. The grid and the top and right-hand edges of the 'box' should be deleted from a graph, except in the rather unusual case where the reader is to take measurements from it.

13.2 *Scientific and mathematical nomenclature*

See also sections 13.3–5 on units, chemistry and biology. The Royal Society's *Quantities, units and symbols* (1) is recommended as a working guide. Points on mathematics are well summarized in (9) pp. 7–41.

A great deal of typographical subtlety is required in the setting of scientific and mathematical matter, and it is very important to ensure that the printer can see clearly how each symbol should be rendered. The Roman and Greek alphabets in various styles, arabic figures, and a vast range of special signs are all used. Useful lists of signs available in Monotype are given in (7), (8), (10) pp. 18–19, (11) pp. 95–102.

Variables (including geometrical 'points' and algebraic 'constants' such as constants of integration) are set in sloping (italic) type, except in typewriter setting where upright (roman) may be used; operators, such as d, representations of pure numbers such as e and i, chemical symbols and symbols for units of measurement are set in upright characters. Bold (or bold italic) is used for variables having a vector property. The upright/sloping distinction may be carried through to Greek symbols, and bold Greek faces are available. Standard symbols for variables are given in (1) pp. 12–20, (10) pp. 21–7.

Unless there are ambiguities, the spacing of mathematical symbols is best left to the printer (for examples of spacing see (9) pp. 32–5). The spacing of unit symbols does need marking: see p. 234.

The marking of italic

Where batches of typed material are predominantly of the same kind (e.g. mainly mathematics or mainly chemistry) many printers can be relied upon to realize this and to set them appropriately without any marking by the publisher; in that case the *exceptions* need to be pointed out, by underlining the occasional variable that occurs within chemistry, or marking 'rom' against the occasional operator or unit symbol within mathematics; it is better to give, at appropriate points, reminders of the system being used, rather than to over-mark, as long as it is clear that these *are* reminders and not exceptions. However, for this system to be safe one needs to know one's printer; and if in doubt *all* italic everywhere should be marked, whereupon the printer will take anything unmarked to be roman.

Italic symbols should remain italic when they occur in an italic heading or headline.

The marking of bold

Vectors and tensors are traditionally distinguished from their scalar equivalents by the use of bold type. If the author has not marked the vectors he should be asked whether he wishes bold to be used – he may not have felt that the distinction was worth making (or perhaps, from the reader's point of view, labouring). If any marking is needed, or if there is any doubt about the consistency of the author's marking, you will probably need to return the typescript to him, as it takes an expert eye to tell whether scalar or vector quantities are being used. If one is familiar with the rules of vector multiplication, it is worth checking the balance of bold symbols in equations.

The Royal Society recommends the use of bold italic rather than the bold roman which has hitherto been more commonly used. Because this more neatly ties up each vector with its corresponding scalar value, italic bold should be suggested to the designer; but there are various typographical reasons why he may want to adhere to roman: for example, there may be bold roman headings keyboarded simultaneously with the text; or, in a typeface which has a rather light bold, the extra distinction afforded by roman may be helpful. This must be decided before the book is estimated.

If second-order tensors are to be distinguished from other vectors they are set in bold sans serif – again italic, if bold italic is being used for vectors.

Superiors and inferiors

A list of recommended symbols is given in (1) pp. 11–12.

Italicization of modifying superiors and inferiors follows the same rules as for other symbols: they should be italic only if the modifier is itself a variable, hence '$X_n = Y$ for $n = 1, 2, 3$', but '...where P_e is the output per editor and P_c the output per copy-editor'. Capitalized inferiors should be full capitals (i.e. *not* marked as 'small capitals'). They need to be fully marked: if all are italic or all roman a blanket instruction will suffice for many typesetters, but if mixed then the italic ones should always be underlined.

Where superiors and inferiors occur together, three distinct renderings are possible: $X_a{}^2$, X_a^2 and $X^2{}_a$. The second ('over and under') has the same meaning as the first and is the neater: in filmsetting this presents no difficulty but in hot metal it is more expensive on account of the handwork involved – with the exception of Times 'four-line' mathematics (Monotype series 569) which can only be used for displayed material. The desired alignment should be marked – even if it is as typed – or, if frequent, a blanket instruction given to the printer. Certain symbols such as the asterisk and the prime are related to the variable in a way that necessitates the inferior *following* the symbol if they are staggered at all, and therefore a blanket instruction may be dangerous. (Asterisks and primes are not strictly superiors, and it can be confusing to mark them as such.) In most cases, though, the third alternative $(X^2{}_a)$ should have its distinction made unambiguous by the use of parentheses: $(X^2)_a$.

The system to be used – overs and unders or staggers – should be specified when the book is estimated. The author should be consulted if it differs from that typed.

If it is not clear that superiors or inferiors are such, they should be marked by a V-shape in pencil. Double superiors or inferiors should be marked by a double-V.

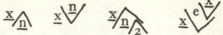

Awkward expressions may be dealt with in the following way:

$$x^a, \quad \text{where} \quad a = z^{4\pi r^2}.$$

The difficulty increases as the size of type decreases, and complicated mathematics of any kind should be avoided in footnotes.

Ambiguous symbols and their clarification

Make sure that all badly written or typed symbols and misleading spacing are elucidated.

Complicated expressions are often clearer to the printer when neatly handwritten than when typewritten, as the typewriter has no subtleties of spacing or sizes of characters, though in handwriting one has to be more careful to avoid possible capital/lower-case ambiguities.

It may in some cases be clearer to underline or ring different alphabets in coloured pencil: see British Standard 1219: 1958 *Proof correction and copy preparation*. If used, this must be done *totally* within each batch (i.e. marking even unambiguous letters) and the meaning of each colour explained in the margin at the beginning of each batch.

Ambiguous mathematical signs should be identified by their names or, if no further confusion is possible, just by the indication 'sign'. It is dangerous to use the Monotype matrix numbers (as found in (7) pp. 26–9), unless it is clear that only *similarity* is desired (e.g. 'sign like s9573'), for a printer may then feel obliged to order a matrix even though he already has a quite adequate alternative.

The following list summarizes many sources of ambiguity, the commonest being capital/lower-case and roman/italic.

a, α, $\propto$ (proportional)
A, Λ, $\wedge$ (vector product)

B, β

c, C, $\subset$ (contained in), ((parenthesis)

d, δ, ∂. Differential operator d preferably set roman, not italic

e, ϵ, ξ, $\in$ (element of). Exponential e preferably set roman, not italic; e represents an electron as a particle, e its charge

g (grams), g (acceleration due to free fall). When the latter has vectorial significance it may be set bold roman or italic, **g** or $\boldsymbol{g}$

h (hours), h (possible mathematical variable). Planck's constant may have a stroke, $\hbar$ ($\hbar = h/2\pi$)

i, ι. i is preferably set roman when it denotes $\sqrt{(-1)}$

j is preferably set roman when it denotes $\sqrt{(-1)}$

k, K, κ, k (kilo-)

l, I, 1, | (modulus), l (litre). ln (natural logarithm) is set roman

L, $\angle$ (angle)

m (metre), m (variable, e.g. for mass)

n, η, $\cap$ and $\cap$ (intersection)

o, O (these may be used to denote 'order of magnitude' as in $o(1)$ and $O(1)$), 0, Greek o, σ, θ, Θ, sign o. Note especially the need to indicate a zero when superior or inferior

p, P, ρ, p (pence)

r, τ, Γ

s, S, $\int$, s, (seconds), ς (terminal sigma)

t, T, τ, Γ, r, + (plus)

u, U, μ, v, $\cup$ and $\cup$ (union)

v, V, ν, $\sqrt{}$

w, W, ω

x, X, ψ, χ, $\times$ (multiplication)

y, Y, γ, Υ

z, Z, 2

Δ, Λ, A, Δ (sign), $\wedge$ (vector product)

θ, ϑ (alternatives which may or may not have a distinction intended), Θ, $\ominus$ (sign)

π, Π, Π as a product sign

Σ, Σ as a summation sign

ξ, ζ, ρ

ϕ, φ (alternatives which may or may not have a distinction intended), Φ, $\varnothing$ (empty set), zero in computer printout, Scandinavian ø, Ø

ψ, Ψ

ω, ϖ (curly pi)

superior 1, ' (prime or minutes)
superior 0, O, o, ° (degree)
decimal point, multiplication point; either may be high or low (see below)
= (equals), C=C (double bond)
− (minus), - (hyphen), – (en rule), — (em rule), C—C (single bond)
|, /, \ (signs)
∥ (parallel), ∥∥ (double modulus)
∠ (angle), < > (signs), ⟨ ⟩ (angle brackets), ≺ ≻ (signs)
∤ (does not divide), deleted modulus or solidus
≏ ≃ ∼ ≈ ≅, ⩽ ⩾ ≦ ≧, ≠ ≢ (various approximation and inequality
  signs). Check that any differences in usage are intended

Miscellany

Decimal point. This should always be preceded by a figure, if necessary a zero. The point is now usually on the line (see next paragraph).

Multiplication point. This is an en point (see glossary), and the Royal Society now recommends a medial point only. It should be possible to avoid any confusion over the significance of a point: a multiplication point should be necessary between numerals only in somewhat exceptional cases like $5! = 5 \cdot 4 \cdot 3 \cdot 2 \cdot 1$; and no sign of multiplication should be needed between letter symbols (except between vectors). The important thing is to ensure that, wherever it *is* used, there can be no ambiguity. Medial multiplication point/low decimal point (or vice versa) should be specified as an instruction to the printer, and any ambiguous ones in the manuscript marked individually.

High plus and minus signs (as opposed to the usual medial ones) have been used, rather rarely, when the sign is a property of the number rather than an operator. Hence: $^{-}2 + {}^{+}3 = {}^{+}1$. The signs are larger than the usual superior plus and minus.

Large numbers. It is usual to have a small space (say a ninth of an em) rather than a comma in numbers of 10 000 and above. Similar spaces should be inserted to the right of the decimal point at intervals of three digits if there are more than four. This should be marked, a light pencil stroke sufficing after the first in each batch.

Colons. If it is not obvious that a colon is indicating a ratio, it should be clarified. The spaces each side of the colon should look the same, and may be indicated by space before as well as after the colon, using vertical pencil lines. The colon is not equally spaced in the representation of a set, $\{x : x \geqslant 0\}$, or a function, $f : A \to B$.

Brackets. Where several brackets have to be used in a mathematical expression the sequence should be $[\![\langle\{[(\dots)]\}\rangle]\!]$ but it is unlikely to be worth changing a consistent system so long as it is one of different *kinds* of bracket; only one *size* of bracket may be used for a given depth of mathematical expression. In much scientific work – crystallography for instance – different kinds of brackets have precise significances and should not then be changed. Note that it is possible to have asymmetrical expressions, as in $\langle x|$ and $|x\rangle$.

Vincula. In filmsetting, vincula ($\sqrt{}$), superior bars, and underlining can be used if necessary, but in letterpress this is awkward and expensive. When a vinculum is removed, parentheses may need to be inserted to maintain the sense; and further rearrangements may help to make the expression clearer:

$$\sqrt{1+x} \quad \text{becomes} \quad \sqrt{(1+x)} \quad \text{or} \quad (1+x)^{\frac{1}{2}}$$

$$\sqrt{1+x}\sin x \quad \text{becomes} \quad (1+x)^{\frac{1}{2}}\sin x.$$

and $1/\sqrt{1+x}$ could become $(1+x)^{-\frac{1}{2}}$ or even $(1+x)^{-1/2}$. Consult the author if many such changes will be needed.

Fractions. Purely numerical fractions can be set within a line's height, though in hot metal all but the common ones have to be made up by hand. Fractions containing letters or other symbols must either occupy two lines or be reduced to one with a solidus. For economy of composition (and the look of the page) the latter alternative should always be used in running text; in displayed equations the two styles should not be mixed in a single equation or group of equations. This is not always the case for typewriter-set books: some methods can cope with one-line fractions and others find even simple numerical fractions difficult; if $2\frac{15}{16}$ must become 2 15/16 mark space between whole number and fraction. When changing fractions to the solidus form, insert sufficient parentheses to avoid ambiguity or alteration of meaning, e.g. $1/(x+1)$ not $1/x+1$; and thought should always be given to rearrangements, such as $3x/2$ rather than $(3/2)x$ for $\frac{3}{2}x$. Even simple numerical fractions such as $\frac{1}{2}$ could use the solidus when occurring as superiors: superior two-line fractions are very small. More examples of rearrangements of mathematics are given in (9) pp. 14–16, (10) p. 10, (11) pp. 27–8.

Two-line fractions can be marked for conversion to one-line by sloping marks at the ends of the rule: $\dfrac{x}{y}$, one-line to two-line similarly: $x\!\big/\!y$.

Exponential. Because the invariable use of e for exponential may commit one to very complicated expressions set entirely in superiors, exp should be substituted for anything containing superiors or inferiors to the superior expression. This should be used consistently through a sequence of expressions, but not necessarily throughout the whole book. Explain the system to the author.

Limits. Bear in mind that, when they have limits, integral signs, summation signs and product signs will require the lines containing them to have extra space above and below. If limits in running text can be set after the symbol, as in Σ_0^n, this will enable the expressions to be set within the line.

Matrices and determinants. Check that the correct nomenclature has been used by the author, and that it is unambiguous. Matrices have large parentheses or square brackets to left and right; determinants have straight vertical rules to left and right (in manuscript, confusion between very large square brackets and rules is easy). Note also that a determinant must be square (i.e. have the same number of rows as columns) whereas a matrix need not be. Elision of missing terms is represented by *three* dots (horizontally, vertically or diagonally as appropriate); terms may be grouped within a matrix or determinant by dashed lines, and if these become complicated in a letterpress book they may need to be artwork. Check that the alignment of different-size expressions on the same line is consistent. It may be worth reminding the printer that the matrix $\binom{3}{2}$ is not supposed to be a fraction.

Ambiguous sorts in mathematical setting. In Monotype series 327 (Times) there is an alternative v to avoid confusion with the almost identical greek ν: warn the printer if relevant. Monotype series 101 (Imprint) has an alternative $\mathcal{J}$ which may be worth specifying. In sans serif faces I and l are totally ambiguous and this may necessitate alternative nomenclature or the spelling-out of abbreviations. In some faces alpha and a are virtually indistinguishable.

Vectors. The 'cross product' should be consistently either $\times$ or $\wedge$.

Ligatures. It may be worth reminding the printer not to use, for example, the ligatures fi, fl for $f \times i, f \times l$.

Elision of any kind should always be by *three* dots.

Theorems, corollaries and lemmas are often difficult to separate off adequately from the text. The use of a line space at the end is not always obvious when there is much displayed mathematics. Indention of the whole (by an em) may be better. Mathematicians often use a symbol such as ☐ to indicate the finish and this is recommended; even so, if space precedes the theorem it should also follow it. Make sure that the end of the theorem is clearly indicated in the typescript.

13.3 *Units*

SI units should nowadays be used for all scientific and technological books (see (1) pp. 22–9). The SI base units are the metre, kilogram (preferred to 'kilogramme'), second, ampere, kelvin, candela and mole. There are however a few units widely used in particular fields which are likely to be retained for a considerable time – for example the ångström unit (Å), the bar, and wavenumber (ν in cm^{-1}).

The names of units are given in lower-case, even when they are derived from a proper name. Plural forms of full names (but not of symbols) may be used. Symbols (i.e. abbreviations of units) are set in roman, without points, and do use initial capitals when derived from a proper name. Hence: 1 watt; 3 W; 3 watts. Abbreviations like amp and amps should be discouraged: the correct forms are 4 amperes and 4 A.

If the author quotes other workers' results their units may be inconsistent with his own; this is especially likely to happen in tables and figures. Other things being equal they should be made consistent with the style of the book, but possible exceptions are that the matter is being quoted essentially for its historical interest or the conversion would imply a different order of accuracy and it could appear odd if readings were 'taken at intervals of 0·3048 m' rather than every foot. Decide individual cases on their merits.

Multiplication by powers of ten in table column heads and on graph axes can easily be ambiguous: it should always be clear how the factor is related to the units, and is best incorporated in the statement of the units.

Symbols

For the division of units the index is better than the solidus, but the use of the solidus for simple cases only, e.g. m/s but J g^{-1} deg^{-1} s^{-1}, may be adopted. The Royal Society recommends that where a solidus *is* used, it should occur only once: J/g deg s and not J/g/deg/s. There is a case for keeping the solidus for books at school level.

Figures should always be used with symbols: never 'five kg', for example.

The space between the numerical value of a quantity and its units symbol is usually (though this varies between printers) a quarter of an em and that between multiplied units symbols a ninth of an em: space should be indicated if none has been left by the typist.

Per cent or % should be used consistently throughout the text, but the former does not preclude the use of the sign in tables and in matter quoting large numbers of percentages in succession.

Temperatures

The Royal Society recommends that the symbol K be used for both temperature and temperature interval. However, °K is still sometimes used and °C will continue to find wide application; and where these forms are used it should be noted that they refer to actual temperature only and the unit for temperature interval is then deg. In scientific work it is not necessary to add C after deg. The ° is part of the unit and should be closed up to the K or C, the standard space coming between figures and °: this should preferably be marked by the copy-editor. Unattached ° signs are unnecessary and should be avoided, the alternatives '2, 3 and 4 °C', and '2 °C, 3 °C and 4 °C' being quite adequate.

Magnifications

× 300 should be used in preference to 300 × . The multiplication sign may need to be identified. In illustrations scales are preferable to magnifications in the caption.

13.4 *Chemistry*

The *Handbook for Chemical Society authors* (2) (especially the summary on pp. 6–7) may be used as a standard guide. This gives the IUPAC recommendations in full. The IUPAC recommendations for the naming of organic and inorganic compounds are available separately, (3), (4). Also useful is (1) pp. 34–42.

Nomenclature

The symbols for the elements are set in roman type. This will be understood by the printer, but any italic characters occurring should be marked. Generalized radicals, metals, etc. (R, M, etc.), may be italicized if the author insists, but the preferred style is now roman.

Superiors and inferiors are deployed as follows: $^m_a X^c_n$ where m = mass number, a = atomic number, c = electrical charge, and n = number of atoms per molecule. This should be adhered to as closely as possible, and in particular the common mistake of X^m for isotopes avoided.

Chemical names should be spelt out wherever practicable, unless the symbolic formula is graphically useful; hence ions *are* generally preferable as symbols: Cu^{2+} ion rather than cupric ion (use Cu^{2+} and not Cu^{++}, to avoid Mn^{++++} or worse).

Prefixes

Many prefixes are used in chemical names and a good deal of variation is possible. If an author has a consistent system follow it gratefully; the Chemical Society has rationalized its own system ((2) p. 8) as: *italic* to be used for prefixes which define *positions* of named substituents or which are used only to define stereoisomers, but not for other prefixes; *hyphens* to be used with italicized (but not with roman) prefixes of more than one letter and with *all* single-letter prefixes, figures and symbols. Hence *ortho*-xylene, *o*-xylene, *cis*-isomer, *N*-methyl, which denote substitution at particular atoms; but isobutane, pentamethyl, cyclobutane. (Note that the abbreviations *o*-, *m*-, *p*- are preferable to *ortho*- etc., and that t- is preferable to tert.) For further examples see (2) p. 8.

In general the order of names in an alphabetical list should be determined by the roman part of the word – the italic ignored – but authors may have reasonable alternative systems of their own: two examples noted recently are the indexing of mRNA etc. under r and *cis*- and *trans*- under c and t.

Structural formulae

In all cases, but especially where they occur in running text, complex formulae should be simplified as much as possible. It is often unnecessary to portray single or double bonds: where they are retained and any ambiguity is possible, identify them for the printer as 'bond' (see p. 237). Structural formulae could be changed to $CH_3.CO.OCl$ or $CH_3C(=O)OCl$ for example. Grouping points should be consistently medial or (preferably) low. Hexagons could be replaced by Ph or Ar. But consult the author before making significant changes.

The larger a structural formula is, the less likely it is to appear just where required on the page, and if there are many of them in the book it will probably be worth using a numbering system, and altering text references appropriately: make sure that the altered sentences are still grammatically complete. If a formula is in the middle of a paragraph in the typescript, link the ends of text with a loopy pencil line or write 'run on' at the side.

Any sensible numbering system of the author's may be used: the most common one is still roman numerals in one sequence throughout the whole book, even though this can result in some inconveniently long numbers; when using this system the numbers should be small capitals within parentheses, and the number dealt with as part of the illustration rather than as a caption. Arabic numbering, typographically distinguished from equations by, for example, square brackets or bold type, is less cumbersome: this should be decimally by chapter if other numbering systems are.

The number of structural formulae that will have to be drawn will depend on the printing process, and even the individual printer: consult the production department, giving a list of folios on which formulae occur if there are not a great many, or pointing out some examples to illustrate the range to be covered if they average one per folio or so. In a *letterpress* book, anything containing a diagonal line, or anything complicated even though all the lines be vertical and horizontal, might be made into blocks: those that certainly will be should be photocopied so that the originals can be put with the artwork (the copies being included in the typescript with the block areas ringed), and the others can be left for the printer to deal with as appropriate. Books printed by lithography are more flexible – and therefore even more unpredictable – and simple diagonals etc. will probably be drawn by the printer, only the more complicated formulae needing a draughtsman.

Miscellany

Isotopes. These should be written as ^{14}C or carbon-14 as appropriate. Square brackets, closed up against the name, are used to indicate labelling: $[^3H]$water, $[\gamma-^{32}P]$ATP.

Molarity is indicated by a small capital M, normality (now obsolete) by N. The former is sometimes confused with number of moles – which should only be abbreviated to mol. In typewriter setting, full capitals may be used.

Oxidation states are indicated by small capital or superior capital roman numbers, thus: manganese(IV) or Mn^{IV}. Note that in the former case the parentheses are closed up against the name.

pH; *pK$_a$*. pH is set in roman; pK_a has a roman p but both the K and the inferior *a* are italic.

Steroids. Small capital A, B, etc., are used for labelling the rings of steroids.

Stereoisomers. *d, l* and *dl* are now no longer used, and should be replaced by $(+)$, $(-)$ and $(\pm)$ respectively. Absolute configuration is denoted by small capital D, L and DL.

Identification of carbon atoms. The best way of referring to carbon atoms in a molecule is by C-1, C-2, etc., using a roman C and a hyphen. An alternative but less desirable system is $C_{(13)}$ etc.; in this case the parentheses are necessary to avoid ambiguity.

Arrows rather than equals signs should be used in chemical equations. (These will normally be 2 ems long.)

Orbitals. The Royal Society recommends that the quantum symbols s, p, d etc. be set in roman. The author may however have feelings of his own about this.

Bonds in molecules should always be marked for the printer. Some printers use em rules, but a special sort is available and it is best to mark 'bond' against every one (or the first of each batch if many). In the phrase 'C—CH$_3$ group' mark the line as a 'bond' since the expression is a graphical representation; but in 'C–C bond' it could be marked as an en rule, since it is equivalent to 'carbon–carbon bond'. On the same basis, 'carbon–carbon double bond' could be represented by 'C–C double bond' (using an en rule), but it may be felt more desirable to compromise and use the double bond sign, 'C=C bond'. An inconsistency in appearance should be avoided.

13.5 *Biology*

Biology books make particularly extensive use of Latin and Greek names (or words derived therefrom) for species, the taxa (or groups) into which they fall, aspects of their structure, the way they function and the kind of environment in which they live.

Biological classification and nomenclature

Main groups. The basic nomenclatural groups or taxa, in descending order, are: phylum or division, class, order, family, genus and species. All group names from family upwards are Latin names with plural endings. They should be written in roman with an initial capital (e.g. Coleoptera, Ericales). Genus and species names are always set in italic and have singular endings. The generic name has an initial capital but the specific name does not, thus *Lophophora williamsii*. These two names constitute the scientific name of a species and are together known as the binomen (zoology), binomial (botany) or the binary combination (bacteriology). I use 'binomen' below to cover all three.

The binomen should be given in full at the first mention; thereafter the genus may be abbreviated to its initial letter (hence *L. williamsii*). This abbreviation may be preserved through changes of the specific name so long as there is no ambiguity. Hence *Bacillus subtilis...B. subtilis...B. megaterium*. Avoid partial abbreviations.

While generic names may be referred to separately (e.g. *Homo*) the specific name must normally be qualified by the generic name (i.e. *Homo sapiens*, not *sapiens* alone). A specific name may, however, stand alone if it occurs in a key or a section covering only a single genus in which the specific names are used repeatedly. A species within a genus may be referred to in general terms by the roman abbreviation sp. (plural spp.) after the generic name (e.g. 'some *Spirorbis* spp.').

Useful tables giving the plant and animal kingdoms down as far as orders are to be found in *Chambers dictionary of science and technology* (appendix).

Authorities. The name of the worker who originally classified the species will sometimes follow the binomen in roman, especially if there is some controversy about the classification. Many biologists recommend that the authority appears at the first mention of each species, even in works not concerned with taxonomy. The best-known authority is Linnaeus, whose name may be abbreviated to L. (e.g. *Parage aegeria* L.) and others may be partially abbreviated (e.g. Lamarck to Lam.). If the authority is written in parentheses this is a significant distinction, denoting that the species has been moved to a genus different from that given by the original authority. Botanists and microbiologists then follow this with the new authority (not in parentheses), for example *Shigella dysenteriae* (Shiga) Castellani & Chalmers. Zoologists do not do this. In some books it may be necessary to include the date of classification after the authority.

Subdivision of species. In zoology the subspecific name (also lower-case italic) may be added to the binomen. In cases where the specific and subspecific names are identical the former may be abbreviated to the first letter, for example, *Lagopus s. scoticus.* Botanists set out the sub-species as *Veronica serpyllifolia* L. subsp. *humifusa* (Dickson) Syme. Note that subspecies should be abbreviated to subsp. not ssp. Its plural form is subspp.

The botanical code of nomenclature recognizes such subordinate taxa as subspecies, varietas (abbreviated to var. or v.), subvarietas (subvar. or subv.), forma and subforma. These are treated like the subspecies above.

Names of cultivated varieties of plants (cultivars) are printed in roman type with single quotes and positioned after the binomial, for example *Pisum sativum* L. 'Marrow fat'. The abbreviation cv. may be inserted before the cultivar name. The provenance is often indicated with plants thus: *Picea sitchensis* (Bong.) Carr. provenance Queen Charlotte Islands.

Headings. Italicized biological names may become roman or remain italic when they occur in italic headings or headlines. One system should be applied consistently.

Common names

The English or common names of plants and animals, of structures, of diseases and anglicized forms of Latin names (e.g. crustaceans, aphid, orchid) should be lower-case roman. They are capitalized if proper names are involved, hence 'Malpighian tubules', and sometimes authors capitalize common names if ambiguity is possible through common adjectives being used as part of the name, e.g. 'Blue Whale', 'Spotted Orchid'. There may be borderline cases which must be discussed with the author.

Where the generic name is used in a general, anglicized sense, it is neither capitalized nor italicized, e.g. petunia, bacillus.

If a common name has two parts, one being a 'group name', the latter will be a separate word only when used in a sense which is systematically correct, i.e. house fly but butterfly, silkworm: the house fly is a true fly, but the butterfly is not, nor is the silkworm a worm.

American terminology

Various biochemical names have different spellings, and sometimes totally different forms, in American. For example, American has estrogen for oestrogen and epinephrine (or the trade name Adrenalin) for adrenaline. In international symposium typescripts, particularly, both may appear, and it may be worth asking the symposium editor to check consistency of usage. Cross-references may be needed in the index.

Other biological nomenclature

Bacterial strains. Bacterial and viral species are often subdivided into strains. They are usually denoted by roman capital letters, which may have a number or subscript number, for example, the *Escherichia coli* bacteriophage T4 or T_4. (See also p. 99.)

There are specific nomenclature and abbreviation lists for such subjects as respiratory physiology and immunology in (5) and various handbooks; but conventions in specialized fields change, so consult the author or follow his system if consistent.

Genetic terms. Genes and chromosomes are denoted by lettered symbols. Genes should be italic, either upper- or lower-case. Chromosomes are denoted by roman capitals (the best-known being the sex chromosomes, X (female) and Y (male)). Generations are referred to also by lettered symbols in roman capitals: the parental (P), the first generation (F_1 or F1), the second generation (F_2 or F2) and so on. The letter *n* used to denote the chromosome complement of a cell may be (consistently) roman or italic, and may be preceded by an arabic figure.

Blood groups. The groups (A, B, O etc.) are set in roman capitals, and so are the antigens after which the groups are named. The genes which determine the antigens may be denoted by the corresponding italic letters (*A* gene produces A antigen and A blood group). Rhesus is abbreviated to Rh (without a full point).

Biochemical abbreviations. Complicated organic compounds are frequently abbreviated to initial capitals without full points. All except the most obvious (this will depend on the level of the book) should be explained at first mention by being spelt out in full and followed by the appropriate abbreviation in parentheses. The following may be well-enough known to require no explanation in specialized texts.

ADP (adenosine diphosphate)
ATP (adenosine triphosphate) and its relations GTP, UTP, CTP

DPN (diphosphopyridine nucleotide)⎰ but these are now superseded by
TPN (triphosphopyridine nucleotide)⎱ NAD and NADP
DNA (deoxyribonucleic acid)
RNA (ribonucleic acid)
EDTA (ethylenediamine tetra-acetic acid)

Messenger, transfer and ribosomal RNA are denoted by a lower-case roman m, t and r which is either hyphenated or closed up: m-RNA or mRNA. RNase (not RNAase or RNAse) is used for the ribonuclease enzyme (similarly DNase). Abbreviations for nucleotides and amino acids are all roman.

13.6 *Representation of computer languages*

There is a certain amount of flexibility in the typographical imitation and layout of displayed material, but this must be decided in consultation with the author. The conventions of the language itself must not be altered in any way by, for example, changing or adding to the punctuation. Fortran and Algol only will be discussed here, being illustrative of the problems of most other computer languages. Note, incidentally, that 'program' is an American word and is always so spelt.

Typeface
It may be that the text type itself is quite adequate, but this should be discussed with the author (see the sections on Fortran and Algol). In a litho book, the displayed matter could be produced by photographing typescript; computer printout itself may be too fuzzy, though many computers have associated photo-composing machines or daisy-wheel printers that produce clear copy. The limitation of photographed typescript or printout is that it is difficult to deal with such matter within running text. For that reason the computer matter is better set in type throughout. Monotype series 82, 100, 105, 127 and 235 imitate typewriting; this has the added advantage that as all characters are of the same width, alignments (as in Fortran) are facilitated. If distinction from the text, but not alignment, is desired, any sans serif face could be used.

Sorts. A variety of symbols are arbitrarily used for the representation of 'oh' and zero: in printout these may take forms such as 0, ☐ and Ø. With the author's approval, usage should be standardized to two of these. The decimal point, the full point and the dot will all share the same character, usually a low point.

Fortran

Fortran is usually represented, in both text and display, by a typeface distinct from the text. The peculiarities of punctuation and other conventions must be followed: 2. and 2.0 are the same but *not* the same as 2 and .2 should not be changed to 0.2. A centred asterisk represents multiplication and $*\,*$ an index $(A*\,*B \equiv A^B)$. Word breaks and the size of word spaces are unimportant: terms like GO TO and GOTO may be made consistent. An exception to this is FORMAT statements, where spaces are important and may be represented by $\sqcup$ signs.

The vertical alignment is important (see fig. 13.1), representing punched cards bearing columns of one character width. The first five columns are used for the statement number (ranged left or right), the sixth is blank, the statement itself starting in the seventh. When long statements have to break and continue, a character (usually C but any except a blank or zero) appears in the sixth column and the statement continues anywhere to the right. 'Comments' are something of an exception: a C appears in the first column and the comment itself starts in the third, the first-column C being repeated for any continuation line.

```
           1 2 3 4 5 6 7 8 9 10 11 12
Statement:   1            A = A + 1


or:                     1  A = A + 1



Continuation:            2   B + D = A + . . .
                         C    + A + A

Comment:           C  T H I S   I S   A   C O M M E N T
```

Fig. 13.1   Simulated computer printout.

This is summarized in the figure. Typographical representation must preserve the alignments about the sixth column: otherwise it is sufficient that statements going off to the right range left against this line. If a face with equiwidth characters (such as series 235) is used, this will occur naturally. To help the printer align correctly, draw light vertical lines.

Algol

The language used for typesetting (publication language) differs from that in printouts (machine language): the former uses bold for *some* occurrences (but not all) of words such as **begin** and **end**. Text type is commonly used to represent Algol. The indention and alignment schemes do not have to be followed closely, as they are only conveniences to show the logic in sequences of steps: it is this that should be preserved.

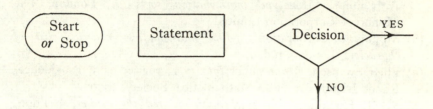

Fig. 13.2   Flow diagram symbols.

Flow diagrams

Flow diagrams will need to be artwork. The boxes are of standard shapes (see fig. 13.2), and may be labelled within in capitals, small capitals or upper- and lower-case; some authors also use capitals or small capitals for these terms in the text. Except when joined in long unambiguous strings they should have arrows on the flow lines. The only words appearing outside boxes are Yes and No, which should be consistently upper- and lower-case, capitals or small capitals.

13.7 *References*

(1) The Symbols Committee of the Royal Society. *Quantities, units and symbols*, 2nd edn, London, 1972

(2) The Chemical Society. *Handbook for Chemical Society authors*, London, 1961; and as subsequently amended by various *Notices to authors*

(3) IUPAC. *Nomenclature of inorganic chemistry*, 2nd edn, London, 1971

(4) IUPAC. *Nomenclature of organic chemistry*, Sections A, B & C, 2nd edn, London, 1971

(5) *Council of Biology Editors style manual*, 4th edn, obtainable from the American Institute of Biological Sciences, Arlington, Va, 1978

(6) The Royal Society of Medicine. *Units, symbols and abbreviations: a guide for biological and medical editors and authors*, 3rd edn, London, 1977

(7) A. Phillips. 'Setting mathematics', *Monotype recorder* (winter, 1956). This includes a list of mathematical signs; an expanded list of signs, together with lists of accented letters, may be found in A. Phillips, *'Monotype' mathematical sorts list*, London, The Monotype Corporation Limited

(8) Monotype Corporation. *4-line mathematics: classified list of characters*, London, n.d.

(9) Ellen Swanson. *Mathematics into type*, revised edn, Providence, Rhode Island, American Mathematical Society, 1979

(10) R. G. Hitchings. *The mathematician and the printer*, London, Hodgson, 1964

(11) T. W. Chaundy, P. R. Barrett & C. Batey. *The printing of mathematics*, Oxford University Press, 1954

14

Other special subjects

14.1 *Classical books*

Many of the problems of copy-editing and printing books containing Latin and Greek arise from the unfamiliarity of the languages and the subject matter; some basic information is listed below. There are also several conventions of style and presentation which require no specialized classical knowledge and which author and copy-editor should be aware of, even if they decide to alter them.

Typefaces

The commonest Greek typefaces used in Britain are Times, Porson and New Hellenic, in which either classical or modern Greek can be set. New Hellenic (shown below) is upright, Porson (shown on pp. 228–9) is sloping; Times has both upright and sloping founts. With Porson one can use either upright or sloping capitals; the sloping ones perhaps look better with lower-case, but the capital alpha slopes so much that the breathing (see below) is a long way from it. All three typefaces have bold founts; emphasized words in Greek are not 'italicized' but letter-spaced or underlined.

Alphabets

There are twenty-four letters in the classical Greek alphabet, including seven vowels:

A α	alpha (a)	Λ λ	lambda (l)
B β	beta (b)	M μ	mu (m)
Γ γ	gamma (g)	N ν	nu (n)
Δ δ	delta (d)	Ξ ξ	xi (x)
E ε	epsilon (e)	O o	omicron (o)
Z ʒ	zeta (z)	Π π	pi (p)
H η	eta (ē)	P ρ	rho (r)
Θ θ	theta (th)	Σ σ	(ς final or C c) sigma (s)
I ι	iota (i)	T τ	tau (t)
K κ	kappa (k)	Y υ	upsilon (u)

Φ φ   phi (ph)   Ψ ψ   psi (ps)
Χ χ   chi (ch)   Ω ω   omega (ō)   (or Ω)

There are also four obsolete characters: digamma or vau (ϝ), stigma (ϛ), koppa (ϙ or ϛ), and san or sampi (ϡ). These occur occasionally in linguistic discussions and were used in classical Greek as numerals (see below). The Mycenaean Linear A and Linear B syllabic scripts are usually reproduced photographically from calligraphy though sorts for metal typesetting are available at the University Printing House, Cambridge; a complete list of the characters in the syllabaries is given in Ventris and Chadwick, *Documents in Mycenaean Greek* (2nd edn, Cambridge University Press, 1973), pp. 33, 41.

The upper- and lower-case forms of several letters in the classical alphabet are easily confused, and where the letters are used singly several are also easily confused with similar English letters. This is particularly relevant in some Aristotle references where Greek capitals are used for book numbers. Identify letters as Greek in cases where doubts could arise, and draw attention to occurrences of the less familiar characters.

There are two forms of the conventional lower-case sigma: ς is only used as the final letter of a word, σ only in some other part of a word. This distinction is not observed when C (capital) and c (lower-case) are used for sigma.

Notice that there is no dot over the Greek iota (ι).

None of the diphthongs in Greek are printed as ligatures. But long vowels (α, η, ω) may have an iota subscript (ᾳ, ῃ, ῳ) which becomes a separate letter when the word is capitalized (ΑΙ, ΗΙ, ΩΙ). The iota is sometimes written as a separate letter even in lower case; but the author should be consistent. With this, as with the lunate sigma (c), it is important to check that the author uses the same convention throughout. Authors sometimes provide photocopies of previously printed texts which use different conventions from their own.

The Latin alphabet is like the English one, except that it has no W or w. I and i are now normally used for J and j (which were in any case later, non-classical forms). The distinction between U, u and V, v is sometimes retained, but V (capital) and u (lower-case) are often used for both vowel and consonant. C (capital) is sometimes used for G (capital) in abbreviations (e.g. C. and Cn. for Gaius and Gneus), and in early inscriptions.

It is rare now to use ligatures for diphthongs like ae in Latin.

See Hart's *Rules*, pp. 113–15, for the division of Greek and Latin words at the end of a line.

Accents

There are no accents in classical Latin, though occasionally stress marks are used to demonstrate pronunciation (and then they are placed over any scansion marks, as in *amícus*). Draw the printer's attention to any such marks or combination of marks. Post-medieval Latin may have accents.

Greek has three accents: grave (ˋ), acute (ˊ), and circumflex (ˆ or ˜). Hart (*Rules*, pp. 111–12) gives some of the basic rules governing their use, but these are extremely complicated and there are many exceptions. When in doubt follow copy.

There is also a diaeresis mark (¨), which indicates that the vowels over which it appears are to be pronounced separately and not as a diphthong. The diaeresis is printed under a grave or acute accent when they fall on the same letter.

Breathings

Greek has a rough breathing (ʽ denoting aspirates) and a smooth breathing (ʼ denoting non-aspirates) on all words which begin with a vowel or a rho (ρ) or where there has been a crasis (fusion of two words, as in τἀγαπά, where the mark is called a *coronis*). Words beginning with diphthongs take the breathing over the second letter. Breathings precede grave or acute accents (when they fall on the same letters), but go under a circumflex. They are not now printed over a double-rho (ρρ) occurring in the middle of a word.

Latin has no breathings.

Punctuation

Greek uses ; for ? and · for ; but is otherwise the same as English (! is often used in modern editions). The apostrophe (denoting an elision, as in English) is easily confused with the smooth breathing; it is printed the same but is never printed *over* a vowel.

Latin is printed with the same punctuation marks as English.

In neither Latin nor Greek is the initial word of a sentence invariably capitalized (usually only at the beginning of a quotation or 'paragraph').

Numerals

The Latin notation up to 100 is familiar. Further signs are D (500), M (1,000), $\overline{\text{X}}$ (10,000), $\overline{\text{C}}$ (100,000). and $\boxed{\text{X}}$ (1,000,000). In inscriptions VIIII is often found for IX.

The Greeks had two different notations: the earlier, 'acrophonic' system, found particularly in epigraphic texts, is tabulated by A. G. Woodhead, *The study of Greek inscriptions* (Cambridge University Press, 1959), pp. 108–10. The later, 'alphabetic' system is set out in Hart's *Rules*, p. 115; it uses the lower-case letters of the classical Greek alphabet plus the obsolete letters stigma, koppa and sampi (see above), accented to distinguish units, tens, hundreds and thousands (thus β' = 2, ,β = 2,000).

Dates

The Greeks named years by Olympiads (quadrennially from 776 BC) or by archonships.

The Romans named them by consulships or counted them AUC (*ab urbe condita* = from the foundation of Rome, 753 BC).

Use BC or AD where there could be any doubt which is intended. The correct form is 250–245 BC, AD 245–50; do not elide BC dates except a year of office in the form 449/8 BC.

Symbols

In textual or epigraphic studies there is a system of signs (the Leiden system) used to indicate the state of the original text and the extent and nature of the editor's own restorations. (A text in its original form usually does not have word spacing, accents, or punctuation, and is written in majuscules; if it is an early text it may even be written from right to left, or alternately left to right and right to left.) These conventional signs include double and single upright lines, parentheses, square and angle brackets, braces, dots and dashes: Woodhead (*Greek inscriptions*, pp. 6–11) gives a useful short explanation of them. The Leiden system is generally accepted, but there are (as always) idiosyncratic usages, and the conventions an editor is using should be explained in the note on 'sigla' which precedes most editions (where the editor also gives the abbreviations he is using for the various MSS and families of MSS).

In lexicographical and etymological works symbols like asterisks and daggers are used very variously and should be explained. Typical usages can be found listed in the larger Latin and Greek dictionaries.

Solidi separating parallels and analogues should be spaced: e.g. *cupiditas | cupido.*

Abbreviations

The *Oxford classical dictionary* and the larger Greek and Latin dictionaries (Liddell and Scott, *Greek–English lexicon*, Lewis and Short, *Latin dictionary*) give conventional abbreviations of classical authors and their works and also of standard 'modern' textbooks. Soph., Eur., Aesch., etc., are preferable to S., E., A., etc. Authors sometimes forget to italicize the appropriate part of an abbreviation (e.g. Soph. *OC* = Sophocles, *Oedipus Coloneus*, and *SVF* = *Stoicorum Veterum Fragmenta*).

The following miscellaneous abbreviations often occur in classical books:

ap.	*apud*, quoted in
AUC	*ab urbe condita*, from the foundation of Rome
EM	Early Minoan, a historical period; also LM and MM for Late and Middle Minoan
fr.	fragment
h.l.	*hic locus*, this passage
h.v.	*haec verba*, these words
init.	*initio*, at the beginning
schol.	*scholion*, an ancient commentary
str.	strophe, part of a choral ode, often printed alongside the relevant part of a text
s.v.	*sub voce*, under the heading
temp.	*tempore*, in the time of
var. lect.	*varia lectio*, variant reading

See further in the lists of abbreviations of the larger dictionaries, and under *References* and *Transliteration*.

References

Classical works: where possible, references should be to the conventional division of the work into books, sections or lines, rather than to the page numbers of a particular edition. Where there is no one standard division or arrangement of the text, the reference should include the name (often abbreviated to a capital letter) of the relevant edition: thus Aeschylus, fr. 26 (N), also written fr. 26N (full capital).

There are various acceptable styles for the punctuation of figures in a composite reference. The two commonest are in the form Horace, *Odes* 4.2.3 (the numerals referring to book, poem, and line respectively), Vergil, *Aeneid* 2.6 (book and line), and Horace, *Odes* IV.2.3, Vergil, *Aeneid* II.6. Both are preferable to Vergil, *Aeneid* 2,3 where the comma is ambiguous.

It is now usual to refer to books of Homer's works by figures not Greek letters (thus Homer, *Odyssey* 2.5–9 not *Odyssey* β, 5–9).

References to Plato and Aristotle usually give section, subsection (denoted by an English letter, usually lower-case), and line: thus Plato, *Republic* 496a5–7 and Aristotle, *EN* 1107a2–b7.

There is no need to mention the work where an author wrote only one (or where they are all collected under one title): thus Herodotus 1.95 (book, section), Thucydides 7.24 (book, section), Catullus 24.18 (poem, line), Demosthenes 46.24 (speech, section), etc.

See also under *Transliteration* and *Indexes*.

Contemporary works: a widely used set of abbreviations of classical journals and periodicals is given in *L'Année philologique*. A Greek word or phrase occurring in the title of a book or article is sometimes printed in capitals, but for aesthetic reasons this practice should be discouraged.

Transliteration

Classical names may be anglicized, latinized or hellenized (Virgil, Sophocles, Odysseus); but attempts to do one of these things absolutely consistently lead to very odd results, and it is probably best just to use the most familiar form in each case (see, for example, the usage in the *Oxford classical dictionary*). There are many borderline cases, and internal consistency is the only rule which can be applied to these. Avoid using one form of a name when it refers to a person and another form when it is part of the title of a book (e.g. Oidipous and *Oedipus Coloneus*), or latinizing some of an author's works and anglicizing others (e.g. Aristophanes, *Aves* and *Ranae*, but *Clouds* and *Wasps*).

Metrical analysis

The commonest scansion marks are ⁻ (long), ˘ (short), × or ⏒ (anceps), ⏖ (resolved long), x̄ (long anceps), and single or double vertical bars ('feet' and 'periods'). But there are various other signs and combinations of signs to which it may be worth drawing the printer's attention since he is unlikely to hold all sorts in all sizes. See further L. M. Dale, *Lyric metres of Greek drama* (2nd edn, Cambridge University Press, 1968) and the *Oxford classical dictionary, s.v.* Metre.

Uprights are preferable to oblique strokes to show line breaks in quotations of Greek and Latin verse which run on in the quotation.

Texts and editions

Most editions of prose and verse texts have an apparatus criticus, which is a summary of variant readings and suggested restorations. It is printed beneath the text in smaller type and is keyed in by line numbers which are usually printed in bold. Various fixed spaces indicate the subdivisions within each entry.

Editions of Greek plays are usually preceded by 'hypotheses', which are introductions to the plays (sometimes themselves in verse) by other ancient writers. The section of hypotheses normally starts a fresh page, and the text starts another.

The ranging of lines of verse may require particular attention. Hexameters are normally ranged left, while elegiacs have alternate lines indented; but there are many complicated versification schemes, particularly in the choruses of Greek plays, which may require special layout and where it may be important to distinguish turnovers from indented new lines. The author should make this clear.

The headlines to a text normally have author left and title right (both in Greek or Latin). There is no real need for headlines except in anthologies.

Commentaries

Commentaries normally make a section after the text in smaller type (i.e. as endnotes), but they may exceptionally be printed beneath the text when they are very short or when there is not a full critical apparatus; see, for example, J. Adam, *The Republic of Plato* (2nd edn, Cambridge University Press, 1963).

Commentaries are usually keyed to the text by section and/or line numbers followed by lemmata (catchwords). The lemmata are normally set in bold and followed by a colon (also in bold) with the commentary running straight on. Stretches of commentary are often preceded by a summary (usually with a centred subheading).

The punctuation and accentuation of lemmata can cause problems;

the following rules are used in the Cambridge University Press series, Cambridge Greek and Latin Classics:

(1) Punctuate lemmata in the following way:

1209 φονᾷ 'is intent on death'.
1213 This line is highly suspect.
1214 πῶς: Jebb takes the view...
1219 σοι is an ethic dative.

(2) For the purposes of accentuation, lemmata in the commentary should be treated as separate headings, complete in themselves, so that what was a final grave in the text will become an acute in the lemma, and accents will not be absorbed from enclitics which do not themselves appear in the lemma. This rule applies also to entries in indexes, but not to entries in the apparatus criticus. In the 'text' of the commentary the rule should be generally applied to isolated Greek words or phrases, except when the accentuation is itself the subject of the note.

(3) Where the last Greek word in a lemma is elided in the text, elide it also in the lemma (even though the next word is not repeated).

Running headlines, indicating the lines or sections under commentary, are the most informative.

Indexes

There is often an index locorum and an index nominum as well as a general index. In the index locorum it is necessary to use some device to distinguish clearly between the locus and the page references to it.

One system is to separate off part of the locus by parentheses:

> Horace, *Odes* 1 (2.1), 34–7, 46–7; (3.6), 45–8, 67–9, 78–9
> 2 (5.1), 45, 64–7

Here the first number in the line refers to the book, the figures in parentheses refer to the poem and the line, and subsequent figures give the page references.

In a less complicated entry the whole of the locus can be placed in parentheses:

> Euripides, *Alcestis* (112 f.), 34–7, 47; (192), 48
> *Medea* (55–9), 11–14

For further examples see the indexes of W. K. C. Guthrie, *A history of Greek philosophy*, vols. I–VI (Cambridge University Press, 1962–81).

Another system is to range right all the page references so that they are physically separated from the classical references; see, for an example, G. E. R. Lloyd and G. E. L. Owen, *Aristotle on mind and the senses* (Cambridge University Press, 1978).

14.2 *Books on law*

References to statutes

Before 1963 titles of statutes were punctuated with a comma between the name and the year (e.g. the Finance Act, 1962), but from 1963 the comma was dropped (Finance Act 1963). In references to statutes, however, the distinction is not copied: the comma should be omitted from all titles, both before and after 1963. Titles should always be set roman, not italic.

Session and chapter references of statutes are often given in tables of statutes (see below) and sometimes in footnotes. Every statute is classified by chapter number within the parliamentary session in which it was passed, and up to 1963 parliamentary sessions were identified by regnal year: thus for example the Act of Supremacy 1558, which was the first chapter in the parliamentary session in the first year of Elizabeth I's reign, is numbered 1 Eliz. I c. 1 (the monarch's numeral can alternatively be arabic). Where a parliamentary session extended from one regnal year to the next, two regnal years are cited, e.g. 12 & 13 Will. III c. 2 (the Act of Settlement 1700). In regnal year references the monarch's name should be abbreviated as follows: Edw., Hen., Ph. & M. (Philip and Mary), Eliz., Jac., Car. or Chas., Will., Geo., Vic. or Vict.

From 1963 regnal year references were replaced by calendar years: thus the Finance Act 1962 is numbered 10 & 11 Eliz. II c. 44, but the Finance Act 1963 is simply 1963 c. 25.

Statutes are subdivided into sections, subsections, paragraphs and subparagraphs, identified respectively by arabic figures, arabic figures in parentheses, italic lower-case letters in parentheses and roman lower-case numerals in parentheses: e.g. Representation of the People Act 1949, s. 63 (1) (*c*) (i). Check that the author uses the correct terminology when referring to subdivisions. Phrases such as 'Subsection 1 of section 63 states...' are better rewritten 'Section 63 (1) states...'

Rules (such as the Rules of the Supreme Court) are divided into Orders and rules, Articles (e.g. Articles of Association) into clauses and articles. The following abbreviations may be used, the ones given in parentheses being the more old-fashioned forms:

	Singular	Plural
section	s. (sec., sect.)	ss. (secs., sects.)
subsection	subs., sub-s.	subss., sub-ss.
paragraph	para.	paras.
subparagraph	subpara., sub-para.	subparas., sub-paras.
Order	O. (Ord.)	Orders (Ords.)
rule	r.	rr.
clause	cl.	clauses
article	art., §	arts., §§

These abbreviations should normally be used in references to specific subdivisions, except at the beginning of a sentence, where they should always be spelled out; and they should be spelled out where the reference is non-specific: thus 'according to s. 63' but 'Section 63 states' and 'according to this section'.

References to statutory instruments

The titles of statutory instruments (delegated legislation such as Orders in Council, Regulations) may be followed by the year and number in parentheses or they may be referred to by year and number alone: thus 'according to the Town and Country Planning (Planning Inquiry Commissions) Regulations 1968 (SI 1968 No. 1911)', or simply 'according to SI 1968 No. 1911'.

References to Command Papers

See p. 175.

References to cases

The name of a case is given as, for example, *Smith* v. *Anderson*, the names of the plaintiff and defendant being set in italic and the v. (for versus; vs. is an alternative old-fashioned form) roman.

Where the plaintiff is the state, the abbreviation R. (not Reg.) is used for both Rex and Regina. The names of companies should be styled consistently Co. Ltd or Co., Ltd (the former is preferred nowadays). Ampersands are frequently used in the names of companies but should not be used to join the names of two parties: thus *Smith & Co. Ltd* but *Smith and Jones* v. *Anderson*.

In general books cases may well be referred to simply by name followed by the year in parentheses, e.g. *Smith* v. *Anderson* (1880). But full references quoting the volume and column/page of the law reports in which the case appears are normally given in specialized books on law. There are three different kinds of reference, arising from the different ways in which report volumes are numbered: (1) where there is one volume per year and the year forms the number of the volume, the year is given in square brackets, e.g. [1962] AC 209; (2) where there are several volumes per year, the year is given in brackets followed by the volume number within that year, e.g. [1958] 2 All ER 733; (3) where the volumes are numbered independently of the year, the year is given in parentheses before the volume number, e.g. (1965) 109 Sol. Jo. 70.

References to English law reports should always conform to one of these styles. The rules apply to many non-English reports as well, but some have different styles of references: for example the place or name of the court may be given in addition to the name of the reports, or the order of items in the reference may differ.

References to Scottish cases are styled differently. Cases reported in the Session Cases reports are styled as, for example, *Hughes* v. *Stewart* 1907 SC 791; cases in the Justiciary Cases reports as, for example, *Corcoran* v. *HM Advocate* 1932 JC 42.

There may or may not be a comma between the name and reference of a case (though one or other style should be used consistently for all cases). If a comma is used it should be placed *before* dates in square brackets, *after* dates in parentheses. In Scottish case references the comma precedes the date. There should never be a comma between the name of the report and the column/page number. However, some authors prefer to cite the first page of the complete case as well as the page or pages specifically referred to; here there should be a comma between the two (sets of) numbers, e.g. *Re Richmond Gate Property Co. Ltd* [1965] 1 WLR 335, 342–4.

Quoting from statutes and cases

Extracts from statutes must be quoted exactly. Authors may even want to retain the typographical conventions of the original, such as em rules after colons and double quotation marks. If possible extracts should follow the original in layout.

In ordinary books on law in which extracts from cases are introduced as quotations, alterations to such extracts should normally be limited to typographical conventions (as for quotations in general). But in case-books where the extracts form the body of the text the author may be willing for you to standardize such things as capitalization, italicization and forms of abbreviation.

Names of judges

In law reports the names of judges are set in capitals and small capitals. Extracts from cases quoted in books on law normally follow the same style, though small capitals throughout are preferred to capitals and small capitals nowadays. Some authors prefer to have judges' names set in (small) capitals wherever they occur, in the text as well as in quotations.

The title of a judge is written in abbreviated form after his name: thus for example Chief Justice Lord Parker is given as LORD PARKER CJ, and Justice Harman as HARMAN J (plural JJ, as in HARMAN and SARGANT JJ).

Tables of statutes and cases

Almost all books on law include tables of statutes and cases. These are always set as the last two items in the preliminary pages, and copy for them should be sent to the printer at the same time as the index copy.

Statutes are listed by title and chapter number (see above); they are conventionally given in alphabetical within chronological order, though the alternative of chronological within alphabetical is acceptable.

Cases are always listed alphabetically. Here the use of italic and roman is usually the reverse of that in the text; thus for example *Foss* v. *Harbottle* in the text becomes Foss *v.* Harbottle in the table of cases.

Italicization

The *Cambridge Law Journal* suggests that italic should be used for all Latin words and phrases except bona fide, prima facie, ultra vires, intra vires and dictum/dicta. Some other candidates for roman rather than italic are: caveat, gratis, habeas corpus, mala fide, mandamus, nisi, subpoena. There is no set rule about this, but the appearance of the page is improved if italic is kept to a minimum.

Capitalization

Act is always capitalized even in non-specific references in order to avoid ambiguity, but bill can be lower-case: thus 'the Act' but 'the bill'.

Unless a court is referred to by name, court is normally lower-case, as are assizes, bench, judge, sessions and so on. Titles of statutes always have the first *and* chief words capitalized.

Bibliographical references
The titles of some major textbooks include the name of the original author, e.g. *Williams on Wills*. The name of the editor of such a work need not be given provided the edition is identified by number.

References to journal articles are generally given in the style of case references, e.g. G. Hughes, 'Sale or return, agents and larceny' [1963] Crim. LR 312, 401; P. Higgins, 'Trade-ins and hire-purchase agreements' (1965) 6 *Australian Lawyer* 17; or even (for first and subsequent references) simply Hughes [1963] Crim. LR 312, 401; Higgins (1965) 6 *Australian Lawyer* 17.

14.3 *Music*

The first part of this section covers simple song books; the second (p. 262) includes some additional points that occur in monographs about music.

Style
1. *Music*
Dynamics (expression indications such as *diminuendo, f*) usually appear in bold italic lower-case; any abbreviations, such as *dim.*, should be consistent, as should the use of full points. Dynamics may appear above or below the stave to which they refer.

Tempo directions (e.g. fast, allegro) are usually set in bold roman upper- and lower-case, and above the stave.

Names of parts (e.g. alto or chorus) should be set full out left, or above the relevant bar if they start in the middle of a line. These often appear in small capitals and may be abbreviated after the first mention. See that the abbreviations are unambiguous; the standard abbreviations are:

S	soprano	Bar.	baritone
A	alto	B	bass
T	tenor		

Names of groups of instruments (e.g. strings) are often set full out left in upper- and lower-case, with individual instruments – usually abbreviated after the first mention – above the relevant note. Otherwise, names of individual instruments are set upper- and lower-case full out left. Watch that the abbreviations for parts and instruments are unambiguous (e.g. 'tr.' could be either 'trumpet' or 'trombone'). A list of standard abbreviations may be found in British Standard 4754 *Specification for the presentation of bibliographical information in printed music*.

Optional parts (e.g. descants) are printed as smaller notes. These should be distinguished in the MS by being written either smaller or in red. Give the necessary instructions.

Guitar chords are indicated by single letters (sometimes capital letters for major chords, lower-case for minor) or a letter and a number, e.g. G7.

Bars may be numbered, or letters may appear at intervals, so that a particular bar can be found easily ('bar 35' or 'the third bar after F'); the British Standard prefers bar numbers. An incomplete first bar is not included in the numbering.

If the author has lines of unequal length in his MS in order to keep certain phrases on one line, tell the printer to follow the MS and leave the right-hand edge ragged.

In an edition including only one part (e.g. a chorus edition) which has long periods of silence, it is usual to include cue notes – a bar of the most obvious piece of orchestration etc. preceding the entry of the part or chorus – so that the performers do not have to rely entirely on counting many bars' rest in order to know when to come in. The cue notes should be smaller, and labelled with the instrument or voice to which they refer.

2. *Words*

In a song, the words of the first verse (or first two verses) are printed between the staves, the other verses being printed after the music. If the words between the staves are not completely legible, type out the wording; but make it clear that this typed version is for identification and that these verses are not to appear twice.

In the verses between the staves, syllables are hyphenated, so that each one is below the relevant note(s). The author should insert these hyphens, but check that the breaks are sensible and that it is clear which syllable belongs to which note. Additional information about syllables can be given throughout the words by the use of an accent or apostrophe, e.g. 'blessèd', 'giv'n'. If the author does use accents, he should use grave or acute consistently.

Italic should be kept to a minimum; for example it may be used to distinguish instructions (such as 'Repeat verse 1') from the words of a song, or to pick out the words of choruses which are printed only the first time they are sung.

Avoid the use of more than one size of type if possible; if there are to be two sizes, see they are clearly distinguished.

Check the indention scheme of songs; authors sometimes have over-elaborate and inconsistent schemes for indenting rhyming lines, refrains and choruses.

3. *Notes, sources, etc.*

General notes on performance should appear above the music. Any footnotes to the music are probably most unambiguously keyed in by symbols.

The composer's name, and a source such as 'No. 5 of *Twelve Duets for Violins*', may appear immediately below the heading of each piece. The author, translator and source of the words usually appear below the words (or as a note at the foot of the first page if all the words are printed between the staves). If author and composer appear above the music, the author should be on the left and the composer (and arranger, where appropriate) on the right.

Acknowledgements for all copyright material should appear in a list in the preliminary pages or at the end of the book, though some may also have to be included on the relevant page, if the copyright holder insists.

If there is a discography, and individual songs on discs are regularly discussed in the text, use roman with inverted commas for song titles, italic for disc titles.

What the copy-editor should do

Examine music copy closely at the earliest possible moment, in case there are a number of things that the author will have to be asked to do. Look out for the following:

illegibility: words, and also whether notes are clearly positioned on or between the lines of the stave

discrepancies in wording and punctuation if there is more than one edition

whether the words are correctly hyphenated and it is clear how the syllables fit the music

omitted repeat marks. (The position of the repeat in a song may be clear
from the words)

whether there is an indication of speed

spot-check for discrepancies in music between, say, piano and melody
editions (including accidentals, staccato, marks of expression such as
crescendo, f); also discrepancies in accidentals between different parts
in the same bar

spot-check whether there are enough notes or rests in a bar to complete
it. Authors often omit dots after dotted notes or tails from quavers;
and sometimes the split bars where the music repeats (which should
have, say, three beats before the repeat mark, and the fourth at the
beginning of the repeat) do not make up a whole bar

if two parts are written on the same stave, spot-check whether each
part has a complete set of notes; for example when a crotchet is
shared between two parts, it should have two tails. Tails rise from the
right of the note for the upper part and descend from the left for the
lower part

spot-check whether some staccato dots in a group seem to have been
omitted

If the author is going to do some more work on the music, he can
also be asked:

to add slurs (curved lines grouping notes together, used to indicate
musical phrases and also in songs to show when one syllable covers two
or more notes)

to see that, if he uses accents or apostrophes to show when syllables such
as -ed are pronounced or elided, he does so consistently

to see that a time signature is included for each piece

to see that all clefs are included

to link quavers etc. where appropriate

If he is going to have to rewrite the music he can be asked also:

to use a consistent style for the things mentioned under *Style* above

to use italic sparingly in the words for songs

to be consistent about capitalizing the first letter of each line of verse to
be printed between the staves, in accordance with the style of verses
to be printed below

Paging

Any piece of music occupying an even number of pages should start on a left-hand page, so that the reader does not have to turn more pages than necessary within that piece. If the pieces vary in length, ask the author whether the order can be varied; if it can, ask the printer to suggest the best order from the point of view of make-up.

In a words-only edition, the items can run over from a recto to a verso, but preferably not where there is a chorus which is printed only the first time it is to be sung.

Page numbering

The user does not need page numbers if the items are numbered and there is no endmatter. If there are no page numbers one can vary the length of the page in a words-only edition, to avoid splitting verses, without this variation being so noticeable. Also one can more easily alter the extent of the preliminary pages (usually paginated in arabic) if this is necessary at proof stage to attain an even working.

Whether page numbers are to be printed or not, make sure that the pagination will be clear to the printer, both at this stage and at proof stage. Try to achieve an even working.

If there is more than one edition

It is sensible to use the same typesetting for both editions as far as possible (preliminary pages, headings, words of songs) reducing the material photographically for the smaller edition. Keep variations to a minimum, though the sources and acknowledgements in a words-only edition should cover only the words. See that the relevant notes on performance etc. appear in each edition. If they are to be set separately check that the words (including punctuation etc.) are identical in both editions, and spot-check the music.

Preliminary pages

Preliminary pages are kept to a minimum, and usually paginated in arabic, partly because they are short and partly because the text may start on a verso.

The title page should contain the name of the edition if there is more than one.

The verso of the title page may include a note on performing rights;

and a note on copyright and acknowledgements is often placed there. Check that the copyright notice is correctly worded and suitably qualified if your firm does not hold the copyright in the music.

The contents list may not contain page numbers if the items are numbered, unless there is some endmatter such as a discography or notes on sources.

If the text has to start on a left-hand page, see that it is not preceded by a blank right-hand page. Repeat the book title if necessary.

If the order is to be changed to aid make-up, tell the author, and see that the contents list, item numbers and cross-references are altered accordingly.

Monographs about music

Rules of style for musical titles and terms are briefly covered in Hart's *Rules* (38th edn, pp. 28–9); see also p. 96 above. Time signatures and figured basses should be distinguished from one another, and any conventions (words versus figures, upright versus italic figures, use of oblique or hyphen etc.) should be logical and consistent. For 'common' and 'alla breve' time signatures mentioned in the text, be sure the printer knows whether to set ordinary capitals C and ₵ (the latter is a special sort) or to insert the special music symbols **C** and **₵** (which will have to be artwork).

Warn the designer if ♯ ♭ ♮ are used in the text ('the F♯ chord') as they are special sorts available only in certain founts; if they occur very rarely it may be best to substitute the word ('the F sharp chord'). Other music symbols in the text will normally have to be produced as artwork and stripped in.

Music examples

Music examples without stave lines (e.g. rhythmic patterns ♩ ♫) can appear within a line of text. Any more complex music examples should be numbered 'Ex. 1' etc. and referred to by number in the text, because the printer may be unable to place them exactly where the author wants them to fall (cf. pp. 44, 159–61).

All music artwork should be extracted from the typescript and sent to the draughtsman separately. If examples within the text line are numerous they must be lettered or otherwise keyed, for identification during make-up.

If you or the designer are unfamiliar with music monographs, look at books comparable in size and subject from more experienced publishers; these will suggest 'pattern' features for the music artwork, such as size and indention of the music staves (and may also show pitfalls to be avoided).

The copy-preparation of music examples is generally similar to that of song books etc., covered above. Music historians and ethnomusicologists often use arcane or archaic features of notation: the music draughtsman may be unfamiliar with the symbols or conventions, and in such cases the author may be asked to supply a carefully drawn specimen of each difficult symbol or a photocopy of published versions of conventions he is using.

Musicologists often use small type for editorial additions (e.g. *musica ficta* accidentals) and may indicate this in their manuscript by writing in red. The convention should be explained to the reader in a preface or footnote. The best ways of instructing the draughtsman about this and other features of a scholarly transcription are dealt with in *Editing Early Music*, cited below.

Separate typewritten copy must be supplied for any lettering to be set separately and stripped in (e.g. captions for examples; and occasionally the words of vocal music, though these are more often typed in by the music draughtsman, as are tempo and expression marks).

Useful references

Editing early music: notes on the preparation of printer's copy, London, joint publication of Novello, Oxford University Press and Stainer & Bell, 1963: very useful

New Grove dictionary of music & musicians, London, Macmillan, 1981: the most authoritative source for correct spellings of composers' names, their works, musical terms, etc.

Ross, Ted. *The art of music engraving and processing*, 2nd edn, Miami Beach, Hansen House, 1974: a more practical guide for the draughtsman, which shows the publisher what the draughtsman can be asked to do

15

Reprints and new editions

Perhaps I should start with some definitions.

An impression is a number of copies printed at any one time. When a book is reprinted or reproduced from the same setting of type, with only minor alterations, this printing is a 'new impression' or a 'reprint'. The term 'new [or second] edition' should not be used unless the text has been significantly changed. The word 'edition' is also used to distinguish different bindings (for example a paperback edition) or a reset version even if the text remains unchanged; such uses of the word 'edition' should be distinguished from real new editions, in which the text has been changed.

15.1 *Reprints*

The corrections are usually marked in a copy of the book called the correction copy; it is important that a copy of the latest printing should be used, as an earlier one might not contain all the corrections that have already been made.

The correction copy should be marked as though it were a proof, with each correction in the margin so that the printer can find it easily. However, if some of the substitute passages are more than a line or two the printer may prefer to have those as a separate typescript; if so, the page number should be written above each correction, plus A etc. if there is more than one on a page; the material they replace should be deleted in the correction copy, and 'Substitute A from typescript' written in the margin.

Try to think of any other corrections that follow from those the author has listed: for example, if he alters the spelling of a name, see whether it is mentioned in the index and if so whether it needs to be altered there or on the other pages listed there.

The numbers of the pages on which any change is required, including the preliminary pages, should be entered on the fly leaf, so that the printer need not look at every page.

Preliminary pages. See section 15.3.

Text. See that the new matter is consistent in style with the rest of the book, and that there is room for it. It is essential that each alteration should affect as few lines as possible: substitutions must be the same length, and new material cannot be added unless one can find (or make) room for it. If necessary, two facing pages can become one line longer or shorter than the rest of the book. If you are not sure whether a correction is feasible, ask the production department.

If the book already contains a list of corrigenda or an errata slip, see whether all the corrections can now be incorporated into the text. If all or some are made, the list of corrigenda should be deleted or modified, and the page number entered on the fly leaf.

See whether the index will need revision. If possible, revise it now and add the relevant index pages to the list on the fly leaf.

Illustrations. See section 15.4.

Jacket and cover. See that a copy of the jacket or cover for each edition is corrected. The blurb, author's appointment and series list should be brought up to date; and you may wish to include extracts from reviews, or to advertise different books on the jacket or back cover. See that the relevant ISBN appears, and that your firm's addresses are up-to-date. If genuine cloth will not be used to bind the book change 'cloth' to 'hard covers' in such phrases as 'also issued in cloth'; and see that the price is changed if necessary.

Proofs

Proofs are usually checked by the publisher, unless the author has particularly asked to see them. The proofs may consist only of the pieces the printer has reset (which may be only a few lines from each corrected page). Check them against the copy and see that the corrections do in fact fit into the available space. If they are shown in position on the page, see that they are correctly placed. If you are sent the camera copy itself, it is best not to mark it, but to write any corrections on a photocopy of the relevant page. If you do have to mark the camera copy, use a soft, pale blue pencil.

See that the index has been revised (if necessary) and that any changes to illustrations have been made.

15.2 *New editions*

In most firms new editions are treated like new books; but check the corrections file and reviews file, to make sure that all outstanding points have been raised with the author.

If the copy is not a typescript but a corrected copy of the last impression, and it is not clear whether the book will be reset, consult the production department. Let them know if some alterations are to be made only if the book is to be reset, or whether some corrections will be modified if the book is not to be reset, so as to fit them into the available space. A printer's estimate will probably be obtained before you complete your marking.

If it is decided that the whole book will not be reset, treat it like a reprint apart from the preliminary pages (see below). If it is to be reset, the whole book should be copy-edited. In either case, see that the old and the new material employ the same conventions; and if chapters, illustrations, etc., are renumbered, change any cross-references to those numbers. If the book is to be reset, or altered so much that the author cannot revise the index before the book goes for setting, return the old index to him for revision later.

For illustrations see section 15.4.

15.3 *Preliminary pages*

Half-title and verso
Bring the series list, or list of other books by the author, up to date.

Title page
Bring the author's appointment up to date; if the author has retired or died, add 'formerly' before his appointment; and after some years you may decide to delete the appointment. Add '[SECOND] EDITION' (if applicable). If there is a publication date on the title page, it may need changing.

Verso of title page
Bring the publisher's addresses up to date if necessary.
  Copyright date. The copyright date should never be *altered*, though another date may be added. A reprint or a change in binding does not

justify an additional date; but a new edition in which the content is changed should have one. If this is the first copyright notice – that is, if earlier editions were published before September 1957 or were subject to the US 'manufacturing clause' (see p. 124) – the notice should read '© . . .' and the new date of publication. If earlier editions were published after September 1957, the dates of those editions should be given:

© [copyright holder and date of each substantive edition, *not* paperback edition or reprint, after September 1957]

For example, the copyright notice for a book first published in 1956, with new editions in 1965 and 1974 and reprints in 1967, 1969 and 1971, would read:

© [copyright holder] 1965, 1974

See also pp. 123–5.

ISBN. In a *reprint* the ISBN is changed only if there is a change in the binding; for example a paperback ISBN should be added if the original edition was only in hard covers and the reprint is wholly or partly paperback. ISBNs will have to be added to books that were first published before ISBNs were introduced; and the group identifier (see p. 125) will have to be added to early Standard Book Numbers, so that:

Standard Book Number: 521 05875 9
becomes   ISBN   0 521 05875 9

Alter 'clothbound' to 'hard covers' if appropriate.

A *new edition* has new CIP data and a new ISBN for each binding. The ISBN(s) for the preceding edition should also be given:

ISBN 0 521 20304 X   2nd edition
(ISBN 0 521 05679 9   1st edition)

Printing history. The date of each edition and reprint published by your firm should be included.

First published 19—
Reprinted 19—, 19—
Second edition 19—

or, if appropriate,

Reprinted with corrections [where there are more alterations than in an ordinary reprint but not enough to justify calling it a new edition]

Reset	[if the type has been reset for reasons other than extensive changes to the text (which would be a new edition)]
Paperback edition	[if there is a change in binding but not extensive changes to the text]

Printer's imprint. If the book is being reprinted (but not reset) by a different printer, some publishers alter 'Printed' to 'First printed' and add below it 'Reprinted in Great Britain [or other country] by . . . '. In any case the new printer's name and town must be given; if you do not know who is reprinting the book, ask the production department. A new edition has a new printer's imprint.

Contents list
Add any new material and make any alterations necessary to chapter titles, etc., and to page numbers.

Preface
In a new edition there should be a preface explaining how this edition differs from the last, so that those who already own the book can decide whether they should buy the new edition. If there is a new preface, alter the title of the old preface to 'Preface to the first edition' above the preface, in the contents list and in the headlines. The preface to the second edition normally precedes the preface to the first edition unless it is just a few lines about the changes that have been made. Change the page numbers on the preliminary pages, where necessary; the pages which have only a change of page number should be listed on the fly leaf with the rest.

If you are in any doubt as to whether additional preliminary material can be fitted into a reprint, ask the production department.

15.4 *Illustrations*

Placing, etc. Sometimes reprints are imposed differently from the original impression; sometimes plates are grouped instead of being scattered, or are reprinted by litho on text paper; if the reprint is to be a paperback, plates and pullouts may be omitted. Alter the contents list and/or list of illustrations and acknowledgements if necessary; also skim through the text looking for references to those illustrations.

If the author wants to add a text illustration in the middle of the book, and you are not resetting, it is best to call it, for example, fig. 56a (even if it is not closely connected with fig. 56) rather than have to renumber all the later figures, check all the cross-references and reset all the affected lines.

If the plate or figure numbering is altered, check all the text references.

Originals. If the author wants to use some of the old half-tones in a new edition, ask the production department whether the printer has a printing image of them. Line illustrations can be reproduced from a copy of the book, but any alterations will be more easily carried out on the original artwork if this is still available.

Permissions. Some copyright owners require an additional fee when a new edition is published, or when more than a certain number of copies of the book have been printed. (In particular, this applies to the use of Ordnance Survey maps.) If there is any additional material that may require permission, see that permission has been obtained and that any acknowledgement has been added.

Checklist of copy-editing

This list is not exhaustive, so read the relevant section of the book: the relevant chapter or section number is given beside each heading (or individual item).

An asterisk indicates things that should be done or considered at estimate stage, a dagger those that may be dealt with by your designer or production department, or covered by general instructions to the printer.

GENERAL

Completeness and organization (3.4)

*check that no folios missing

*number folios in one sequence. If extra folio added after 66, change 66 to 66a, number the new folio 66b, and on 65 say '66a, b follow

*mark where arabic pagination begins

*mark 'run on', 'fresh page', 'fresh recto', 'verso blank', where appropriate. (†A general note saying whether chapters start fresh pages, fresh rectos, or run on, is also useful.)

if extent has changed since estimate, tell production department; give details if cuts or additions localized

Legibility and ambiguous characters (3.4, 13.2)

see all handwriting is legible

identify capital O/zero, l/1, minus/em rule/en rule, x/multiplication sign, decimal/multiplication point, Greek letters etc. where necessary

identify superscripts, subscripts where not clear in typescript and diagrams. Say whether they should be aligned or staggered if superscripts and subscripts appear together

mark up bold

*warn production department of any unusual characters that printer may not have in stock; see whether something else could be used instead. If not, make it clear exactly what is wanted, and say whether each unusual character is used more than once or twice and if so whether it occurs throughout or only in one or two sections (2.1)

check printer's list of special sorts, to see that he has identified them correctly; pass any queries to author

Numbered or lettered paragraphs

are cross-references unambiguous? (6.3)

if numbers or letters are necessary, they should be consistently with or without parentheses, and preferably not with closing parenthesis only

similar kinds of paragraph should have similar indention (3.4):

(*a*) xxx	*or*	(*a*) xxxx
xxxxxxxx		xxxx

Breaks in text where no subheading (3.4)

mark each 'space' or $\supset\!-$

if spacing between paragraphs is erratic, say 'extra space only where marked'

where large spaces have no significance, draw line across them

Space or close up

mark abbreviations etc. to be spaced or closed up according to your house style (6.1)

Specimen page (2.3)

copy sent with typescript should be amended throughout (if necessary) and identified as master copy

Copyright (3.6)

check that all sources (quotations, tables, line drawings and half-tones) are acknowledged, and that acknowledgements comply with copyright holder's stipulations about wording, position of acknowledgements etc.

Books with offprints (12.1)

each paper should probably start on a right-hand page

if notes and references are to be printed at end of each paper, put copy with individual papers

acknowledgements must be within paper

figure and table numbering usually starts afresh in each paper. Give number of figures and tables on first folio of each paper, and put caption copy with paper illustrations and caption copy should be identified by contributor's name if numbered separately

if plates in one group, try to arrange it so that plates from different papers are not printed on the same leaf

Author's argument

obscure, misleading or ambiguous sentences

non sequiturs

mixed metaphors

grammar, and punctuation for grammar (see also below)

paragraphing

libel and obscenity

errors of fact (names, dates, etc.)

inconsistencies and contradictions in author's argument

safety (6.15)

HOUSE STYLE (6)

(*not* to be implemented in book, article and journal titles, or in quotations except author's own translations)

stet first occurrence (in each type size and in the prelims) of optional spellings and of departures from normal style

Abbreviations (6.1)

? unfamiliar ones explained in list in prelims or at first occurrence

? consistent, e.g. % or per cent

? consistent in use of capitals or small capitals and omission or inclusion of points in USA etc.

remove points in St and other contractions that include last letter of singular

consistent inclusion/omission of commas with 'i.e.', 'e.g.', 'etc.'

avoid 'l' (line) if lining figures used

Capitalization (6.2)

mark all capitals where confusion is possible

mark all small capitals, e.g. for vol. nos., abbreviations where appropriate (e.g. AD, BC), except in typewriter-set books, in sans serif, italic and bold, and where lining figures are used

? capitalization of special terms consistent

Cross-references (6.3)

consistently capital/l.c., abbreviated or not

above, below rather than *supra, infra*

if footnotes to be numbered by page, change reference to footnote from 'n. 61' to 'p. ooo, n. o'

change folio numbers to two or three zeros so that author and reader pick them up at proof stage

check table, figure, equation numbers; change roman to arabic where necessary

Dates (6.4)

consistent style. Avoid arabic numbers for months, even in footnotes, as 1.4.71 means 1 April in Britain, 4 January in USA

Italic (6.6)

check that correctly and consistently used

plural 's' italic, possessive 's' roman

Numbers, units etc. (6.9)

spelling-out, elision (quantities should not be elided)

space or comma to indicate thousands

change decimal comma to point; say whether decimal points are to be low or centred

remove point and plural 's' after abbreviated units

add zero before decimal point if no digit there at present

Parochialisms and stereotypes (6.10)

change 'this country' etc.; spell out abbreviations likely to be unfamiliar to overseas readers; watch out for stereotypes

Punctuation (6.12)

hyphenation

stet hyphens at end of typed lines, where appropriate

mark spaced en rules for parenthetical dashes

mark any (unspaced) en rules needed for sense, e.g. 'input–output ratio', if you think the distinction is needed

possessives, e.g. Thomas' or Thomas's

comma at end of clause if one at beginning

Spelling (6.13)

correct spelling errors

stet first occurrence (in each size of type) of optional or US spellings

make use of accents consistent. Tell printer if accents needed on capitals. No accent on capital A unless author particularly wants it

mark oe, ae ligatures in French and Old English. Tell printer if they are needed

check spelling of proper names, especially those which have two accepted forms. Is author consistent in use of native/anglicized forms?

consistent use of ü/ue etc. where appropriate

PARTS OF A BOOK

Preliminary pages (7; for reprints and new editions 15.3; for works in more than one volume 12.2)

see that copy is complete (i.e. *all* wording supplied) and that order of items is clear. If one item is not available, give exact or approximate length. (If necessary warn production department that preliminary pages should not be imposed with rest of book, at any rate until proofs are passed for press)

*mark fresh pages and rectos

say where arabic pagination to begin

half-title: list of preliminary matter for printer if not all items are in contents list (e.g. series list, dedication, epigraph)

provide series wording if necessary; are series editors etc. still the same?

verso of half-title: ? list of books in series, or author's other books, needed. Provide up-to-date version

title page: title, author and his position should be as on any brief for the jacket

verso of title page: Check copyright notice: ? right owner and date(s). Should it be qualified or omitted?

? notice about information retrieval

publication history

publisher's and printer's names and addresses

obtain CIP data. Is ISBN correct?

dedication: ? placing

contents list: ? complete (e.g. preliminary matter and index included). ? too full (query if more than first grade of subheading included), or not full enough. Check that it tallies in numbering (preferably arabic), wording, spelling, capitalization (where appropriate), hyphenation and order with prelims and text

†mark up for style

list(s) of illustrations: ? necessary. ? tally with captions, but each contains minimum necessary for its purpose

list of tables: ? necessary. Check against table headings

all lists: remove 'list of' from heading, put 'o' opposite first item. Delete point at the end of each item

preface: add initials and date if your house style. If series preface or note to reader, does it apply fully to this volume?

acknowledgements: ? available and complete

list of abbreviations: ? needed. Check order, and use of italic and points

note on notation, system of transliteration etc. needed?

Headlines or running heads (9.2)

make sure each headline will fit across page

say whether capital initial for all main words or only for first word and proper names

say whether printer is to use new or old section title if new section starts below top of page

supply list if contents list cannot be followed exactly, e.g. if short forms needed or quotes round words italicized in the text

if first section title does not come at beginning of chapter, give chapter title as first right-hand headline

Subheadings (9.3)

*? too many kinds

? numbers/letters can be deleted

*code each kind (excluding chapter heading)

mark capitals in u. and l.c. headings

no full point if broken off, ? full point if run on

*marginal headings taken into type area?

add quotes to words or phrases usually distinguished by italic, if necessary

Footnotes and endnotes (9.4)

check that all notes have text reference and vice versa

number throughout chapter if endnotes or Linotype, Intertype or filmset footnotes; if already numbered throughout chapter, check that complete sequence with no gaps or additional numbers

move text indicators to break in sense

say where copy for notes begins

footnotes: ? too long; if so can they be moved into text?

†tell printer whether a footnote which runs over on to another page should have a rule or 'continued' line to divide it from the text on the second page

endnotes: headlines should probably say 'Notes to pages ooo–o'

Tables (9.5)

*indicate extent of table and notes if not clear in typescript

mark approximate positions in margin, if separate in typescript

if some have titles, should they all?

check numbering. Unless there are very few, all tables over 4–5 lines should be numbered in case they have to be moved

change 'as follows' to 'as in table 5'

if table of over 4–5 lines is in middle of paragraph, mark text to run on

identify any vertical rules that are essential

check that table and column headings include *minimum* necessary wording, and that units are identified

check totals and any other figures that can be cross-checked; do spans overlap?

add zero before decimal point if no digit there at present

change decimal comma to point

comma or space to indicate thousands; space in four-digit numbers if there are also five-digit ones

delete full point at end of item

remove ditto marks

see that table notes are consistent, keyed differently from footnotes or endnotes

†say whether setting may be unjustified in narrow columns

†say whether turnovers flush left or indented (and if so how much)

say how items in column should be aligned: flush left in each column, or decimal or units aligned

large tables: if it occupies more than one folio, make clear how it runs on (sideways or downwards)

if too big for a page, where can it be split?

†give instructions about 'continued' lines for table titles and column headings, and about placing of any notes with indicators in the table

Other tabulated material

punctuation at the end of broken-off phrases should, within reason, be consistent (or consistently omitted)

remove ditto marks

do not use small type if this would imply that displayed material was quoted from elsewhere

Appendixes (9.6)

*mark fresh page or run on

*mark small type for whole or part of appendix, where applicable

Glossary (9.7)

should one be compiled?

check alphabetical order, use of italic, punctuation. Avoid (or explain) use of foreign alphabetical order

spot-check coverage

Index (8)

is coverage satisfactory?

check that entries concise but informative

check alphabetical order of entries

check order and punctuation of sub-entries and sub-sub-entries. Should they be run on or broken off?

check cross-references. Information in one place, with cross-reference (or in both if few page references). Never half in each place

check capitalization and use of italic

elide pairs of numbers

check consistency of references to notes

†say whether and where 'continued' lines should be inserted

†say how much turnover lines and broken-off sub-entries should be indented

Author index cum list of references (8)

? add cross-references from second etc. authors

? have '*et al.*' authors been indexed

BIBLIOGRAPHICAL REFERENCES (10)

References in text

author–date system (10.2): check names and dates against list of references, make use of &/and consistent, also use of *et al.*, punctuation between name and date, between two references, between date and page number: a in 1960a to be consistently italic or roman

numbered references (10.3, 10.4): check complete sequence of numbers

*should numbers be in parentheses or square brackets to distinguish them from superscripts used in the text?

References in footnotes

? consistent system for first and subsequent mentions

check wording, spelling, capitalization, date, etc., against bibliography; standardize capitalization system unless good reason for not doing so.

remove *op. cit.*, *loc. cit.* except soon after full citation, substituting short title where necessary

ibid. etc. consistently italic or roman, preferably not followed by comma, to avoid double punctuation

? *ibid.* correctly used

do not try to make Command Paper abbreviations consistent

standardize punctuation, use of vol. and p.; use pp. if referring to more than one page. Close f, ff up to number

mark roman volume numbers (but not page numbers) to be small capitals except in typewriter-set books, passage set in sans serif, italic or bold or where lining figures are used

mark space between 'p.33' etc. if none in typescript

mark sources such as IV. ix. 6, 6.4 to be consistently closed up or spaced if inconsistent in typescript

standardize use of parentheses

? are abbreviations (e.g. for documents, journals) explained somewhere, if necessary

Bibliography or list of references

*? is bibliography easy to use or too much subdivided

check alphabetical order of authors, order of publications by one author, pair of authors, etc.

check convention for titles by same author: usually indention where author(s) exactly the same, repeat names where any change

check completeness, order, punctuation within each item. If text references
are 'Smith 1960', date should follow immediately after author's name

mark italic and capitalization

check consistency of abbreviations

mark arabic volume numbers for journals to be bold (where appropriate)

mark roman volume numbers to be small capitals except in typewriter-set
books, or in sans serif, italic or bold passages or with lining figures

are publication places consistently anglicized/not anglicized? Should native
names be followed by English name in square brackets?

are quotes consistently included/omitted round article titles?

LITERARY MATERIAL

Quotations (11.1)

*if there are only a few, consider whether use of small type is necessary

*mark any quotations that are to be distinguished from main text by indention
or use of small type

mark following line of main text full out or new paragraph

should first line of displayed quotations start full out or indented?

double to single quotes

remove quotes from beginning and end of quotations set in small type.
(? Retain quotes if quotations are to be indented text type)

ellipses: ? standardize number of points (usually three) plus full point if
required

punctuation to introduce quotation, and position of punctuation with closing
quotes. Punctuation at the end of displayed quotation changed to fit
surrounding sentence, e.g. so that sentence does not end with a comma

square brackets for editorial interpolations

spot-check for accuracy

check all items that are quoted twice (i.e. phrases from a longer quoted
passage) for consistency

check that all quotations have sources, and that sources are placed in best
position

spot-check sources for accuracy; are right number of lines given (e.g. 4 lines
not called 101–5)?

Poetry (11.2)

mark 'prose' or 'verse' if not obvious, e.g. Latin verse with no capitals for
new lines, German prose with capitalized nouns starting lines

make sure that stanza breaks are clear

HALF-TONES AND DIAGRAMS (4)

separate illustrations from the text

check that originals are complete, and clearly and correctly identified; all illustrations should be numbered for identification, even if numbers not to be printed; folio numbers may be used for unnumbered figures

provide separate lists of captions. (First and last page of each group of illustrations to be printed separately from the text should be labelled '*facing p. 000*' below the caption if there is no list of illustrations in prelims.) Points consistently included or omitted at end of captions. Ring figure or plate numbers if not to be printed

†say whether each caption is to be the same width as the illustration (if so give the width of each one) or text measure; also whether turnover lines are to start flush left, to be indented or to be centred

mark approximate position of text illustrations in margin (provide list of folio numbers if illustrations are few or localized). For a book requiring a paste-up, see that a duplicate of this information is provided if necessary

check that content is consistent with text and captions

Half-tones (4.4)

see that top is identified, scale provided and trim marked if necessary

All diagrams (4.2)

see that lettering is legible and consistent with text. Mark capitals. Identify superscripts, subscripts, italic, etc. Remove as much as possible to caption

see that roughs are intelligible

if any figures are included in typescript, photocopy for draughtsman and ring in text

provide notes for draughtsman

Graphs (4.3)

see that axes are adequately and consistently labelled. The labels of vertical axes should read upwards

Maps (4.3)

see that author has provided typed list of place names with separate columns for towns etc., or compile one yourself; check spelling and coverage against text

SCIENCE AND MATHEMATICS (13)

identify Greek, script and bold letters. Differentiate between roman and italic within maths and chemistry, and mark italic in running text

identify 1/1, cap. O/zero, x/multiplication sign, en rule/em rule/minus; clarify confusion between mathematical signs, letters, etc., e.g. ϕ and $\varnothing$, ϵ and $\in$. (See fuller list on pp. 228–30)

identify multiplication points and say whether to be centred or low

identify superscripts, subscripts, where not clear in copy

number and punctuate equations, if necessary; say whether punctuation is to be retained. Move equation numbers from left to right, if appropriate. Check numbering if already numbered

add brace and centre equation number if one is necessary to make clear that group of equations shares one number

check correct sequence of brackets

? system of solidi/indices for units consistent

spacing between number and unit symbol(s)

spaces/commas for thousands

? abbreviations, for both special terms and units, consistent

spelling-out of numbers

two-line fractions in running text changed to one-line where possible. See that brackets are inserted where necessary, and that sequence of brackets is correct

? change exponential 'e' to 'exp' where appropriate

mark inclusion/omission of vinculum with square roots, adding parentheses where necessary

†say whether limits must be set below and above characters or may be set beside them.

Chemistry

? spell out abbreviations for elements and compounds

mark en rules, em rules, bonds etc.

mark small caps. for N and M (normality, molarity), L and D (laevo, dextro)

? italicization and hyphenation of prefixes in names of chemical compounds consistent

? artwork needed for structural formulae. ? simplification possible

give instructions about use of dotted or dashed bonds

Biology (13.5)

check abbreviation/spelling-out and italicization of generic and specific names

? strains of organisms used in experiments always typed in the same form

watch out for capitalization in common names

REPRINTS (15)

Text and illustrations

*get corrections from author, corrections file and reviews file. Are all corrections necessary; will they fit into the available space?

mark corrections, in style consistent with rest of book, in a copy of the latest printing

make consequent changes, e.g. in cross-references, index

Preliminary pages

update series list, ? series editors

? update author's/contributors' appointments

update publisher's address(es)

update printing history

add full ISBN(s), including preliminary zero, if missing or incomplete; change 'cloth' to 'hard covers' where appropriate

change page numbers if something has been added or material has been squeezed up

add any additional material to contents list and alter page numbers where necessary

Jacket/cover

add review quotes

is ISBN correct and complete?

update information about author

update series list

? new back copy for jacket

change price(s) if necessary

NEW EDITIONS (15)

Text and illustrations

find out whether book is to be reset

*see that all corrections in corrections file are included

see that new and existing material is consistent

obtain permission for new copyright material

if numbering of illustrations etc. changed, correct all cross-references

arrange for revision of index

Preliminary pages

update series list, ? series editors

update author's/contributors' appointments

update publisher's address(es)

add new copyright date

add new ISBN (followed by ISBN for previous edition)

update printing history

see that contents list and other lists are complete and tally with text

should be a preface explaining how new edition differs from old (if this is not
self-evident). Alter title of old one to 'Preface to the [first] edition' in
heading, headlines and contents list

Jacket/cover

update blurb, add review quotes of earlier edition

substitute new ISBN

update information about author

update series list

? new back copy for jacket

new price(s)

Book sizes

	Trimmed page size in millimetres	Untrimmed page size/board size in millimetres	Trimmed size equivalent in inches (to nearest $\frac{1}{16}$)
Standard sizes			
Metric Crown 8vo	186 × 123	192 × 126	$7\frac{5}{16} \times 4\frac{7}{8}$
Metric Crown 4to	246 × 189	252 × 192	$9\frac{11}{16} \times 7\frac{7}{16}$
Metric Large Crown 8vo	198 × 129	204 × 132	$7\frac{13}{16} \times 5\frac{1}{16}$
Metric Demy 8vo	216 × 138	222 × 141	$8\frac{1}{2} \times 5\frac{7}{16}$
Metric Demy 4to	276 × 219	282 × 222	$10\frac{7}{8} \times 8\frac{5}{8}$
Metric Royal 8vo	234 × 156	240 × 159	$9\frac{1}{4} \times 6\frac{3}{16}$
Metric Royal 4to	312 × 237	318 × 240	$12\frac{3}{8} \times 9\frac{3}{8}$
A5	210 × 148	216 × 151	$8\frac{1}{4} \times 5\frac{13}{16}$
A4	297 × 210	303 × 213	$11\frac{5}{8} \times 8\frac{1}{4}$

Countries of Africa

Present name (1987)	Old name	Date of independence
Algeria	Algeria	1962
Angola (People's Republic of)	Angola (Portuguese)	1975
Benin (People's Republic of)	Dahomey	1960
Botswana (Republic of)	Bechuanaland	1966
Burkina Faso	Upper Volta	1960
Burundi	part of Ruanda-Urundi	1962
Cameroon (United Republic of)	French British Cameroons	1961
Central African Republic	Ubangi Shari	1960
Chad	Chad	1960
Congo (People's Republic of)	French Congo	1960
Djibouti (Republic of)	French Somaliland, then Afars and Issas	1977
Egypt (Arab Republic of)	Egypt	1922
Equatorial Guinea	Spanish Guinea	—
Ethiopia	Abyssinia (also includes Eritrea)	centuries ago
Gabo(o)n	Gabo(o)n	1960
(The) Gambia	Gambia	1965
Ghana	Gold Coast	1957
Guinea	Guinea	1958
Guinea-Bissau	Portuguese Guinea	1974
Ivory Coast	Ivory Coast	1960
Kenya	Kenya	1963
Lesotho	Basutoland	1966
Liberia	Liberia	1847
Libya	Libya (Kingdom of)	1951
Malagasy Republic	Madagascar	1960
Malawi	Nyasaland	1964

Present name (1987)	Old name	Date of independence
Mali (Republic of)	French Sudan	1960
Mauritania (Islamic Republic of)	Mauritania	1960
Morocco	French and Spanish Morocco, and Tangier	1956
Mozambique	Mozambique (Portuguese)	1975
Namibia	South West Africa	—
Niger	Niger	1960
Nigeria	Nigeria	1960
Rwanda	part of Ruanda Urundi	1962
Senegal	Senegal	1960
Sierra Leone	Sierra Leone	1961
Somalia (or Somali Democratic Republic)	{ British Somaliland Protectorate / Somalia	1960
South Africa (Republic of)	South Africa (Union of)	1960
Sudan	Sudan	1956
Swaziland	Swaziland	1968
Tanzania	{ Tanganyika / Zanzibar	1961
Togo (Republic of)	Togo	1960
Tunisia	Tunisia	1956
Uganda	Uganda	1962
Western Sahara	Western Sahara	1976
Zaïre (Republic of)	Belgian Congo	1960
Zambia	Northern Rhodesia	1964
Zimbabwe	Southern Rhodesia, then Rhodesia	1980

Phonetic symbols

The following table shows some of the most common phonetic symbols and accents. When phonetic characters in a typescript are not clear, it is often helpful to send the printer a photocopy of this table, ringing the symbols used by the author and identifying them in the typescript by the reference numbers in the table.

	a	b	c	d	e	f	g	h	j
1	ä	ɑ	ü	ã	ɒ	ɐ	æ	ḅ	β
2	ɓ	ʚ	ɔ	ʔ	ɔ̃	đ	d̥	ɖ	ḍ
3	ḍ	ɗ	dʒ	ð	ə	ë	ę	ẽ	ɚ
4	ɜ	ɝ	ɛ	ę	ẽ	Ẽ	ɡ	g̊	ɠ
5	ʄ	ɟ	ħ	ɦ	ɥ	ɨ	ï	i̥	ɨ
6	ɪ	ʟ	ɾ	j̥	ǀ	ɫ	ɬ	l̩	ɭ
7	ɬ	ɮ	m̩	ɱ	ɯ	ɰ	ɰ	n̩	ɳ
8	ŋ	ɳ	ɲ	ŋ	ŋ̊	ŋ̊	ɳ	ö	ǫ
9	ø	θ	ö	ʘ	œ̃	ɾ	ɽ	ʈ	ɽ
10	ɹ	ɟ	ɹ̥	ʀ̥	ʁ	ʁ	ʂ	ṣ	ṣ
11	ꞩ	ʃ	ɛ	ʈ	ɹ	ʈ	ʈ	tʃ	ü
12	ʉ	ʮ	ü	ʊ	ʊ	ʏ	ʏ	ʌ	ʍ
13	ʏ	ʎ	χ	ɣ	ɣ	χ	ƻ	ʑ	ʐ
14	ʒ	ẓ	ɸ	ʔ	ʕ	ʡ	C	ƶ	
15	ː	ˌ	˅			ˇ		ˈ	ˉ
16	˙	ˋ	ˌ	ˈ	ˉ	ˇ	ˇ	ˆ	˜

ɪ = ɩ

ʊ = ꭒ

The Russian alphabet

				Trans- literation						Trans- literation
А	*А*	а	*а*	a		Р	*Р*	р	*р*	r
Б	*Б*	б	*б*	b		С	*С*	с	*с*	s
В	*В*	в	*в*	v		Т	*Т*	т	*т*	t
Г	*Г*	г	*г*	g		У	*У*	у	*у*	u
Д	*Д*	д	*д*	d		Ф	*Ф*	ф	*ф*	f
Е (Ё)	*Е (Ё)*	е (ё)	*е (ё)*	e (ё)		Х	*Х*	х	*х*	h or kh
Ж	*Ж*	ж	*ж*	ž or zh		Ц	*Ц*	ц	*ц*	c or ts
З	*З*	з	*з*	z		Ч	*Ч*	ч	*ч*	č or ch
И	*И*	и	*и*	i		Ш	*Ш*	ш	*ш*	š or sh
Й	*Й*	й	*й*	j or ĭ		Щ	*Щ*	щ	*щ*	šč or shch
К	*К*	к	*к*	k		Ъ	*Ъ*	ъ	*ъ*	” or ″
Л	*Л*	л	*л*	l		Ы	*Ы*	ы	*ы*	y
М	*М*	м	*м*	m		Ь	*Ь*	ь	*ь*	’ or ′
Н	*Н*	н	*н*	n		Э	*Э*	э	*э*	è or é
О	*О*	о	*о*	o		Ю	*Ю*	ю	*ю*	ju or yu
П	*П*	п	*п*	p		Я	*Я*	я	*я*	ja or ya

The use of a prime ′ rather than an apostrophe avoids confusion with a closing inverted comma.

Old English and Middle English letters

Name	l.c.	Capital	Approx. sound	Remarks
ash	æ	Æ	h*a*t	There are two forms of italic lower-case ash – *æ* and *œ*. The former is preferable, but it does not usually matter provided the printer is consistent
eth	ð	Đ	*th*is	But used interchangeably in OE and ME
thorn	þ or þ	Þ	*th*in	Printers sometimes read thorn as p, so identify them if they are rare or look like p
wynn	ρ	ρ	*w*ynn	But w more often used in printed texts, to avoid confusion with thorn
yogh	ʒ	ʒ		In OE usually printed as g. In ME both yogh and g were used, g being equivalent to the stop (get, go) and yogh being used for the sounds y (ʒeer = year) and h, or rather gh (kniʒt from OE cniht). (Yogh sometimes appears in ME texts as a scribal error for z, e.g. ʒeferus = Zephyrus.)

7 is used in OE as an ampersand. In a text there would need to be a capital version (7) as well as a lower-case one (7), but in quotations one form is used throughout, to save expense.

French and German bibliographical terms and abbreviations

FRENCH		
Abbreviation	Full form	Meaning
ap(r). J.-C.	après Jésus-Christ	AD
av. J.-C.	avant Jésus-Christ	BC
c.-à-d.	c'est-à-dire	that is to say
ch(ap).	chapitre	chapter
Comptes Rend.	Comptes Rendus	Proceedings
conf.	confer (Lat.)	compare
exempl.	exemplaire	copy (of a printed work)
inéd.	inédit	unpublished
in pl.	in plano (Lat.)	broadsheet, flysheet
l. c.	loc. cit. (Lat.)	in the place cited (*not* lower-case)
liv.	livre	book (usually in the sense of a division of a volume)
m. à m.	mot à mot	word for word, sic
p. e.	par exemple	for example
pl.	planche	full-page illustration
rel.	relié	bound
s. d.	sans date	no date (of publication)
s. l.	sans lieu	no place (of publication)
sq. (sqq.)	sequens (Lat.)	following
s. (ss.) ⎱ suiv. ⎰	suivant	following
t., tom.	tome	book – may be a volume or a division of a single volume
v.	voyez, voir	see
vol.	volume	volume

GERMAN

Abbreviation	Full form	Meaning
a. a. o.	am angeführten Ort	loc. cit.
Abb.	Abbildung	fig.
Abt.	Abteilung	part, section
Anm.	Anmerkung	note
Aufl.	Auflage	edition
Ausg.	Ausgabe	revised edition
Bd., Bde.	Band, Bände	vol., vols.
bes.	besonders	especially
Bl.	Blatt	leaf or perhaps fascicle
br., brosch.	broschiert	sewn, in pamphlet form
bzw.	beziehungsweise	respectively, or
ca.	circa	circa, about
d. h.	das heißt	that is to say, *viz*
d. i.	das ist	that is
ebd.	ebendaselbst ⎫ ebenda ⎭	ibid.
Erg. Bd.	Ergänzungsband	supplementary volume
Evg.	Evangelium	gospel
geh.	geheftet	sewn, in fascicle form
Hft.	Heft	part
hrsg.	herausgegeben	edited by
Hs., Hss.	Handschrift, Hand- schriften	MS, MSS
K., Kap.	Kapitel	chapter
Lfg.	Lieferung	instalment, issue, part etc.
m. E.	meines Erachtens	in my opinion
m. W.	meines Wissens	as far as I know
n. Chr.	nach Christus	AD
Nr.	Nummer	no., number
o.	oben	above
o. ä.	oder ähnlich	or something similar
o. J.	ohne Jahr	no date (of publication)
o. O.	ohne Ort	no place (of publication)
R.	Reihe	series
s.	siehe	see
S.	Seite	page, p., or pp.

GERMAN (cont.)

Abbreviation	Full form	Meaning
SA	Sonderabdruck	offprint
s. a.	siehe auch	see also
s. o.	siehe oben	see above
sog.	sogenannt	so-called
s. u.	siehe unten	see below
u. a.	unter andern	among others
u. ä.	und ähnlich	and such like, and so on
u. ä. m.	und ähnliches mehr	
u. s. f.	und so fort	etc.
usw.	und so weiter	
V.	Vers, Verse	verse, verses
v. Chr.	vor Christus	BC
verb.	verbessert	revised
Verf., Vf.	Verfasser	author
vgl.	vergleiche	cf.
z. B.	zum Beispiel	e.g.
z. T.	zum Teile	in part

Other bibliographical terms

Abhandlung(en)	article, essay or transactions (of a learned society)
Auswahl, ausgewählt	selection, selected
Beiheft	supplement
gesammelte Werke	collected works
Herausgeber, herausgegeben von	editor, edited by
Teil	part
Übersetzung, übersetzt von	translation, translated by
Verlag, im Verlag von	publication or publishing house, published by
Verlagsrecht	copyright
Zeitschrift	journal

APPENDIX 8

Contents of standard Monotype matrix case for mathematics

ALPHABETS

A *to* Z &   *A* to *Z*

a *to* z *and* fi ff fl ffi ffl   *a* to *z* and *fi ff fl ffl ffi*

, . ; : - - — ... ! ? ' '

SIGNS

I *to* o   · (dec. pt.)

+ = − × ± √ < > ≤ ≥ ∼ %

→ ← ∞ ∂ ∇ ( ) [ ] { } | / § * ' °

FRACTIONS

$\frac{1}{4}$ $\frac{1}{2}$ $\frac{3}{4}$

SUPERIOR LETTERS

a b c k l m n p q r s t x y z

INFERIOR LETTERS

a b c k l m n p q r s t x y z

SUPERIOR FIGURES

1 2 3 4 5 0

INFERIOR FIGURES

1 2 3 4 5 0

SUPERIOR SIGNS

. . ' / + − ( ) [ ] ∞

INFERIOR SIGNS

. . + −

GREEK CAPS

Γ Δ Θ Λ Σ Φ Ω

GREEK L.C.

α β γ ζ η θ λ μ π ρ σ φ χ ψ ω ϑ

293

Glossary

The entries are restricted to words, and meanings, that a copy-editor is likely to meet fairly frequently. In order not to introduce more technical terms, the definitions are perhaps oversimplified; books on printing and binding will explain the various terms and processes more fully.

Alphabetical order is letter by letter.

AH: *anno Hegirae*, in the year of the Hegira, i.e. from the flight of Mohammed (mid AD 622 by the Christian reckoning). Used to identify Muslim dates.

angle brackets: ⟨ ⟩

apparatus criticus: materials for the critical study of a document, usually variant readings.

art paper: coated paper used for printing fine-screen half-tones (q.v.). 'Imitation' art is the most common variety.

artwork: a picture suitable for reproduction.

ascender: the part of such letters as d and h which extends above the height of the letter x (see fig. G.1). *See also* descender.

author–date system: a system of bibliographical references, in which a particular work in the list of references is referred to in the text etc. by the author's name and the date of publication, e.g. 'Smith, 1960'. See section 10.2.

a/w: artwork (q.v.).

backed plate: a leaf which has half-tones on both sides.

bastard title (or half-title): the first printed page of a book, preceding the title page and containing the title of the book.

b.f.: American abbreviation for bold face (q.v.).

bleed: to bleed is to extend an illustration beyond the trimmed edge of a page; *the bleed* is the amount by which the illustration extends beyond the trimmed size to allow for variations in trimming, normally 3 mm or $\frac{1}{8}$ in.

blind blocking: see blocking.

block: a relief printing surface, normally produced by photography and

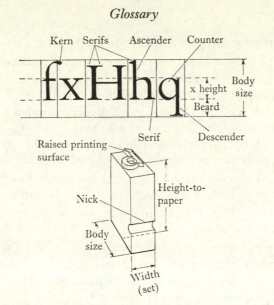

Fig. G.1   Type nomenclature.

chemical etching; the term is usually used of metal blocks of illustrations, either line or half-tone (q.v.). The US term is 'cut'.

blocking: impressing a design or lettering on a book cover. (The US term is 'stamping'.) The blocking may be in ink or metal foil, or it may be *blind blocking*, to produce a recessed surface without the addition of ink or foil.

blockpull: a proof of a block, usually taken by the blockmaker on coated paper. It gives a much better idea of the quality the printer will attain in the printed book than does the printer's own proof, which is pulled on inferior paper and is intended only to show position and wording.

blow up: to enlarge photographically.

blurb: a description of the book for the jacket, cover or publicity material.

boards: sheets of strawboard, millboard, etc., used in hard-cover binding. Also heavy paper or light card used for paperback covers.

body: in Monotype the shank of a piece of type (see fig. G.1); the measurement of the rectangle from back to front (i.e. from top to bottom as you look at the printing surface) remains constant throughout the fount and gives the point size of the type. However, type can be cast on a larger body (e.g. 11 pt on 12 pt), to give the same space between the lines as would a separate lead.

bold (face): a type with very thick strokes, a thickened version of another typeface.

BP: before the present (1950). Used in prehistoric dates.

brace: may be a curly bracket } or ⌒; used mainly in tables.

bracket: to a printer a bracket is a square bracket; a round one is called a parenthesis or paren. *See also* angle brackets, brace.

brass: a brass die used for blocking (q.v.). Brasses are wholly or partly cut by hand and are considerably more costly than Chemacs (q.v.). *Brass repro* is a repro pull (q.v.) of lettering to be used for making a Chemac or brass. (The word 'brass' may be used loosely to refer to both brasses and Chemacs.)

break off: to begin something on a separate line rather than running it on within a paragraph, e.g. subheadings and index sub-entries.

breathing: one or other of two signs in Greek to show the presence or absence of the aspirate (see section 14.1).

broadside page: a landscape page (q.v.).

bulk: thickness of a book, estimated in advance in order that the jacket, cover and blocking die can be designed with the right spine width; also thickness of a sheet of paper.

caesura: a pause in a line of verse, usually near the middle.

camera copy: material ready for photographing, usually for reproduction by litho. It should not be marked except lightly with a pale blue pencil.

cancel: reprinted leaves (e.g. a four-page cancel) to be substituted in bound copies and sheet stock, when a serious error is found after a book has been printed.

caps.: capitals, upper-case letters.

caps. and s.c.: capitals and small capitals.

caps. and smalls: capitals and small capitals.

caption: wording set below an illustration; also called a legend or underline.

caret: an insertion mark.

case: a 'hard cover' for a machine-bound book, consisting of front and back boards and spine. *See also* lower-case, upper-case.

cased: bound in hard covers by machine.

cast-off: a calculation of the number of printed pages that the copy will occupy when set in a given typeface and measure.

catchword, catchphrase: a word or phrase from the text, repeated at the beginning of a textual note or gloss at the foot of the page.

chapter opening: the beginning, or first page, of a chapter.

chase: in letterpress printing the metal frame in which type and blocks are locked. The frame, type and blocks are together called a forme.

Chemac: a kind of copper die, used for blocking (q.v.).

CIP: Cataloguing in Publication (see p. 127).

clothbound: bound in hard covers. As non-woven material is sometimes used in place of cloth, this kind of binding is best described as hard covers or hardback.

club line: the first line of a paragraph at the foot of a page.

cold composition or cold type: filmsetting or typewriter setting (qq.v.), as against hot-metal typesetting (q.v.). It is also used to mean typewriter setting only.

collate: (1) more correctly to *conflate,* i.e. to transfer corrections from one proof to another, say from another proofreader's proof to the author's corrected proof; (2) to gather the signatures (q.v.) of a book in the correct sequence; (3) to check the signatures to ensure that they are all there and are in the right order.

collotype: a method of printing illustrations from a gelatine image. No screen is used for reproduction of photographs, and an almost continuous gradation of tone is achieved.

colophon: an account of the book's production, or printer's imprint, at the end of a book. Incorrectly used of a publisher's device on a title page.

colour-coding of corrections: see section 5.5.

composed: typeset and paged.

composition cost: the cost of printer's marking-up, setting, paging, proofing and proofreading the book.

compositor: a printing craftsman skilled in setting up type by hand and correcting it, making up pages and correcting them.

contraction: an abbreviation which includes the first and last letter of the full form of the singular (e.g. Dr, Mme, St); it is not followed by a full point.

copy: raw material such as typescript, photographs, rough drawings, etc.

copy-preparer: a person employed by the printer to translate the designer's typographical specification into instructions on the typescript.

corrigenda: a list of corrections printed in a book, as against a separate errata slip (q.v.); however, an errata slip may be called a corrigenda slip.

cropping: 'cutting down' or masking an illustration, such as a photograph, to remove extraneous areas. Better called masking (q.v.) to avoid the risk of the cropping being done with a sharp instrument. *Crop marks* are placed on the back of an illustration or on an overlay, to show what is to be omitted. (The term is also used to describe the variable growth of crops visible in aerial photographs, which often indicates the presence of an archaeological feature.)

cross-head: a centred heading or subheading.

cut: a US term for a block (q.v.).

cut lines: the edges of pieces of paper from which a paste-up is compiled, appearing as lines on a proof.

descender: the part of such letters as g and y which extends below the baseline or foot of the letter x (see fig. G.1). *See also* ascender.

diacritical marks: accents, dots and bars below or above letters etc.

diaeresis: two dots placed over a vowel, to show that it is pronounced separately, e.g. naïve, Brontë.

diecase: a matrix case (q.v.).

displayed: set on separate lines, and distinguished from the text by being set in a smaller or larger size or by its position in relation to the margin (full out, indented or centred). Displayed matter is usually preceded and followed by a little extra space. Examples of displayed matter are headings, long quotations and mathematical equations.

diss, dissed, dissing: see distribution of type.

distribution of type: originally the return of type to the type case, though machine-set type is now normally melted down. Often abbreviated to 'dissing'.

double-page spread or *spread:* an illustration or table extending across a pair of facing pages.

dummy: a dummy book, which may or may not be bound, made up of the correct number of signatures (q.v.) of the paper to be used for the book, to show the thickness or 'bulk'.

duplexed: Linotype matrices (q.v.) are usually duplex, i.e. each has two characters punched into it. These characters are said to be duplexed with one another.

edition: one or more printings (or impressions) of the same version of a book in the same kind of binding. The term 'new [or second] edition' should not be used unless the text has been changed so much that libraries which already have the book will need to buy the new version. Issues with only minor corrections are called reprints or impressions. The same text issued in a different binding or at a lower price may be called a paperback edition or cheap edition.

electro: an electrotype, i.e. a duplicate letterpress printing plate made by electrolytically depositing copper on a mould taken from the original plate or type and backing with a lead alloy. *See also* stereo.

elision: the running together of pairs of numbers, e.g. 38–39 becomes 38–9 and 213–218 becomes 213–18.

ellipsis: three points used to indicate an omission.

em: the square of any size of type, i.e. a 10 pt em is 10 points wide, though the width of a 10 pt letter M will depend on the set (q.v.); 12 pt (or 'pica') ems are used to measure the width and depth of the text area on a page, irrespective of the size of type in which the page is set. If copy is set to '24 ems' or '24 picas' it is approximately 101 mm or 4 inches wide, since 72 pts = approx. 25.33 mm or 1 inch.

em rule: a rule occupying the full width of the square of any type size. For the use of em rules see section 6.12.

en: a measurement half the width of an em (q.v.). *See also* en point, en rule.

endmatter: the material that follows the text proper, e.g. appendixes, bibliography and indexes.

endnotes: notes which follow the appendixes or text (or, more rarely, the relevant chapter) rather than appearing at the foot of the relevant page of text.

endpaper: a folded sheet, one leaf of which is pasted to the front or back cover. The other leaf, known as the flyleaf, is pasted along the folded edge to the first or last page of the book.

en point: a point set midway along a piece of type as wide as an en, so that the point will appear with space either side of it; it may be medial or low.

en rule: a rule half the width of an em rule (q.v.). For the use of en rules see section 6.12.

epigraph: a quotation in the preliminary pages or at the beginning of a part or chapter.

erratum (or *errata*) *slip:* a slip of paper containing a list of corrections and pasted into, or placed in, a copy of a book.

estimate: an estimate of the cost of producing a book; an estimate of length is called a cast-off (q.v.).

even small caps: small capitals without full capitals.

even working: a multiple of the number of pages that will fill one sheet of paper of the size to be used for printing the book. Usually a multiple of 32 octavo pages.

extent: the length of a book in terms of the number of pages.

extract: a term used by some printers to refer to displayed quotations.

face: the printing surface of a piece of type; *see also* typeface.

figure: (1) an illustration printed in the text; (2) an arabic numeral.

film feed: the distance in points by which the film in a filmsetter is advanced between lines. Also called film advance.

filmsetting or *photo-composition:* typesetting by photographic means.

flatbed: a flatbed printing press with a horizontal printing surface such as type; *see also* rotary press.

flexible plate: a plastic or rubber relief plate (q.v.).

flush left, right: adjoining the left or right margin.

flyleaf: see endpaper.

foldout: a pullout (q.v.).

folio: (1) a sheet of typescript or leaf of manuscript; (2) a printed page number; (3) in book sizes 'folio' traditionally indicates a sheet folded in half, i.e. twice the size of quarto.

font: see fount.

foredge: the outer edge of a book, opposite the spine.

foreword: introductory remarks about a book or its author, often written by someone else.

format: the trimmed page size; the term is loosely used to distinguish between different styles of binding, or to describe the style of production.

forme: paged metal type and blocks, together with the metal frame (called a chase) into which they are locked ready for printing.

foul proof: an earlier corrected proof.

fount: the characters of one size of the same typeface, including alphabets of capitals, small capitals, lower-case, figures, punctuation marks, etc.; sans serif founts have no small capitals. A titling fount consists of capitals, figures and punctuation only. The proof correction *wrong fount* indicates that a letter of the wrong design or wrong size has been included in the text.

Fraktur: a specific German fount; often used as a generic name for any 'black letter', 'gothic' or 'old English' face. Occasionally used in mathematics.

frontispiece: an illustration facing the title page; usually, but not always, a half-tone (q.v.).

full out: adjoining the left or right margin. If a passage starts full out it is not indented.

full point: a full stop.

furniture: various lengths and widths of metal, wood and plastic used for filling the blank spaces in a forme (q.v.) or the white spaces between type and blocks, etc.

galley: a flat metal tray, with raised edges on three sides, used for holding type; *galley proofs* are proofs taken on a long slip of paper from the type-matter while it is still in the galley. The typematter may be divided into pages, in which case the proofs are called 'page on galley'. (See p. 59.)

gloss: an explanation of a difficult word, either in the margin or in a note.

gravure: photogravure (q.v.).

guillemets: special quotation marks used in French and some other foreign languages. See Hart's *Rules* (38th edn), p. 100.

gutter: (loosely) the inner margins of a book; really the inner, folded edge, also called the back.

half-title: (1) the first printed page of a book, preceding the title page and containing the title of the book; (2) a subsidiary title page sometimes used to introduce each of the parts into which the book may be divided; the recto contains the number and title of the part, and the verso is blank or may contain a map or introductory note.

half-tone: a process by which various shades of grey, from black to white, are simulated by a pattern of black dots of various sizes (except in photo-gravure (q.v.)). The image is photographed through a grid or 'screen' which breaks the picture into dots. Screens of various gauges can be used to suit the paper on which the half-tone is to be printed: e.g. a screen of 65–85 lines per inch is suitable for letterpress printing on newsprint (q.v.), a screen of 150 for letterpress printing on good art paper (q.v.).

hanging indention: the first line of the paragraph starts at the left margin, and subsequent lines are indented, as in this glossary.

Harvard system: a version of the author–date system of bibliographical references.

headline: the headings set at the top of each page except over chapter openings, etc., in most non-fiction books and some novels. Also called pagehead or running head, though some publishers use 'running head' to mean a head-line which changes from page to page rather than remaining the same throughout a chapter or section; 'page headline' is a better term for head-lines that are different on each page.

histogram: see p. 53.

hot-metal typesetting: Monotype, Linotype or any other typesetting in which type is cast from molten metal, as distinguished from typewriter setting and filmsetting.

ibid., ibidem: 'in the same place'. (See p. 178.)

idem or *id.:* 'the same', used to mean the same author as before.

impose: see imposition.

imposition: the arrangement of pages of type etc. in such a way that they will appear in the right order and with the correct margins when the printed sheet is folded.

impression: a number of copies printed at any one time; a new impression is a reprint with only minor corrections. *See also* edition.

imprint: the publisher's or printer's imprint is his name and address, which is usually on the verso of the title page.

indention: beginning a line further in from the margin than the rest of the passage. *See also* hanging indention.

indicator: a footnote indicator is the number or symbol in the text which indicates that there is a footnote to the word or sentence.

inferior: a small letter or figure set beside and/or below the foot of a full-size character. Also called a subscript. *See also* superscript.

insert: (1) a small group of pages (often half-tones) inserted so that half appears, for example, between pp. 4 and 5 of a sixteen-page signature, and the other half between pp. 12 and 13 (see fig. 5.4, p. 78). *See also* inset.

inset: a small group of pages (often half-tones) inserted in the middle of a signature, e.g. between pp. 8 and 9 of a sixteen-page signature (see fig. 5.4, p. 78); sometimes called an insert.

inset map: a small map inserted in a corner of a larger map.

insetting: (1) the placing of the signatures (q.v.) of a book one inside the other; (2) *see* inset.

ISBN: International Standard Book Number (see p. 125).

italic: sloping characters.

justified setting: setting in which the space between words is varied from line to line, so that the last letter or punctuation mark in each complete line reaches the right-hand margin.

kern: the part of certain letters which overhangs the body of the type (see fig. G.1); a feature of certain italic or sloping types.

keyboard: the rows of keys on a typesetting machine; to *keyboard* is to 'type' the characters on these keys.

key in: to key in illustrations is to indicate their approximate position by a note in the margin of the typescript.

landscape: the shape of an illustration or book is referred to as 'landscape' when its width is greater than its height; a *landscape page* is a page on which tables, illustrations, etc., are turned to read up the page, so that their foot is at the right-hand side of the page.

l.c.: abbreviation for lower-case (q.v.).

leaders: a series of dots leading the eye from one column to another, e.g. in old-fashioned contents lists.

leading: the spacing between lines of type. The space can be added by inserting strips of lead between the lines or by casting extra metal on the body of each character (Monotype) or line (Linotype) or by increasing the 'feed' or film advance in a filmsetter.

leaf: two pages which back on to one another.

legend: a caption (q.v.).

lemma: a headword such as a quoted word at the beginning of a textual note; in mathematics a preliminary proposition used in the proof of a mathematical theorem.

Letraset: a system of dry transfer characters, used in preparing artwork.

letterpress: the process of printing from a raised surface.

letterspacing: the addition of small spaces, usually between capitals or between small capitals, to improve their appearance. In German and Greek texts, lower-case letters may be letterspaced for emphasis.

ligature: two or more letters joined together and combined in a single matrix, e.g. ff, fi, ffi, fl.

line drawing: a drawing which consists of black lines, shading and solid areas, but no greys. Grey may be simulated by using a suitable tint (q.v.).

lining figures: arabic numerals of equal height, usually the same height as capitals (see p. 99). *See also* non-lining figures.

literal: a mistake made by a compositor or keyboard operator when setting up type; used mainly of mistakes affecting only one or two letters. The US term is 'typo'.

lithography: see photolithography.

logarithmic graph: see fig. 4.2, p. 53.

lower-case: the small letters as distinct from capitals and small capitals.

M: see em.

machining: printing.

magazine: a container in which Linotype matrices are stored.

make-ready: adjustment necessary to ensure that an even impression will be obtained from every part of the printing surface.

make-up: the making-up into page of typeset material. It also includes the insertion of headlines, passages in small type, footnotes, tables, illustrations, captions and page numbers.

marked proof: the proof on which the printer's reader marks his corrections and queries.

masking: indicating the unwanted areas at the edge of an illustration such as a photograph, either by means of an opaque cut-out overlay or by lines marked lightly on a transparent overlay or on the back of the illustration.

mat, matrice: a matrix (q.v.).

matrix: a mould for casting the printing surface of a piece of type; in film-setting a photographic image to be projected on to photo-sensitive film. A *matrix case* is a frame containing a large number of matrices.

measure: the width to which a complete line of type is set; usually expressed in 12 pt ems (or picas).

Monotype: a method of casting single type characters. The keyboard perforates a paper tape which in turn controls the caster (the machine which casts the type).

N: see en.

net book: a book with a fixed UK price.

newsprint: a cheap paper used for printing newspapers etc.

non-lining figures: arabic numerals which have ascenders and descenders. Also called old style figures. (See p. 99.)

octavo: a page one-eighth of the size of the traditional sheet.

oddment: a sheet containing fewer pages than other sheets in the book.

offprint: a printed copy of a single article from a book or journal; also called a separate or, less accurately, a reprint.

offset: offset lithography (q.v.).

offset lithography: a lithographic printing method in which the flat image is printed on to a rubber roller (blanket) from which it is transferred to paper.

old style figures: non-lining figures (q.v.).

op. cit.: abbreviation of *opere citato*, 'in the work cited'. (See pp. 167, 178–9.)

opening: a pair of facing pages.

original: a photograph, drawing, etc., provided by the author as copy for an illustration, as distinct from a proof etc.

overlay: a transparent flap covering the front of a photograph or other illustration (see p. 47).

overrunning: the rearrangement of lines of type caused by a correction which makes a line longer or shorter. The insertion of a word in the first line of a paragraph may mean overrunning as far as the end of the paragraph, i.e. taking a word or two from each line to the next and altering the word spacing accordingly.

Ozalid: a method of making photographic copies, used for making paper proofs from film.

pagehead: a headline (q.v.).

page-on-galley proofs: proofs pulled from typematter which has been paged but not imposed (q.v.). They may be sent out with two or three pages on a galley proof, or each page may be on a separate sheet.

pagination: page numbering.

paperback: a book bound in paper or card.

paren: a parenthesis (q.v.).

parenthesis: a round bracket; to printers a 'bracket' is a square bracket. *See also* brace.

part: a group of related chapters, with a part number or title or both.

paste-up: a paged layout with galley proofs of the text pasted in position, and the size and position of the illustrations shown by outlines drawn on the layout, as a guide to the printer. If the paste-up is camera copy (q.v.), repro pulls (q.v.) are used in place of proofs, and any instructions about placing the illustrations etc. must be in pale blue pencil.

perfecter: a printing press that prints both sides of a sheet of paper in one operation.

period: a US term for a full stop.

permission: permission to reproduce copyright material.

photogravure: the process of printing from a surface in which ink is contained in recessed cells of various depths. Gravure half-tone 'dots' are all the same size, the variation in shade being effected by the different amount of ink in each cell.

photolithography: the process of printing from a photographically prepared metal plate on which the non-printing areas are protected from the greasy ink by a film of water. Offset lithography (q.v.) is the commonest printing method.

photo-offset: offset lithography (q.v.).

pica: a measurement, 12 pts, i.e. approx. 4.21 mm or $\frac{1}{6}$ inch.

pie-ing or *pi-ing:* dropping type, so that all the pieces become muddled up.

plate: (1) an illustration printed separately from the text, on a separate sheet, e.g. a letterpress half-tone printed on art paper; (2) any one-piece printing surface, such as a lithographic plate which prints the whole of one side of a sheet, or a flexible plastic or rubber letterpress plate which prints one page of the book and is therefore mounted on backing with the other plates needed to print one side of a sheet.

point: (1) as a measurement, approx. 0.35 mm or $\frac{1}{72}$ inch; (2) a dot, e.g. a full stop ('full point').

portrait: (1) the shape of a book or illustration is referred to as 'portrait' when its height is greater than its width; (2) if a table is 'set portrait' it is set upright on the page and not turned to read up the page. *See also* landscape.

preface: a personal note by the author, explaining how he came to write the book.

prelims: preliminary pages, which contain half-title, title page, contents list, preface, etc. (see chapter 7). The US term is 'front matter'.

press proof: the proof that is last read before printing, and authorizes printing.

print run: the number of copies printed.

proof: a photocopy or roughly printed copy, for checking and correction; also called a 'pull'. *See also* repro pull.

pull: a proof (q.v.).

pullout or *foldout:* a folded insertion in the text, which when opened extends beyond the normal page size. Also called a throw-out.

quarto: (1) a page one-quarter of the size of the traditional sheet; (2) a size of stationery, 10×8 inches in Britain, a little larger in the USA, now being replaced by A4, an international size, 297 × 210 mm.

quotes: inverted commas.

range: to align.

rebind: the binding of a second or subsequent batch of printed sheets.

recto: a right-hand page. *See also* verso.

reduction: the amount by which an illustration is to be photographically reduced before reproduction (see pp. 40–1).

references: (list of) bibliographical references.

register: the accurate superimposition of colours in multicolour printing; the exact alignment of pages so that they back one another precisely.

registration marks: pairs of marks, often a cross in a circle, to show the relative position and exact orientation of two pieces of artwork that are to be superimposed, or to ensure accurate register (q.v.) in colour printing.

reprint: (1) a number of copies reprinted from the same setting of type, with only minor corrections; also called a new impression (*see also* edition); (2) loosely, an offprint (q.v.).

repro pull (reproduction proof): a high-quality print on paper suitable for photographic reproduction.

retouching: handwork on photographic prints or transparencies, to remove blemishes, to obtain more accurate colour reproduction, etc.

reverse left to right: to reproduce an image so that it is reversed like a mirror-image.

reverse out: to reverse black to white when making a plate or block, so that the final appearance is of white printed on black (or another colour) rather than black on white.

revise: the revised, or second, proof.

rotary press: a printing press in which the printing image, as well as the impression surface, is cylindrical.

rough: the author's rough sketch, or any drawing that will have to be redrawn.

routing: cutting away the high parts of a block which are not required for printing.

royalty: a payment to an author (or someone else) for every copy sold.

rule: a strip of metal used to print a continuous line, e.g. in a fraction or at the top and foot of a table; hence any line to be printed, whether set in metal or not.

run: see print run.

running head: see headline.

running text: continuous text, as against displayed equations, note form, footnotes, etc.; used in such phrases as 'chemical symbols should be spelt out in running text'.

run on: continue on the same line, rather than starting a fresh line or new paragraph. Chapters run on if each one does not start on a fresh page.

sans serif: a typeface with no serifs (q.v.).

s.c.: small capitals.

screen: see half-tone.

script: a typeface based on handwritten letterforms; used in mathematics.

section: (1) *see* signature; (2) a subdivision of a chapter.

semi-bold: a typeface with strokes midway in thickness between ordinary roman and bold.

separate: an offprint (q.v.).

serif: a small terminal stroke at the end of a main stroke of a letter (see fig. G.1).

set: to set words is to produce the metal type or filmset or typewritten image of the characters that make up those words. *The set of a letter* is its width across the shank (see fig. G.1). *The set of a fount* is the measurement of the width of the widest letter.

set-off: the accidental transfer of ink from a freshly printed sheet on to the back of the next sheet.

sheet: a printed sheet; the term is usually used of sheets which have not yet been folded, and which may comprise several signatures.

short-title system: a system of bibliographical references which employs a shortened form of the book title after the first mention (see section 10.1).

sig: signature.

signature: (1) a folded section of pages in a book, i.e. one sheet or part of a sheet. Some people prefer the term 'section' but I have used 'signature' in this book to avoid confusion with the second meaning of 'section' (q.v.). (2) The identification letter(s) on the first page of each signature.

SI units: Système International units. For a list of the fundamental units see p. 98.

sizing: deciding the reduction or final size of an illustration original.

slip: a slip of paper on which galley proofs or page-on-galley proofs are proofed; colloquially a galley proof.

slug: a line of type cast in one piece.

slugset: typeset in slugs (q.v.).

small capitals: capital letters similar in weight and x height (q.v.) to the lower-case letters, and cast on the same body. They are not available in typewriter setting or in bold, italic or sans serif type.

small type: type intermediate in size between the main text and the footnotes.

solid: if type is set solid, it is set without additional space between the lines.

solidus: an oblique stroke, /.

sort: a single character of type. *See also* special sort.

special sort: a character that the printer does not have in stock; more generally, a character that cannot be keyboarded with the rest of the text, or a character not included in the standard fount of type.

specification: the designer's specification for a book, listing typeface and size, style for headings, etc.

specimen: sample page(s) set to show the various type sizes, headings and other typographical complications. (See section 2.3.)

spread: see double-page spread.

s/s: same size; an illustration so marked will be reproduced the same size as the original.

s/t: small type (q.v.).

standing type: type stored after a letterpress book is printed.

stereo: a stereotype, i.e. a moulded and cast duplicate block or plate. *See also* electro.

stet: an instruction that the letter or word with a row of dashes below it is to remain unaltered or to be restored if already deleted or altered.

strip in: to combine two pieces of film or paper.

strike-on composition: typewriter setting (q.v.).

strip in: to insert corrections or illustrations in camera copy or filmset matter.

strong: a page is described by some printers as strong if it has too many lines of type on it.

subheading: a heading to a section of a chapter or of a bibliography.

subscript: a small letter or figure set beside and/or below the foot of a full-size character. Also called an inferior. *See also* superscript.

sub-title: an explanatory phrase forming the second part of a title.

superior: a superscript (q.v.).

superscript: a small letter or figure set beside and/or above the top of a full-size character. Also called a superior. *See also* subscript.

swash letter: an ornamental italic character, usually a capital.

symposium: (1) a conference; (2) a volume of papers presented at a conference.

text area: see type area.

text type: the size of type in which the main text of the book is set.

throw-out: a pullout (q.v.).

tilde: the diacritical sign over an n in Spanish to indicate the sound *ny*, i.e. ñ; the sign is also used in mathematics.

tint: usually a *mechanical tint*, i.e. a ready-made dotted, hatched or other pattern, available in various densities, which can be applied to an illustration by a draughtsman, blockmaker or printer. Also a solid panel in a second colour.

tip in: to paste a plate or pullout to the adjoining page.

transliterate: to transcribe something in letters of another alphabet.

transpose: to change the order of letters, words, etc.

ts: typescript.

turned: a turned table or illustration is one which is turned on the page so that its left-hand side is at the foot of the page.

turnovers: the second and subsequent lines of a paragraph; the term is used in phrases such as 'turnovers indented 2 ems'.

two-page spread: a double-page spread (q.v.).

type area: the area occupied by text and footnotes on a page; it should always be made clear whether the area does or does not include the area occupied by the headline and page number.

typeface: strictly the printing surface of a piece of type; hence the design of that surface.

typewriter setting: typesetting carried out on a more or less sophisticated type-writer which may produce justified or unjustified setting (q.v.). Also called strike-on composition or cold composition, or (if an IBM machine is used) IBM setting.

u. and l.c. or u./l.c.: upper- and lower-case, i.e. a mixture of capitals and lower-case letters rather than all capitals.

unbacked: printed on one side of the paper only.

underline: a caption (q.v.).

unit system: a counting method developed by Monotype and now used for some typewriter setting and all filmsetting systems to measure in units the width of the individual characters and spaces being set in order to total the accumulated units and determine how much space is left for justification.

unjustified: unjustified lines have even word spacing and a ragged right-hand edge. *See also* justified setting.

upper-case: capitals.

verso: a left-hand page. *See also* recto.

virgule: a solidus (q.v.).

w.f.: wrong fount, *see under* fount.

white line: a line of space the same depth as a line of words.

widow: the short last line of a paragraph at the top of a page. Printers try to avoid starting a page with a short line, but they may have to respace several lines in order to make the paragraph longer or shorter, and this is expensive.

word break: splitting a word at the end of a line.

working: see even working.

wrap-round: a small group of pages (often half-tones) wrapped round one signature of the text, so that half the group appears before the signature, and the other half 16 or 32 pages later (see fig. 5.4, p. 78).

wrong fount: *see* fount.

x height: the height of the letter x. The x height of a lower-case alphabet is the height of the printing surface of a lower-case x, i.e. a lower-case letter without ascender or descender (see fig. G.1).

Select bibliography

For books relevant to science and mathematics books and to classical books, see section 13.7 and 14.1 respectively. For lists of abbreviations for journal titles, see p. 189.

BRITISH STANDARDS

1629: 1976 *Bibliographical references*

1749: 1969 *Alphabetical arrangement and the filing order of numerals and symbols*

3700: 1976 *The preparation of indexes to books, periodicals and other publications*

4148 *Abbreviation of titles of periodicals*, Part 1: 1970 *Principles*. Part 2: 1975 *Word-abbreviation list* (now withdrawn; recommended for use instead is *The international list of standard title word abbreviations*, published by the International Centre of ISDS, Paris)

4754: 1971 *Presentation of bibliographical information in printed music*

4755: 1971 *Presentation of translations*

5261 *Copy preparation and proof correction*. Part 1: 1975 *Recommendations for preparation of typescript copy for printing*. Part 2: 1976 *Specification for typographic requirements, marks for copy preparation and proof correction, proofing procedure*. Part 3, not yet written, will cover mathematical material and replace the remainder of BS 1219: 1958

5605: 1978 *Citing publications by bibliographical references*

BOOKS

Anderson, M.D. *Book indexing*, Cambridge Authors' and Publishers' Guides, Cambridge University Press, 1971

Book production practice, London, British Printing Industries Federation and Publishers Association, 1978

Butcher, Judith. *Typescripts, proofs and indexes*, Cambridge Authors' and Publishers' Guides, Cambridge University Press, 1980

Carey, G. V. *Mind the stop*, 2nd edn, Cambridge University Press, 1958. Now a Penguin Reference book

Cavendish, J. M. *A handbook of copyright in British publishing practice*, London, Cassell, 1974

Copinger and Skone James on copyright, 12th edn, London, Sweet and Maxwell, 1980

Fowler, H. W. *A dictionary of modern English usage*, 2nd edn, revised by Sir Ernest Gowers, Oxford University Press, 1965

Gowers, Sir Ernest. *The complete plain words*, 2nd edn, revised by Sir Bruce Fraser, London, HMSO, 1973. Now also a Pelican

Hart's rules for compositors and readers at the University Press, Oxford, 38th edn, Oxford University Press, 1978

Jennett, Sean. *The making of books*, 5th edn, London, Faber and Faber, 1974

Manual of style, 12th edn, University of Chicago Press, 1969

MHRA style book: notes for authors, editors and writers of dissertations, 2nd edn, London, Modern Humanities Research Association, 1978

MLA handbook for writers of research papers, theses and dissertations, New York, Modern Language Association of America, 1977

Names of persons: national usages for entry in catalogues, definitive edition edited by A. H. Chaplin and Dorothy Anderson, Sevenoaks, International Federation of Library Associations, 1967

Oxford dictionary for writers and editors, Oxford, Clarendon Press, 1981.

Rees, H. *Rules of printed English*, London, Darton, Longman and Todd, 1970

Scarles, Christopher. *Copyright*, Cambridge Authors' and Publishers' Guides, Cambridge University Press, 1980

Williamson, Hugh. *Methods of book design*, 2nd edn, Oxford University Press, 1966

INDEX

references (*cont.*)
165, 187, 191; page numbers
referring to, in author index, 144
see also bibliographical references
reprints of books, 264–5, 282
ringing
of full points and colons in proof
correction, 65
of matter not to be set, 24, 65, 74
of typescript folio numbers in list of
contents, etc., 128
Roman Catholic Church
numbering of Ten Commandments
by, 176
translations of Bible used by, 176
roman numbers, 99, 102, 247
for acts and scenes of plays, 202–3
in biblical references, 175
in index, 208
not elided, 102
for numbering preliminary pages, 28,
102, 120
for numbering structural formulae, 236
in references to journals, 182
roman type, marking for change of
italic to, 26
Royal Society: recommendations of,
on units of measurement, 222,
225, 230, 233, 234, 237
rules
above footnotes that extend to more
than one page, 77
to show line breaks in quotations,
194, 205, 251
in tables, 163
see also em rules, en rules, solidi
Russian language
alphabet of, 95, 288
bibliographical references to books
in, 177

s
long, 206
plural and possessive, for words in
italic, 96, 273
safety, checking practical instructions
for, 117–18
Saint, Sainte, in French proper names,
95, 105
sales and publicity department of
publisher, 121, 122
sans serif typeface, 241
ambiguity in, 232
no small capitals in, 90

scales
for illustrations, 45, 46, 57, 225,
234; checking of, 77
logarithmic, for graphs, 53
for maps, 51–2
for photomicrographs, 225
scansion, indications of, 200, 250–1
scenes of plays, numbering of, 202–3
science, books on, 222–4, 281
copyright acknowledgements for
illustrations in, 38
nomenclature in, 224–33
units in, 98, 233–4
see also biology, chemistry, mathematics
Scientific, Technical, and Medical
Publishers, International Group of
(STM), 37
sections of chapter, 6
headings for, 151
numbering of, 28, 63; in headlines, 91
symbol for, 90
titles of, in headlines, 76, 148, 149
unheaded, space between, 12, 30–1
sections and subsections of statutes, 253,
257
see, 91
and *see also*, in indexes, 141
semi-colons, 111
in index, 132, 141
sentences
abbreviations at end of, 85, 110
positions of words in, 115–16
should not start with numbers, 92, 100
series of volumes, 179
setting, *see* typesetting
sex stereotypes, 103
shading, in figures, 46
'she' or 'it': consistency in use of, for
countries and ships, etc., 34, 115
ships, 96, 115
short-title system of bibliographical
references, 167
bibliography for, 172–5
form of references in notes, 168–71
parts of references, 171–2
SI (Système International) units of
measurement, 34, 98, 222, 233
sic, 206
signatures of books, placing of plates
in relation to, 77–8
slang, parochial, 103
slugsetting (Linotype, Intertype)
bold type in, 182, 189